# THE OFFICIAL
## AMERICAN
## SKI TECHNIQUE

# THE OFFICIAL AMERICAN SKI TECHNIQUE

*New and Revised Edition*

PROFESSIONAL
SKI INSTRUCTOR
OF AMERICA

*Professional Ski Instructors of America (PSIA)*

*To Hannes Schneider, his son, Herbert,*
*The Hannes Schneider Ski School,*
*Toni Matt, Otto Lang, Luggi Foeger, Friedl Pfeiffer,*
*and Benno Rybizka,*
*who have contributed so much to American skiing.*

Copyright © 1964, 1966, and 1970 by Professional Ski Instructors of
    America, Inc. All rights reserved.
SBN 402-12045-0
Library of Congress Catalog Card Number 75-118908
Cowles Book Company, Inc.
A subsidiary of Cowles Communications, Inc.
Published simultaneously in Canada by
    General Publishing Company, Ltd.
    30 Lesmill Road, Don Mills, Toronto, Ontario
Printed in the United States of America

| First Edition | 1964 |
| Second Printing | 1964 |
| Second Edition | 1966 |
| Second Printing | 1967 |
| Third Printing | 1968 |
| Fourth Printing | 1969 |
| New and Revised Edition | 1970 |

## ACKNOWLEDGMENTS

Authors:
  Bill Lash
  Paul Valar
  Willy Schaeffler
  Edward L. Wyman
  René Farwig
  Richard L. Voorhees, M.D.

Art Work:
  Kathy Coomer
  Jackie Steinman
  Sue Elggren
  Ron Edwards

# CONTENTS

# A SKIER'S REMINISCENCE *by Lowell Thomas*

We are told how life is marked by milestones. My first encounter with the real thing was when I was crossing a stretch of the Arabian Desert in 1917. Suddenly we came upon a stone placed there by Roman soldiers nearly two thousand years ago. And then we passed many more as we rode our camels through the Wady Araba on our way to "The Rose Red City" of Petra. While there isn't much connection between the sands of Araby and skiing, I hear there have been a number of major milestones in the history of our favorite sport, especially since World War I. In those days I was first exposed to the sport in the Italian Alps where King Victor Emmanuel's mountain troops were using skis eight and nine feet long, with a single pole. But it wasn't until the Winter Olympics in the Adirondacks in 1932 that I decided here was something I wanted to do. In those days the Olympic ski events were strictly Nordic, cross country, and jumping.

So far as recreational skiing goes here in North America, the first instruction was given by Erling Strom at Lake Placid in the late twenties, four years prior to the '32 Olympics. The big impetus came in 1934 when Katherine Peckett brought the first Austrian pros to America. There were four of them, but the two responsible for our first instruction in Alpine skiing were Kurt Thalhammer and Sig Buchmayr, from Salzburg. They were soon followed by Benno Rybizka, Otto Lang, and others who also came to New Hampshire, and then by a group of their countrymen who were lured to the Sawtooth Mountains of Idaho by Averell Harriman.

This Austrian invasion of course was made possible by the one and only Hannes Schneider as a result of what he had been doing at his school at St. Anton on the Arlberg. Then, in the forties Emile Allais came along with what proved to be an exciting new technique. I'll never forget the dramatic meeting in New Hampshire when Emile was on his first visit to the United States. In Jackson one night after we had all been up to Tuckerman Ravine, I had the pleasure of introducing Hannes and Emile, the two ski giants of those days who had never met. Although there was much rivalry among their followers, even a bit of acrimony, these two obviously had great admiration for each other.

Since those pre-World War II days there have been other

striking advances in skiing, usually brought about by some decidedly uncommon young men most of whom have been my friends and occasional ski companions. Now at long last we are told that what can be termed an "American ski technique" has emerged. Be this as it may it's obvious our American ski schools have been producing tens of thousands of competent and happy skiers, and doing it on a greater scale than on any other continent—this despite the fact that Japan now seems to have more skiers than we have.

One of the difficult-to-explain experiences of my skiing years was at Aspen when I was invited to address the Eighth Inter-Ski International Ski Instructors Congress. Obviously there was nothing important I could tell them, but it was a pleasure to have such an opportunity to express my enthusiasm for skiing and my gratitude to the many ski instructors who have wrestled with the hopeless task of making me "a hot-shot skier." In the White Mountains of New Hampshire, the Green Mountains of Vermont, the Adirondacks, the Catskills, the Berkshires of New York, the Laurentians, I have enjoyed the companionship of these men who have meant so much to American skiing.

I also have roamed the mountains of our western states with them—Colorado, Arizona, Wyoming, Idaho, Utah, Nevada, California, Oregon, Washington. They are on the whole the finest group of men I've ever known. My ski jaunts have taken me to the Alps, the Himalayas, the mountains of Australia and New Zealand, to Japan, and the glaciers of Alaska. Because of the glorious times I have had with ski pros all over the world, it's a pleasure and an honor to be asked to salute them in the foreword to this important book.

# INTRODUCTION

*The Story of Skiing*
*Ski Technique Development*
*Certification of Ski Teachers*

# THE STORY OF SKIING *by Bill Lash*

Skiing may well be over five thousand years old. Not many sports can make that claim. The word "ski" is the Norwegian name for a snowshoe that was used by the northern nations of the old world. The name is derived from an Indo-Germanic root. It is found in the English words skid, skip, skiff, slide, and skate. The Norwegian word *skilober* is a snowshoe. However, a Dr. Fowler wrote in the Year Book, Ski Club of Great Britain, in 1909, that the word "ski" came from a Germanic and Latin word implying splitting. Thus, ski referred to a split or splitting of wood into the ski shape. The Indian snowshoe is different from the ski; thus, the English term "snowshoe" has never been popular in reference to skis and skiing.

In an unbroken area, in glacial areas, from Norway to the Bering sea, skis, sleighs, skates, and snowshoes have helped man cover great distances over snow and ice. These contrivances have been used for thousands of years for hunting, migration, warfare, and sport. Early skis were used to prevent sinking into the snow but not necessarily for sliding. It is in the gliding instruments that we are interested. The so-called Hoting Ski is the oldest found. It was dug up by Swedish archeologists in a peat bog in 1921, and its age is estimated at over forty-five hundred years old. The Hoting Ski is now in the Swedish Ski Museum at Stockholm. It is made of pine wood and is wide and short.

A stone carving uncovered by Gutorm Gjessing in northern Norway, shows a man on skis. This is believed to be at least forty-five hundred years old. Other finds of that age have been found in Scandinavia and in Russia. The Kalutrask Ski, found in a Swedish marsh, is about thirty-nine hundred years old. The ski is 204 cm. long and is 15 cm. wide at the center. It is of pine wood. A stick, with a hollowed-out blade on one end, was found near the ski.

The Ovrebö Ski is in a museum in Oslo, Norway, and is about twenty-five hundred years old. The ski resembles the skis of the 1890s. The Aruträsk Ski, found in Lapland, is fifteen hundred years old.

Prehistoric skis are divided as follows:

(1) *The Northern Arctic Type:* This was wide and short. Straps were attached through vertical holes in the top of the ski. The ski bottom was covered with hide. This ski is still used in Siberia.

(2) *The Southern Type:* This was long and turned up at the top and resembles the skis of the 1930s. They had high side pieces for toe straps and holes for heel bindings. The ski was used in mid-Europe from the Urals to southern Norway.

(3) *The Central Nordic Type:* These consisted of skis of unequal length. The left ski was long and grooved. The right was cov-

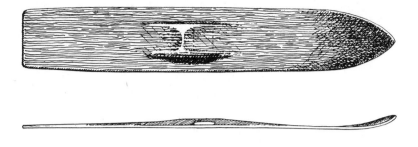

## THE HOTING SKI

This is the oldest ski. Found in a peat bog in Sweden, it is over 4,500 years old.

## THE OVREBÖ SKI

This ski is about 2,500 years old. It is in a museum in Oslo, Norway.

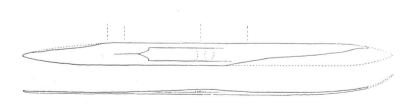

## THE ARUTRÄSK SKI

This ski was found in Lapland and is 1,500 years old.

ered with fur for traction and was called "Andor." The locale where this ski was used is now modern Lapland.

Some of the first skis were frames of pine ash, or birch and covered with leather. Pine skis were tarred on the running surface.

The first written record of a mention of skiing is from the historian Procopuis (526–559 A.D.). He mentioned gliding Finns—Skridfiner—who raced against nongliding Finns. In A.D. 800 Skadi, the goddess of the ski, is mentioned in literature. In 880 King Harfagr praised Vighard who shusses a slope. In 1060 is the first recorded race between Norway's King Harald The Hard and Heming Aslakson The Skier. In 1199 Saxo Grammacticus, the Danish historian, describes how Finns ski and wage war on skis.

From 1200 on, skis are mentioned in Norwegian history. It becomes less evident in history from 1250–1400. The Russians used skis for military campaigns in 1483. In 1525 there is mention of Norwegian postmen on skis. But it was not until the sixteenth century, when the printing press was widely used, that skiing became widely known. The most famous of ski books is one by the Swedish bishop who was exiled in Norway, Olaus Magnus. He published a book about Norway in 1555, which shows an illustration of hunters skiing. The pictures are not really descriptive because they are an artist's woodcuts, and do not represent scenes seen first-hand by Olaus Magnus. Nevertheless, the book is considered a fundamental historical source, and the illustrations are reproduced in many books.

Hunting scene in Norway from a book by Olaus Magnus, 1555.

From book by Olaus Magnus.

Cæte.

Lapp skier published in a Latin work, *Opera Laponia,* in 1673 by Johann Scheffer.

Not until 1650 was a correct picture of a Norwegian ski, of 1644, published. This was published in *Saxo Grammacticus*—a Danish history by Steffanius. An Italian Priest, Francesco Negri, wrote a book describing his travel through Scandinavia in 1663, although the book was not published until 1700. He was the first to describe a turn to a standstill. In 1673 a German, Johann Scheffer, published good pictures of Lapp skiers in *Opera Laponia*—in Latin. It shows the one long and one short ski.

In 1689, Valvasor, the German author, makes first mention of skiing on the continent and relates that the peasants of Krain (Carniola, an Austrian province), were strong skiers. He described the techniques as "They run downhill on short skis, with a stick in their hands, and all the weight of their body well to the rear."

He describes the skis as wooden boards one-quarter inch thick, six inches wide, and about five feet long. They are turned up and have a strap in the center for the feet. Valvasor said he had never seen this invention in other lands—referring to the European continent. In 1795, a German had skis made by a Norwegian and skiing was introduced to central Europe.

A description of skiing, with good pictures of men on skis, appeared in a book of travels by a Dutch ski captain, de Jong. He described a visit to Norway and the book shows Norwegian troops on skis. The first handbook for Norwegian ski troops was written in 1733 by Jens Henrik Emahusen. A description of skiing is found in Sir Arthur de Capell Brooke's *A Winter In Lapland And Sweden,* 1827. He notes that the "machines" are by no means easy to use where the ground is precipitous.

Sondre Nordheim, a Norwegian, introduced ski jumping at the end of a gradient. In 1843, Tromso, the Lapp, won a cross country race using two poles—one with a disk near the stick. The Osier binding was developed by Sondre Nordheim in 1850, and the Norwegian practice of skiing spread all over the world. Norwegian skiers were in Germany in 1853, Australia in 1855, New Zealand in 1857, and John A. "Snowshoe" Thomson was carrying the mail in California. In 1865, Lt. Col. Wergeland detailed a history of Scandinavian skiing. It helped to revive skiing in Norway. The first

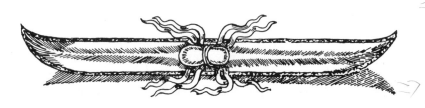

Picture of a Norwegian ski of 1644 published in *Saxo Grammacticus.*

Lapp skiers from Johann Scheffer's *Opera Laponia.* 1673.

ski races were held near Christiania in 1866—with the first big race there in '67. In 1867 the Winter Sports Association of LaPorte, California, held a race; prizes of $75 were given. By 1868, the Telemark skiers appeared in Christiania. Here, Sondre Nordheim jumped eighteen meters without a stick, and he swung to a standstill with a Telemark. Skis of the same length were used. The Norwegian press for the first time discussed ski techniques. In 1870 a downhill race was held in Plumas County, California. The ski club of Christiania was organized in 1877. Meanwhile, in Switzerland (1873), Dr. Herwig used skis in Arosa and Dr. Alexander Spengler was experimenting at Davos. In 1878 the first skiers appeared on the snows of France.

The first exhibition jumping meet was held in 1879 by the brothers Hemmestveit, from Telemark. The brothers then opened the world's first ski school. During the 1880s considerable competition of jumping and cross-country skiing was taking place. The Huseby Hill competitions were held in 1883, and jumping and cross country became separate events. In the United States the first ski club had been formed in 1887, at Ishpeming, Michigan, and a tournament was held. In 1884 German foresters started using skis and Norwegian students were skiing in the Black Forest. Dr. Fridtjof Nansen, a Norwegian, crossed the southern portions of Greenland in 1888. The party used sledges and skis and took forty days to cover a distance of five hundred kilometers. This crossing was the beginning of Alpine skiing in Central Europe.

In 1890 Nansen's book, *The First Crossing of Greenland,* was published and was translated into many languages. We quote the following passage: "Of all the sports of Norway, skiing is the most national and characteristic. As practised in our country, it ranks first in the sports of the world. Nothing hardens the muscles and makes the body so strong and elastic; nothing gives better presence of mind and nimbleness; nothing steels the will power and freshens the mind as skiing. This is something that develops not only the body but also the soul—it has a far deeper meaning for a people than many are aware of and a far greater national importance than is generally supposed." No book has had greater influence upon skiing than Nansen's work. It was descriptive of equipment with drawings and methods. Wilhelm Pauleke (German), Colonel Christopher Iselin (Swiss), Mathias Zdarsky (Austrian), and others were greatly influenced by this book. Nansen experimented with various skis and woods, and the Telemark ski design was to be popular for almost fifty years.

Ski literature is important in the evolution of ski technique. Many techniques have been developed in the minds of their creators. But ideas are not techniques until written down, defined, published, and made readily available.

Mathias Zdarsky (1874–1946) is the father of the Alpine Ski Technique. Zdarsky wrote the first methodical analysis and description of a ski technique in 1896, *The Lilienfelder Skilauf Technik*. Zdarsky laid the groundwork for other early ski technicians. It was the German translation of Nansen's book that transformed Zdarsky into a skier. The first winter after reading Nansen's book he skied alone—never seeing another skier. He experimented with bindings and skis and eventually designed the binding that bore the name of his home town—the Lilienfeld binding. Zdarsky was one of the first to teach skiing on a systematic, regular basis. His school was successful—by 1908 Zdarsky had twelve hundred pupils—and he attributed his success as a ski instructor to discipline.

Zdarsky's skis were short, had no grooves and were unsteady for straight running. He used a single pole without a basket or disk. This was called the stick and was applied during turning and skiing to keep the speed down. Although Zdarsky advocated that the weight of the body should not rest on the stick, he pointed out the trailing of the stick produced a steady position. Zdarsky, his Lilienfeld technique and binding have long disappeared. The short, grooveless ski was never very popular. Neither was the use of the stick as a break. Nevertheless, Zdarsky remains in his position as the true father of all Alpine skiing.

W. R. Rickmers, Zdarsky's principal disciple, was successful in converting many Englishmen to the Lilienfeld technique. The book, *Ski Running,* published in 1903, and revised in 1905, was written by Rickmers, Critchton Somerville, and E. C. Richardson. This was the first ski book written in the English language.

In 1906, Henry Hoek wrote a book, *Der Ski,* based on the Norwegian technique, but utilizing the stem and snow plow from Zdarsky's Lilienfeld system. *Der Alpine Skilauf* written in 1910, by George Bilgeri, presented an analysis of the Norwegian and Zdarsky ski techniques. Bilgeri also had a chapter on ski moun-

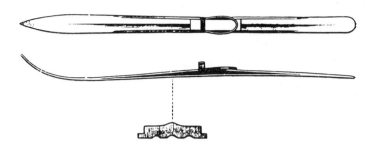

The ski used on Nansen's expedition. This is a forerunner of the Telemark ski.

The boot and binding used by Nansen—the binding was called "Lauparsco." From *The First Crossing of Greenland.*

taineering. It was in 1910 that Vivian Caulfield wrote the first book that analyzed the dynamics of skiing—*How To Ski.* It was an influential book on skiing and appeared in many other editions. In 1910, the *Ski-runner* by E. C. Richardson was published. Also in that year, *Skiing for Beginners and Mountaineers* was written by W. R. Rickmers. It is a pioneer classic on avalanches and mountaineering.

Arnold Lunn wrote his first ski book *Skiing* in 1912. Lunn's book advocated skiing without the use of the single stick for downhill racing. Other books and ski literature have had an impact on skiing. In 1922, *Skiing Turns* by Caulfield was written, and in 1925–26, *Der Wunder des Schneeschuhs* (*The Wonders of Skiing*) was published, written by Hannes Schneider and Arnold

De Jong, a Dutch ski captain, describes a Norwegian ski company in 1797.

Drawing by Mornay showing early nineteenth-century Lapp ski troops at maneuvers.

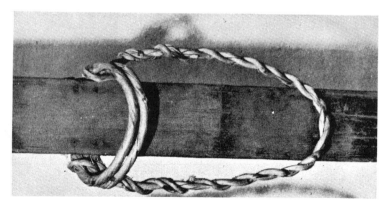

The Osier binding of 1870, developed by Sondre Nordheim in 1850.

English print of 1815—a drawing by Mornay showing Norwegian skiers of about 1790–1805.

Franck. This was a book describing the Hannes Schneider or Arlberg technique. It was translated into English in 1933. In 1927, Arnold Lunn wrote *The History of Skiing*. This was the first comprehensive book on ski history ever written. It is interesting that in 1927 Arnold Lunn and others set the first modern slalom in Austria for school children.

In 1932, F. Schuler wrote a book on ski mechanics in Switzerland. In 1934, Toni Ducia and Dr. Harald Reinl wrote a book on twisting skiing and counterrotation, followed by a similar technique written by Giovanni Testa and Dr. Eugen Matthias—*Naturliches Schilaufen*, in 1936. *Ski Français* was written by Emile Allais, Paul Gignoux, and Georges Blanchon in 1938—an important contribution to modern skiing. This book, describing the French method, was the beginning of the parallel system which was to enjoy popularity until the mid-1950s. The book was revised and reprinted after the war. It was subsequently published in English in 1947, and called *Ski The French Method*. *Ski The French Method* is one of the most beautifully illustrated books on skiing ever published.

In 1937, Hannes Schneider and Arnold Franck wrote the new edition of the *Wonders of Skiing*. This 232-page book with 242 photographs and 1,100 cinema reproductions is must reading.

In the United States in the 1930s, skiers were reading Otto Schniebs and J. W. McCrillis' *Modern Ski Technique,* and *The Complete Book of Skiing* by F. Hallberg and H. Muckenbrunn, was translated into English in 1936. A favorite book on skiing, ski technique, mechanics, and the psychology of teaching was written by Otto Lang in 1936 and '46, *Downhill Skiing*. Benno Rybizka's *The Hannes Schneider Ski Technique*—1938 and '46—was a favorite among ski teachers.

One of the best, and most popular books written on technique and skiing is Fred Iselin and A. Spectorsky's, *Invitation to Skiing*. The new *Invitation to Skiing* sold over 100,000 copies. No technique book has influenced modern ski technique as much as *Oesterreichischer Schilerplan,* by Stefan Kruckenhauser, 1956. Translated into English in 1958, by Roland Palmedo, *The Official Austrian Ski System* is probably the most widely read technique book—this, too, has sold over 100,000 copies throughout the world. In 1957–58, Joubert and Vuarnet came out with *Ski ABC,*

PICTURES FROM *Skiing Turns,* VIVIAN CAULFIELD, 1922.

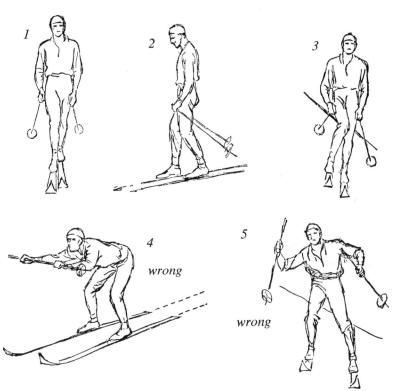

*PLATE I   STRAIGHT-RUNNING NORMAL POSITION*

*PLATE II   STRAIGHT-RUNNING TELEMARK POSITION*

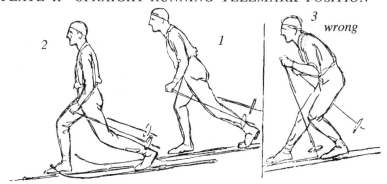

*PLATE III    STEP TURN (Uphill from traverse)*

*PLATE V
LIFTED STEM TURN (Uphill)*

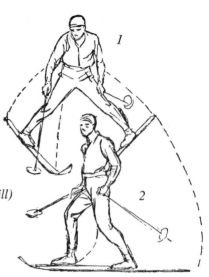

*PLATE IV    PURE STEM TURN (Uphill)*

*wrong*

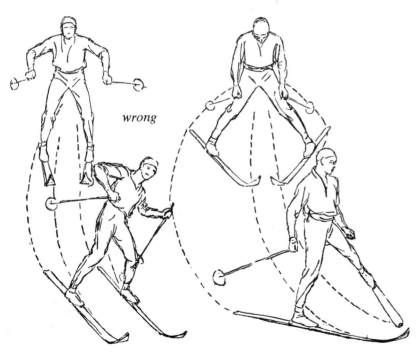

*PLATE VI    LIFTED STEM TURN (Downhill)*

*(1 wrong)*

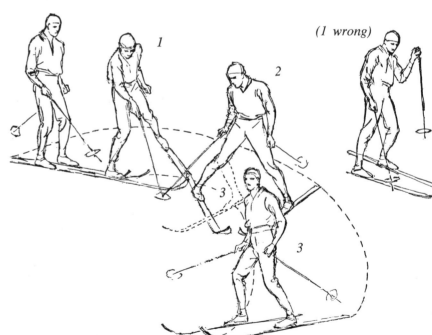

PLATE VII   TELEMARK (Uphill)

PLATE IX
OPEN CHRISTIANIA (Uphill)

PLATE VIII   TELEMARK (Downhill)

PLATE X
OPEN CHRISTIANIA (Downhill)

PLATE XI
JUMP TURN (Uphill from traverse)

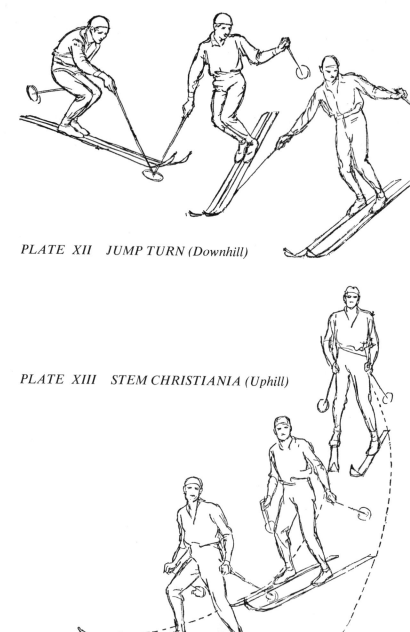

PLATE XII    JUMP TURN (Downhill)

PLATE XIII    STEM CHRISTIANIA (Uphill)

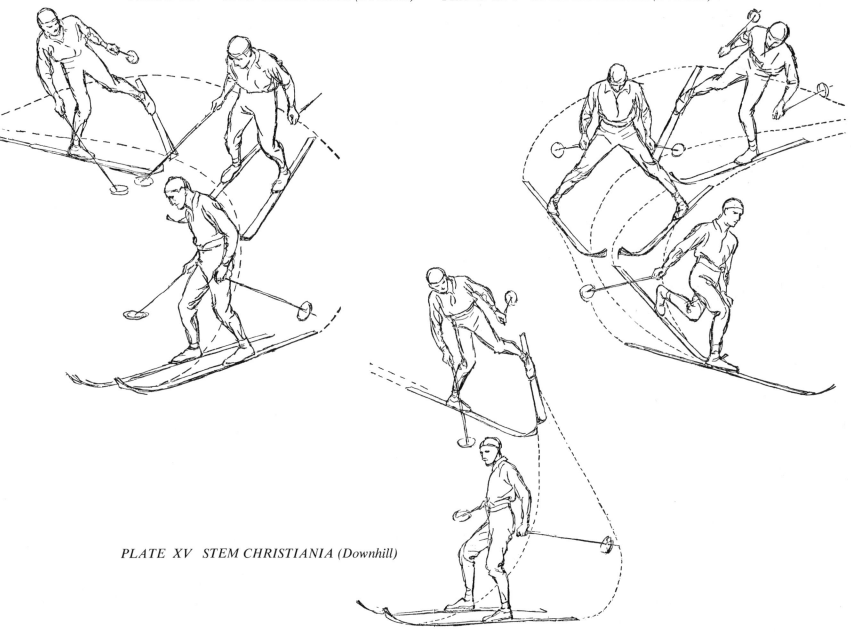

PLATE XIV    STEP CHRISTIANIA (Downhill)      PLATE XVI    STEM TELEMARK (Downhill)

PLATE XV    STEM CHRISTIANIA (Downhill)

Doug Pfeiffer with *Skiing with Pfeiffer,* Bill Lash with *Outline of Ski Teaching Methods,* and in 1960, Willy Schaeffler and Ezra Bowen with *The Sports Illustrated's Book of Skiing.*

Dr. Fritz Reuel said in 1911 that the development of ski technique could be considered completed. This has been said of ski techniques by their proponents since that time. Obviously one should not consider ski technique either as a passing fancy or the ultimate. Ski technique is the result of development and evolution. Modern techniques are a product of individual and collective practical teaching experience, psychology, basic mechanics, and physiological movements.

Ellefsen's patented binding had a strap sewn to the heel to prevent straps from slipping off. 1903.

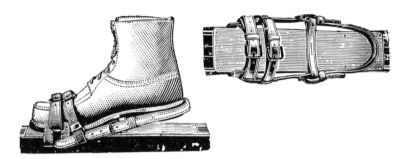

The Huitfeldt binding with iron toepiece and straps. 1903.

The Lilienfeld binding Alpine ski with movable steel sole. 1903.

Torgerson's handy binding with driving belt and straps. 1903.

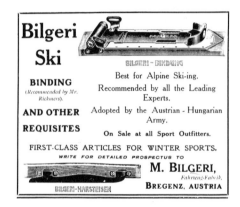
Binding ad in book of 1911.

Ski boot ad in book of 1911.

# SKI TECHNIQUE DEVELOPMENT

The evolution of modern ski technique began about the 1880s:

1880s    The Telemark-turn period began in Norway.

1896     Zdarsky, the father of the Alpine technique, skied with the snow plow and stem turn.

1909     The start of the Hannes Schneider period and the stem christiania.

1910     The Bilgeri Caulfield, Rickmers' influence, the first logical method of ski instruction.

1910–25  The end of the Telemark period.

1915–30  The end of the "Open Christie."

1920s    The English period of ski racing development.

1930     The invention of the metal ski edge.

1932     F. Schuler's *Ski Mechanics* showed the application of physics to skiing.

1933     Swiss ski schools organized and separated technique from methodology.

1934–36  The Seelos influence.

1935–36  Hoschek and Wolfgang introduced the stem swing approach to instruction and method.

1932–38  Ducia, Reinl, Testa, and Matthias introduced talk of a "twisting technique."

1937–48  The French era of parallel ski instruction.

1945–50  The occupation of Austria Tyrol by France. The French technique was studied by the Austrians.

1950–55  The transition to the Austrian system.

1955–60  A period of the Kruckenhauser and Austrian system influence.

1960–70  The evolution to natural positions for teaching systems.

## FACTORS AFFECTING GROWTH

The factors affecting the growth of skiing are many. It has been ski competition that makes the continuous contribution to the development and evolution of ski technique. Without competition, skiing technique would not have advanced. However, competition has not been the only contributing element. Competition and its influences are directly related to factors concerning the general growth of the sport in Europe and the United States.

*SKIS:* The first ski of importance was the Telemarken Ski from Telemarken, Norway. This ski was shorter and wider than skis used previously. It was similar to the shape of skis today; it had a curved tip, and the boot was held with a thong. Modern-day skis are a product of the Telemarken Ski.

Hickory and ash have always been the best wood for skis.

Wood remained popular until the mid-1950s when metal skis received a good share of the market in the United States. Nevertheless, the wood ski is predominantly utilized in the world today. An important advancement in skis and equipment was the introduction of the steel edge in the 1930s. This made possible the skiing of packed slopes and affected the evolution of ski technique. In the 1960s epoxy and fiber-glass skis were widely used.

*BINDINGS:* The design of bindings has changed rapidly since 1890. The first metal binding was made around 1900, by Fritz Huitfeldt in Norway. It was so successful that it was employed in skiing for over twenty-five years. The binding consisted of a piece of iron slipped through a mortise under the ball of the foot and bent up around the toe. An adjustable strap was laced across the toe. Various combinations of long-thongs and buckles were utilized to hold the heel from turning back and forth across the ski. No attempt was made to hold the heel to the ski. Since 1925, many modern advancements in bindings evolved. Probably the development and promotion of the safety binding is the most important safety advancement in equipment.

*BOOTS:* Early boots were of the moccasin type. The boots have advanced with the bindings in direct demand to the needs and/or to the limitations of existing equipment. In other words, as technique became better understood, better equipment was designed to meet the requirements. In 1966, plastic boots were popular.

*POLES:* The Lapps used a single heavy pole as a weapon. One pole was common for skiing until the early 1900s. The pole was placed between the legs. After 1907, two poles became part of the ski technique. The early poles had no rings on the ends. The trend in lengths of poles has changed many times: poles were long until about 1942; short poles became popular and remained so until 1949, and the trend was then toward long poles. The first commercial bamboo poles were introduced about 1900. Since World War II, many advancements in pole design and materials have helped the evolution of modern ski technique.

*CLOTHING:* Improvements in materials and clothing design have helped to popularize skiing as a style sport. After World War II, manufacturers of clothing recognized the postwar revolution in skiing. The shift from mountain-touring to downhill-skiing demanded the design of clothing suited to the new ski techniques.

Famous racers have been the trend setters. The racer's style in skiing and ski wear has often become the gospel. Lightweight, warm clothing has been an important factor in the evolution of ski technique. Because of these new concepts in ski wear, elegance grew out of functional design.

*GEOGRAPHIC:* The geographic comparison of Alpine Europe to the United States has a bearing on the growth of skiing. In Europe the amount of land available for agriculture has been limited for hundreds of years. Therefore, farmers moved to the mountain areas, and this group became the first skiers. This has not been true in the United States. The United States agricultural belt is located primarily in the valleys and the plains. Furthermore, all of Alpine Europe will fit geographically into an area approximately the area in square miles of Colorado, Kansas, and parts of the Texas panhandle.

*ECONOMIC:* Many economic conditions have influenced the growth of skiing. The growth of capitalism in Europe and the United States has made it possible for people to have more spending money. The reduction in the work week and the trend toward family vacations has increased the demand for recreational facilities.

Economic depressions have had an impact. This has been good and bad. During the great Depression in the 1930s, skiing received an important shot in the arm. The Civilian Conservation Corps built roads and cleared ski areas during the thirties and early forties. The CCC cut the first ski trail in the U.S. on Cannon Mountain in Franconia in 1932. Many of the access roads and trails of the western United States were built by the CCC and the United States Forest Service program for ski area discovery and development.

*WARS:* Wars have had an effect on the growth of the sport and on the method and techniques of skiing. Hannes Schneider's experience with troops in Austria during World War I contributed to the knowledge of organization and supervision of ski classes. The aftermath of two wars exposed thousands of troops to skiing as a recreation.

*FACILITIES:* The availability of and access to ski areas naturally has affected the growth of skiing. Similarly, the lack of uphill facilities in Europe and the U.S. until about 1948 has been cause for change in ski techniques. The increase in skiers has caused congestion of facilities and trails and changed the terrain from open, smooth slopes to bumpy moguls. As slope and area conditions change, so does the need for variations in teaching methods.

*PROMOTION AND PUBLICITY:* Skiing has advanced through the individual efforts of men and women who have promoted the sport in countless ways. These people taught others to ski, built tows and lifts, cleared ski areas, organized clubs, promoted and organized ski races, and told the story of skiing whenever anyone would listen.

The popularity of skiing in the 1920s and 1930s in Europe can be attributed to a great extent to the movie industry. Ski movies were made in the twenties; newsreels showed vacationers skiing in Europe. The newsreels also showed competition and promoted the sport. This unfortunately had an adverse effect in that it often depicted skiing as dangerous—especially ski jumping.

The promotion of skiing by resorts and railroads during the 1930s helped to accentuate the growth of skiing. The ski trains in New England created the demand for ski schools and uphill facilities. The Union Pacific's promotion of Sun Valley—"Fun under the Sun"—gave Hollywood-glamour to skiing. This also provided nationwide publicity that was unparalleled in skiing.

The 1932 Winter Olympics and National and International FIS events helped skiing to grow in the U.S. With the growth of skiing as an international sport, ski technique has grown in proportion.

Nevertheless, evolution of teaching methods and techniques has been subject to the rigors of nationalism, individualism, misunderstanding, and the lack of communication because of economic, geographic, and language barriers.

Hannes Schneider said in 1938, there is an old Austrian saying: "Gray is all theory but the grayest the one about the ski."

| DATE | THE HISTORICAL EVENT | THE SIGNIFICANCE |
|---|---|---|
| 1880s | Skiing in U.S. where Norwegian populations are found. Skiing in Montreal and Ottawa. The Norwegian Ski Technique is a straight run, a Telemark turn, and open christiania. | U.S. and Canadian skiing will be years behind Europe. Techniques were adapted to rolling hills—not steep Alpine slopes. No bindings used. |
| 1888 | Father Fridtjof Nansen crossed the southern tip of Greenland on skis with a group of six. | Nansen's book, translated into many languages, had an impact upon skiing. It received worldwide attention, attracted other skiers, *i.e.,* Paulke, Hoek, Iselin, and Zdarsky. |
| 1890 | Nansen's book, *Paa Ski Over Grönland,* is published. | |
| 1890s | Wilhelm Paulke, a German, was the first pioneer of mountaineering. Henry Hoek was one of the first Germans to race and one of the greatest ski mountaineers. Christopher Iselin, father of Swiss skiing, was founder of Swiss Ski Federation. First Swiss ski club formed. | The pioneers were early proponents of skiing, equipment, mountaineering, etc. |
| 1894 | Colonel Bilgeri introduces military skiing to the Austrian Tiroler Corps. | Bilgeri's experience will prove of value later. |
| 1896 | Mathias Zdarsky experimented with the sport with Norwegian skis in the early 1890s, and in 1896 wrote the first illustrated ski manual, *Lilienfeld Schilauf Technik.* He used short skis and one pole. | Zdarsky is the father of the Alpine Technique; he contributed snowplow and stem turn. Wrote first treatise on avalanches. |
| 1901 | Zdarsky is the first person in Austria to have taught skiing on a regular basis. He has 612 pupils. | His technique is called the "Lilienfeld Technique." His military courses for masses extended to Germany and Switzerland. |
| 1901–02 | French Army organizes first military ski classes with Norwegian instructors. Italian ski club formed at Turin. | Civilian skiing is still in its infancy. |
| 1903 | Ski Club of Great Britain is formed. | |
| 1904 | Zdarsky has 1,000 students. Survives an avalanche, in later life, with over eighty fractures; lives to an age of seventy-two. National Ski Association of America is formed by Carl Tellefsen. Victor Sohm holds ski courses in the Arlberg using the Norwegian Technique. | Jumping is popular—NSA has sixteen clubs by 1906. Sohm teaches Hannes Schneider, who is fourteen years old, to ski. |

| DATE | THE HISTORICAL EVENT | THE SIGNIFICANCE |
|---|---|---|
| | *Ski-Running* is written by E. C. Richardson, C. Somerville, and W. R. Rickmers. | First ski book in the English language. |
| 1905–06 | Zdarsky sets a torlauf near Lilienfeld. | Continued race until 1938. It did not have effect on downhill skiing. |
| 1906 | Henry Hoek writes *Der Ski.* | It is Norwegian Technique based on Zdarsky's stem system. |
| 1907 | Schneider receives a call from St. Anton-am-Arlberg to be a ski teacher. | With the sport of skiing so young, Schneider has time to practice and experiment. |
| 1908 | Fritz Huitfeldt describes a type of slalom in a book called *Kria.* | Huitfeldt invented the first bindings with toe irons in 1894. |
| 1909–10 | Schneider invents the stem christiania after he experiments with the Telemark. | Schneider races in Switzerland, wins. Starts his method of instruction. |
| 1910 | Colonel Georg Bilgeri, an Austrian Army officer, who was once challenged to a duel by Zdarsky over a description of a stem turn, writes *Der Alpine Skilauf.* | Bilgeri's book analyzes the Zdarsky and Norwegian ski techniques. |
| 1910–11 | Vivian Caulfield writes *How to Ski;* W. R. Rickmers writes *Skiing for Beginners.* Marius Eriksen uses the Telemark turn to be champion of Norway for ten years. | English begin to show influence upon skiing. Caulfield deals a mortal blow to the single stick (pole). |
| 1911 | C. J. Luther writes *Der Moderne Wintersport.* | He introduces the term, "stem christie." |
| | Editor's Note: Paulke and Caulfield were opposed to the Lilienfeld Technique. So were the Swiss. This amounted to christianias and Telemarks with Alpine skiing. | In time both the Lilienfeld and pseudo-Norwegian techniques were blended into the stickless stem turn and stem christie. |
| 1912 | Schneider has a staff of two instructors. The Telemark turn begins to lose its influence in ski technique. However, it is to be taught for twenty-five years in some parts of the world. | Schneider develops a class system with three stages—beginner, intermediate, advanced. He systematizes the sport so it can be taught. |
| | *Skiing* is written by Arnold Lunn. | Lunn talks of downhill skiing without a stick. |
| 1916–18 | Schneider teaches skiing on a mass scale to Austrian Mountain Troops. The supervision of classes and instructors becomes a necessity of ski school organization. | Schneider discovers need for supervision of instructors and ski classes by director of ski school. |
| 1916–25 | A successor to the Telemark turn was the open christie. This was and still is called the scissor christie. It was seen in this country in part of the West until World War II. | The open christie name came from the Norwegian village of Christiania. |

| DATE | THE HISTORICAL EVENT | THE SIGNIFICANCE |
|---|---|---|
| 1920 | Canadian Amateur Ski Association is formed.<br><br>From 1920–30, ski technique evolution stands still. Turns are made by a stem and weight change. There is little rotation and no sideslipping. Most skiing is in deep snow. The uphill facilities are limited; there are few skiers by present standards. | Modern-day ski racing becomes important in Europe and starts in North America.<br>In the 1920s an Englishman, Sir Arnold Lunn, contributes a lasting significance to skiing. He studies technique and snow, and writes books on mountaineering. Lunn revolutionizes competitive skiing. Sir Arnold Lunn's slalom is adopted into the Olympic program. |
| 1924 | Federation International de Ski (FIS) formed. Ski instructors meet at St. Christoph for a discussion of a ski course.<br>First International Downhill and Slalom and first Parsenn Derby founded. | All instructors and schools adopt the Schneider Arlberg Technique.<br>The rapid development of racing arrives—British influence arises. |
| 1925 | German and Austrian Ski School directors meet at St. Anton. | |
| 1926 | First downhill race held in the U.S. at Dartmouth.<br>Hannes Schneider and Dr. Frank write *The Wonders of Skiing*. | Racing becomes an international sport.<br>The Schneider influence is now written and published. His influence is felt. |
| 1927 | Arnold Lunn writes *A History of Skiing*. He discusses a proposed Arlberg-Kandahar with Hannes Schneider. | History is now recorded for skiing. |
| 1928 | Sir Arnold Lunn organizes the first Slalom Race—the Arlberg-Kandahar.<br><br>Erling Strom is America's first and only ski instructor (at Lake Placid, N.Y.). | <br><br>Strom is one of the pioneers of American and Canadian skiing. He saw the early potential of Stowe. |
| 1928–30 | Rudolph Lettner, an engineer from Salzburg, invents and patents the steel edge. This provides narrow-tracked running and turning. Skiing is started in the Pacific Northwest of the United States. | The steel edge effected the eventual elimination of the deep crouch position in skiing and revolutionized ski technique. |
| 1931 | By 1931, the first ski school in the United States is in operation at Peckett's Inn on Sugar Hill in Franconia, N.H. The school was begun in December of 1929, by Sig Buchmayr. He charged $1 a lesson. | Buchmayr is the first man brought from Europe to teach skiing in the U.S. He taught the Arlberg crouch with extreme down-up-down motion. |
| 1932 | In 1932 F. Schuler's *Ski Mechanics* is published in Switzerland.<br><br>The first ski trail is cut at Franconia. The Third Winter Olympic Games is held at Lake Placid, N. Y. | This will become the basis for the Swiss Technique.<br><br>The games contributed to the interest shown in winter sports in the U.S. |

| DATE | THE HISTORICAL EVENT | THE SIGNIFICANCE |
|---|---|---|
| 1933 | The Swiss ski schools organize and a two-week instructor course is held. Fifty instructors and directors attend. This number will increase to one hundred by 1936.<br><br>The Swiss ski schools decree: That the ski school director has the task of transmitting to his instructors that which is learned in special classes.<br><br>The training of ski instructors begins to take on importance.<br><br>Attenhofer develops the first complete all metal cable binding. | At this meeting is the first attempt to segregate technical knowledge (explanation and demonstration) from methodology. This separation was to enable the teacher to build up lessons logically and in an interesting manner and to pick out the right aspect of the technique and to instruct as individually as possible.<br><br>This will combine with the steel edge to accelerate technique and racing development. |
| 1934 | The first rope tow in the United States is built at Woodstock, Vt.<br><br>Hannes Schneider at St. Anton is teaching the Low Arlberg crouch. | This is the first of many tows in New England.<br><br>The crouch was awkward with the feet apart, etc. |
| 1934–36 | Anton Seelos, Austrian racer and trainer, coaches the French team which includes Emile Allais. Seelos uses a technique with complete body-rotation and counterrotation with an up-unweighting. | Makes an important impact upon skiing. Allais discovers that Seelos uses almost exclusively parallel turns. |
| 1936 | Max Dercum begins a ski school near Dodge Ridge, Calif. | |
| 1935–36 | Dr. F. Hoschek and Professor Freidl Wolfgang start a new approach to teaching skiing. Hoschek's system emphasizes:<br>(1) Rotation.<br>(2) Up-unweighting.<br>(3) Uphill swing (uphill christies) to reach the downhill swing, the parallel swing and the stem swing. | Hoschek's study into the field of instruction would influence methods of instruction in large ski schools by 1938–40. |
| 1936–38 | Rotation will be the established technique for skiing by 1938. However, in 1936, others dispute this theory. Four authors write books on the concept of "twisting skiing." One book by Toni Ducia and Dr. Harald Reinl in Austria and the other by two Swiss—G. Testa and Professor E. Matthias. The "twisting technique" was misunderstood and generally rejected. These people were far ahead of their time.<br><br>Ducia and Reinl help instruct the French team in France. The French do not adopt the Ducia–Reinl technique. They go their own way (the French Allais).<br>(1) Up-unweighting is discarded.<br>(2) Downward and forward movement with accentuated rotation is the chief characteristic of the French technique. | All four authors came from different regions and independent of each other developed the same fundamental principles for their technique and teaching system. The number of skiers who could demonstrate the technique was too small to make it popular.<br><br>The success of Seelos influenced the French. |

| DATE | THE HISTORICAL EVENT | THE SIGNIFICANCE |
|---|---|---|
| 1937 | Austrian ski instructors meet on technique at St. Christoph. Hannes Schneider, Toni Ducia, Dr. Hoschek, Dr. Freidl Wolfgang, and others attempt to explore the teaching situation. | There are too many points to be compromised; the time is not ripe for uniformity. |
| | Otto Schniebs has a ski school at Woodstock, Vt. (started 1935) and Whiteface, N.H.; Hannes Schroll School is at Yosemite; Otto Lang establishes schools at Mt. Rainier and Mt. Baker. Sun Valley is built. | Because of publicity skiing becomes popular in all snow sections of the United States. |
| | Emile Allais, France, wins the FIS downhill and slalom. | Allais' parallel technique startles the ski world. |
| | Canadian Ski Instructors Alliance formed. | |
| | The Swiss Ski Schools feel too much attention is given toward stemming in ski teaching. | A change is coming in ski technique. |
| 1938 | The Swiss by 1938 have eliminated the notion of extreme forward lean and rotation. Swiss eliminate lower stem—keep body in a high position, weight is placed on the stemmed upper or outside ski. | Swiss feel the most important factor in technique is weight shift to the outside ski of the turn. |
| | The follow-through of turns used a forward drop for unweighting and rotation. | |
| | The Arlbergers (Austrians) rotate from the shoulders and use lateral pressure (rotation) to pivot the skis. | Arlberg is extreme forward rotation. |
| | The Swiss use a counterrotary motion but pivot with the direction of the turn and the skis. | Swiss are more or less square to the skis. |
| | A difference erupts between the Arlberg and the Swiss. Swiss emphasize the sideslipping—which the original Arlberg did not. The Swiss find that less body motion achieves the same result as the exaggerated forward swing. The Swiss find that with less rotation there is less recovery between turns. | Technique becomes a subject of discussion and the modern evolution of ski technique begins. |
| | The French School adopts the Allais Technique. | Allais brings important new concepts to ski teaching: |
| | *Ski Français* by Allais, Paul Gignoux, and Georges Blanchon is published. | 1. That in ski teaching methods there can be dynamic changes. |
| | National Ski Patrol is formed. | 2. That these changes often are an indirect result of racing necessities and techniques. |

| DATE | THE HISTORICAL EVENT | THE SIGNIFICANCE |
|---|---|---|
| 1939–40 | The outstanding differences in the Allais approach are:<br><br>1. Discarding of the stem position as the basis of learning christies eliminates the sequence of snowplow, snowplow turn, stem turn, and stem christie.<br>2. Allais begins with sideslipping; he feels that skidding the skis is most important and should be taught first; he teaches the snowplow later.<br>3. Hip blocking is used to convey body rotation to the skis.<br>4. The Allais Technique emphasizes equal weighting of both skis. | The Allais system proves to the ski teaching world the importance of sideslipping, edge control exercises, and uphill swings (christies) in ski teaching methods.<br><br>Edge control exercises are incorporated into ski school methodology. In the Arlberg method—free rotation—the leverage was dispatched into the ankles and feet. The French used hips to convey rotation to the skis. This represented a mechanical advantage. |
| 1939–46 | The war years stop the development of skiing. Some is done in Switzerland, Austria, France, and the United States, but it is limited.<br><br>Skiing plays a military role in some combat areas, and is used for recreation and the transportation of troops.<br><br>Skiing is introduced to thousands of troops during and immediately after the war. It serves postwar recreation for Allied Occupational Forces in Europe and Japan. | The lack of skiing and facilities during the war creates a postwar demand for the sport that is phenomenal. In the United States, neither resort facilities nor ski schools are able to meet demands until late 1940s. |
| 1946–48 | Ski resorts in Austria are occupied by France. French instructors train racers and conduct courses for the military.<br><br>The Austrians feel that the French technique is not as important as the course of instruction.<br><br>Austrian teachers begin to follow the basic thought of Hoschek— "on the direct road to swinging." | The French are studied by the Austrians.<br><br>French use uphill christies and parallels without the stems and plows.<br><br>The Austrians feel that the stem swing is the central point of ski instruction. |
| 1948–49 | Status of ski techniques in 1948 is summarized as follows:<br><br>*Swiss:* Developed each individual student according to ability. The Swiss did not stress standardization of methodology.<br><br>Unweighting is up-down-movement. Uphill stem is used. Turning is done on tips of the skis with unweighted heels. The Swiss use the snowplow and stem turn approach. Shoulder movements are not emphasized.<br><br>*French:* The French technique calls for unweighting with a down movement—followed with a forward lean with rotation. Although | The Swiss deserve more credit for progress in modern ski technique development. They have always stressed sideslipping. In the late forties the Swiss stressed the importance of hips, legs, and ankles as a means of effecting turning power.<br><br>Some advocates of the French overexaggerate the rotation and forward lean. The Ruade is misused. |

| DATE | THE HISTORICAL EVENT | THE SIGNIFICANCE |
|---|---|---|
| | the Allais technique stressed equally weighted skis at the start of the turn, the outer ski is gradually weighted more toward the end of the turn. | The French reach a peak in 1948 with the victories of Couttet and Oreiller at the 1948 Winter Olympics. |
| | *Austrian:* The Arlberg stresses sideslipping but with stemming maneuvers. The system uses upper-body rotation with a lower ski stem. | Arlberg strength was in the transition phases. |
| 1948–50 | The extreme movements of the official French technique does not permit the quick action necessary to change direction through the moguls. The increasing number of skiers since World War II produces moguls in an amount that has never before been experienced. Many new lifts are built in Europe and the U.S. | The need for a great deal of traversing and sideslipping in the French technique makes the technique impractical for teaching at areas with trails only. |
| | Because many of the old teachers have been lost in the war, the new generation of European skiers is largely self-taught. | The Arlberg technique was satisfactory in its day and does not change. |
| | The Arlberg technique, with stems, wind-up, and follow-through, is not adapted to mogul skiing. | |
| 1948–52 | Some of the younger skiers in Europe begin to ski with a relaxed style and use hip and leg action for rotation. Shoulders are held still. | These turns are called counter-shoulder turns. |
| | At the 1948 Olympics, Nogler, Schoepf, and Mall are watched and imitated by many of these going racers and skiers. | Ski school methodolgy and ski technique is in a static state. |
| | The Austrians have watched and imitated the French and see the need to develop a new system of racing that will allow faster movements of the shoulders in the bumpy terrain and in slalom running. | It becomes necessary to ski with the lower body and counterrotation. These early turns were called reverse shoulder. |
| | In 1950–52 Toni Spiess, Christian Pravda, Hans Nogler, and Franz Gabl win international victories. | The new ski technique becomes a basis for the Austrian success. |
| 1950–51 | The "new technique" begins to show up in the form of "mambo and wedeln." It is used by Allais and Stan Tomlinson in 1951, in Chile. Stein Eriksen uses "reverse shoulder" in 1950. | Mambo and wedeln are used by Allais in Squaw Valley. |
| 1951 | The I International Ski School Congress is held at Zurs, Austria, in order to reach an agreement on a unified technique by the Central European ski schools. The congress was called by Austrian initiative, and the Austrian team demonstrated their current "rotation technique." Nothing new develops. No mention is made of the fact that the Austrian experts are developing a new technique based on the natural intuition and elementary reasoning of a natural ski style. | The congress becomes a basic means of international discussion and comparison of ski techniques and teaching methods. |

| DATE | THE HISTORICAL EVENT | THE SIGNIFICANCE |
|------|---------------------|------------------|
| 1953 | The II International Ski School Congress is held in Davos. The Swiss demonstrate their technique based on rotation of the body in the direction of the turn. They show a forward and downward movement of the body toward the tips of the skis.<br><br>Italy, France, and Austria are invited by the congress officials to demonstrate their teaching methods. | The French National School and the Italian National School of Skiing at Sestriere both show uniform techniques, but the Austrians fail to show a unified technique. The new method developed by Kruckenhauser ends in defeat. |
| 1954 | Professor F. Wolfgang, Professor S. Kruckenhauser, Dr. F. Rossner, and other Austrian experts are watching the 1954 FIS "with interest." They analyze slow motion movies of the best racers to help develop the new ski technique. | The new technique with hip and leg action resulting in "the comma" is built into a teaching method by the Austrians. |
| 1955 | The III International Ski School Congress at Val D'Isere brings to view the new development of ski technique by the Austrians. The Austrian contingent show their new technique to be practical, new, and interesting. The Austrians show shortlinked christies. (This system was a new concept that eliminated upper body rotation even in the beginning exercises.)<br><br>The Austrian system shifts the initial turning impetus from the shoulders to the lower body in all levels of learning from beginning to advanced. The technique places emphasis on the forward sideslipping, the stem turn, and the stem swing. These basics—sideslipping, stem turn, and the stem swing (stem christie)—are the central point for ski instruction. These are the basis for advancement to the parallel swings, and the Austrians consider the stem swing the most important turn for the general use by all skiers. This was a theory of instruction method advocated by Dr. Hoschek twenty years before.<br><br>The Austrians publish Professor Kruckenhauser's *Osterreichischer Schilerplan*—The Austrian Ski Teaching System. | The theory of movements of the new technique is not clear, but the Austrian demonstrations create an international controversy over technique. A dispute begins even in Austria over the new technique and rotation. One reason for eliminating rotation in the elementary stages is that it is not always needed in difficult turns that require an advanced inner shoulder. Thus, rotation is not logical to use in the elementary stages. This new development brings ski schools closer together.<br><br>This book makes it possible for the world's ski teachers to study the Austrian technique. |
| 1956–57 | There are different expressions of the new technique:<br><br>1. Austrians lead to parallel turns through a series of stem exercises. Austrians talk of "comma position."<br>2. The French lead to parallel from the parallel sideslip positions. French use the term, "hip angulation." | The American Ski Schools are thrown into turmoil by the "new technique"—the Wedeln. Early translations and articles by Willy Schaeffler, Clemens, Hutter, and others promote the demand for the new technique by the skiing public. |

| DATE | THE HISTORICAL EVENT | THE SIGNIFICANCE |
|------|----------------------|------------------|
| 1957 | The "new technique" confusion in the U.S. is caused by:<br><br>1. Bad and incorrect translations.<br>2. Translations by nonexperts.<br>3. Personality cult among some ski schools and teachers.<br>4. Publicity.<br>5. People writing about technique who are not qualified.<br>6. Experimental theory.<br>7. The instructor or school who "want to be left alone." | The size of the country and the thinking of the progressive ski school heads bring about the demand for some national meetings to discuss mutual problems of technique, method, certification, etc. |
|  | Otto Steiner represents the United States at the IV International Ski School Congress at Storlien, Sweden. | Steiner attends at his own expense, and contributes to the international acceptance of U.S. ski teachers. |
|  | G. Joubert and J. Vuaret publish *Ski ABC* in France describing the French version of "angulation—flexion and recoil." | Translations are soon made in English. The book helps to both clear and confuse the technique question. |
|  | U.S. Division instructor associations and certification groups become conscious of the need for understanding the technique question. Rallies, symposiums, and clinics are held throughout the U.S. | Willy Schaeffler, chairman pro-tem, NSA, Ski Instructors Committee, calls a meeting in Arapahoe Basin in April; committee attempts to form a national instructors group to exchange ideas. |
| 1958 | The Alta meeting: The East and the West meet to discuss and demonstrate technique methods and mechanics. Attending the meeting are: Kerr Sparks, Paul Valar, Jimmy Johnston, George Engel, Jr., Willy Schaeffler, Bill Lash, Alf Engen, Junior Bounous, Ed Heath, Dr. Chuck Hibbard, and Earl Miller. It is agreed to hold annual meetings. This meeting helps to clear the controversy over "the new technique." | First national meeting of the National Ski Association Ski Instructors Certification Committee where all divisions are represented. It is discovered that the national problem is not only certification but technique, recruiting, and training of instructors, and related business problems of ski teaching. |
| 1958–59 | *The Official Austrian Ski System* is translated by Palmedo. Doug Pfeiffer writes *Skiing with Pfeiffer.* Bill Lash publishes *An Outline of Ski Teaching Methods.* Hutter writes books and articles which are published in the U.S. Hugo Brandenberger writes *Skimechanik—Methodik des Skilaufs* in Switzerland. | These works make available studies that are directed to the ski teacher and the student teacher. Pfeiffer and Lash explore the "whole turn concept" of unweighting—edge change and turning power—which was originally discussed in the 1955 Far West Instructor's Manual. |
| 1959 | V International Ski School Congress in Zakopone.<br>1. Austrians strong in their approach to teaching.<br>2. Swiss are not strong but show better balance. | Alpine nations agree to settle all technical arguments by using physical laws. |

| DATE | THE HISTORICAL EVENT | THE SIGNIFICANCE |
|---|---|---|
| | 3. French show "split-rotation"—rotation with uphill shoulder to initiate the turn; shoulders are used in the end phase of the turn.<br>4. Italians show the best style—relaxed with neutral positions. | Progressive thinking comes out of the Congress. Less up-and-down action is seen in demonstrations; misused terms that are lost in translations are cleared up. |
| | Paul Valar, Franconia, N.H., represents the United States at the Zakopone Congress. | National unity on technique seems an apparent evolution. |
| | A National Ski School Meeting is held in Arapahoe Basin under direction of the NSA Certification of Ski Teachers Committee. Valar reports on the Poland Congress. Each division of the NSA fields a demonstration team. A remarkable similarity of national unity on technique seems an apparent evolution. | Instructors from all the divisions begin to work together. |
| 1960–61 | The French: Jean Vuarnet, James Couttet, Paul Gignoux, and Emile Allais develop a natural ski style called "Christiania Leger." In this system the body remains square over the skis at all times.<br><br>The French produce a movie called *Christiania Leger,* which proves to be some of the world's best ski photography. The film is distributed worldwide. | An analysis of French competition styles showed that French racers combined elements of their technique with the "heel thrust" movements of the Austrian technique. Critics claimed that the French had returned to rotation. |
| 1960 | Over seventy-five instructors meet to discuss teaching psychology, technique, etc., at the National Ski School Meeting in Brighton, Utah. | Divisional demonstration teams show that only minor differences exist in these finished school forms. |
| 1961 | In May, 1961, The Professional Ski Instructors of America is formed at the National Ski School Meeting at Whitefish, Mont. All division demonstration teams show final technical forms of skiing. | Bob Parker of Denver takes and studies hundreds of photos of the Whitefish skiers and proves that in end forms skiers look similar. |
| | Instructors of the U.S. ask for a clarification of ski techniques. In November, 1961, PSIA is incorporated in the State of Minnesota. | Parker suggests that an American Ski Technique exists. |
| | PSIA becomes accepted by organized skiing and the United States ski industry. | Allais and Perillat demonstrate at Whitefish for the American teachers. |
| 1962 | VI International Ski School Congress is held in Italy at Monte Bandone. Six nations demonstrate: French show split-rotation (turn is started with rotation and finished with a reverse). Austrians show less extreme; all nations show a trend toward normalcy in demonstrations. | The United States fields a team under the direction of PSIA.<br><br>The United States and PSIA receive international recognition. |

| DATE | THE HISTORICAL EVENT | THE SIGNIFICANCE |
|---|---|---|
| | The French fail to agree on a basic presentation of their technique, while the other nations show modified forms of the classic Austrian system. | |
| | The Italian demonstration team takes the Congress by surprise with their smooth demonstration of the "Italian Modern Technique." | The Italian technique had been modified slightly by the French influence. |
| | The PSIA, at its convention meeting in Alta, Utah, studies the films and reports of the VI Congress at Bandone. The American Ski Technique is demonstrated at the Alta convention. | The American Ski Technique receives national acceptance. |
| | The Board of Directors of PSIA defines the Finished Technical Forms based on a three-year study of demonstrations at national meetings. | The technique is separated into three parts: Finished Technical Forms, Ski Mechanics, and Methodology. |
| 1964 | The PSIA publishes *The Official American Ski Technique*. | |
| 1965 | The VII International Ski School Congress is held at Badgastein, Austria. Twenty-two nations attend. | The American team does well. American technique depicts natural positions, total motions, and emphasizes the importance of the traverse. |
| | Alpine demonstrations are given by Americans, Canadians, Austrians, Japanese, Germans, Italians, and French. | USA, PSIA to host the Eighth Interski at Aspen, Colorado in 1968. |
| 1966 | PSIA publishes *The Official American Ski Technique*. | Complete revised book shows that PSIA accepts evolution as part of the American ski technique. |
| 1967 | Georges Joubert and Jean Vuarnet publish *How to Ski the New French Way* (English translation). | This is the first book outlining the advanced skiing maneuvers so completely. |
| 1968 | Eighth Interski at Aspen. Seventeen nations see American skiing. The theme: Skiing is for Everyone. Best Congress, with one thousand attending. | Splendid organization. Americans have outstanding performance and choreography in demonstration. Austrians introduce wide-track; French, advanced skiing; Swiss, trick skiing. Lectures given on short skis, graduated length method. Karl Gamma, Swiss, proposes an international technique. |
| | International Professional Ski Instructors Meeting in Zermatt. | Further international effort to arrive at a universal ski technique. |

| DATE | THE HISTORICAL EVENT | THE SIGNIFICANCE |
|---|---|---|
| 1969 | International Professional Ski Instructors Meeting at Cervinia, Italy. | Continuation of progress at the international level. Nations agree to some compromise. |
| | PSIA alters basic principles to allow for down-unweighting and some rotation (axial motion). | Allows for advanced skiing maneuvers. |
| | PSIA meets with Canadian instructors at Toronto. | A further step toward unification and international cooperation. |
| 1970 | Revised edition of *The Official American Ski Technique* is published by Cowles Book Company of New York City. (Earlier editions sold thirty thousand copies.) | Includes basic technique, advanced skiing. Greatly expanded. |

# CERTIFICATION OF SKI TEACHERS

A need for an examination for ski instructors became apparent in Europe after the end of World War I. But it was not until 1928 that the Austrian State Ski Teacher Examinations were decreed.

The examinations were a result of examples set by guilds of Alpine guides, encouragement of European amateur ski organizations, and a desire of ski teachers for recognition. First examinations gave diplomas that granted teachers the "right to teach." It was at this time that ski instruction in Austria was made subject to law, and a state-examining commission was appointed.

In the early examinations a preliminary test or precourse was given to weed out candidates whose ability was below the necessary average. Examination requirements included: general skiing information, history, mountaineering and snow, teaching ability, equipment, touring, doctrine of instruction and training, skiing ability, health and first aid, and a written examination covering theory.

In the season of 1937–38, the Board of Directors of the United States Eastern Amateur Ski Association admitted that a serious situation had developed concerning ski instruction. Many phonies were teaching in the East. At the same time, true professionals such as Benno Rybizka and Sepp Ruschp were also teaching. The Eastern Board felt that unless something was done the promotion, reputation, development, and growth in the sport of skiing would be affected. Dr. Raymond S. Elmer, USEASA President, realized that the organization could not certify instructors without the help of the professional teachers. He therefore appointed Ford Sayre the Certification Chairman as well as committee members Roland Palmedo and Bjarne Langslett. The first exam was conducted in February, 1938.

The term "certification" was used, not "licensing." Licensing means "permission from a legal authority." The plan was designed to protect the skiing public from unqualified and incompetent instruction and to assure them of a high standard of approved instruction of uniform quality everywhere. The National Ski Association of America's convention in Milwaukee, December 5, 1937, approved the certification project.

The National Ski Association eventually established a Ski Teachers Certification Committee. The association members never were certified or examined instructors, and no mention of ski teachers or ski teacher certification ever appeared in the by-laws or constitution of NSA. The committee later evolved into a coordinating group of the division certification plans.

The eastern plan has always been comprehensive, impartial, and very strict, and it was soon introduced to other divisions as a model plan. It was in 1942 that plans for certification of instructors was adopted by the Pacific Northwest Ski Association and the Rocky Mountain Ski Association. The standard cost of exams in 1942 was $15. In 1946, Charles Proctor and Cortland T. Hill held a ski instructors' meeting at Sugar Bowl, California. The purpose was to drill the instructors in proficiency, to demonstrate, to teach, and to conduct a certification examination. Hill was named Chairman of Certification of Ski Teachers for the California Ski Association, and in 1947 he was the first chairman of the National

Ski Association Certification Committee. Hill was an early advocate of "teach the same system." In 1946, the Southern Rocky Mountain Association gave a ski teachers' test at Berthoud Pass, Colorado.

W. S. "Slim" Davis in 1947 was Chairman of the Southern Rocky Mountain Association Certification Committee. He stated: "Through the combined forces of public opinion and Forest Service cooperation, unqualified instructors were effectively kept from our ski areas during the season. Also, our tests are slightly different from those given by other divisions. We are looking forward to the day when a standard national certification procedure for ski instructors can be established." It was Davis who helped write the original Special-Use Permit requiring certified instructors on national forest lands.

It was in 1947 that the Intermountain Amateur Ski Association had its first certification plan, and the California Ski Instructors Association was working with the California Ski Association with Otto Steiner as the instructors' representative. The California Certification Committee stated at that time: The functions were to plan and work with the National Committee for unified national certification objective. In 1947, the Pacific Northwest Ski Association had revised their plan for certification of teachers. And in this year the East had reactivated the ski teacher's certification and the policy included a one-week training, precourse for the exams. The East now formed: (1) a Certification of Professional Ski Instructors, and (2) the Certification of Amateur Teachers. It was in this year that the Professional Instructors of New York State formed "The Empire Unified System."

In 1948, Dot Hoyt Nebel, Joseph J. Berry, Jr., and the New York Professional Ski Instructors published the *Empire Unified Technique,* which was probably one of the first instructor manuals in this country. The New York group felt that unification, adoption of a modern technique, and certification of the best trained instructors combined with a university of ski teachers that would meet once a year to consolidate new ideas and methods was necessary. This was an early attempt to separate technique from method.

In April of 1948, the California Ski Instructors Association was formed at Mammoth Mountain, California. The group incorporated an official technique and attempted to develop a na-

tionally recognized guild of Professional Ski Instructors, and it passed a resolution to organize a National Federation of Ski Instructors. The original California organization was later called the Far West Ski Instructors Association.

Cortland T. Hill, NSA, Ski Teachers Certification Chairman, attended the Southern Rocky Mountain Ski Instructors Exam at Berthoud Pass, Colorado, in December, 1948. Of the twenty-one candidates who took the exam, three passed: Gordon Wren, Jack Snoble, and Willy Schaeffler. The results were violently protested. The candidates thought the exam was too strict. But it was Hill's opinion that a strict exam would produce a higher quality of teachers, and so the results of the exam stood.

In February, 1949, Hill published an article in the *American Ski Annual,* and stated: The functions of the National committee were: (1) to bring about in each division an organization for the certification of ski teachers, and (2) to work out a procedure for national certification in addition to the divisional certification—as soon as the divisions have started to operate effectively. By 1949, many of the divisions were starting their certification programs, yet the Central and Northern Rocky had none. Hill was premature. The divisions did not have a national meeting and discussion until 1958.

Hill planned a meeting at Alta of the national committee. He said the problem of technique would be discussed, and he wanted to establish a similar meeting in the eastern and central divisions. He said, "It is your chairman's desire that all [7] divisions will be able to standardize examination procedures, qualifications of applicants, and the categories of classifications of instructors." Hill could not accomplish any national organization because no effective organization existed on all divisional levels.

In December, 1949, the Pacific Northwest Ski Association held its first large-scale examination. The use of the instructor and apprentice class of certification came into being.

By the 1950s, the United States Forest Service became an important factor in the certification of ski teachers. The Forest Service realized that there was delay, red tape, different methods of certifying, and too much difference in standards. They threatened to do their own certifying of ski teachers in those areas under permit. Most of these areas were in the Western United

States. In 1949, less than 5 percent of the ski areas operating in the East were under United States Forest Service Special-Use Permit.

The Rocky Mountain Ski Instructors Association and the Intermountain Ski Instructors Association formed their own independent groups in the season of 1950-51. This was done because of the suggestion of Bob Johnstone, President of Sun Rocky Mountain Ski Association, and F. C. Cozial, the Intermountain Division Certification Chairman. Both felt that it was time that instructors ran their own affairs.

The National Ski Association Committee for Certification of Ski Teachers Chairman, Ken Cuddeback, proposed provisions for certification by the NSA on April 23, 1952. Officers of the Far West Ski Instructors and Intermountain Ski Instructors Association met in Squaw Valley, California, to discuss a Western Federation of Instructors. This is the first time that a serious communication concerning national certification became apparent. The National Certification Committee met in June, 1952, in Estes Park, Colorado, to discuss Cuddeback's national plan. The plan did not allow for existing instructors associations, and a national instructors association was to be seriously discussed. At the Estes Park meeting were: Gordon Wren, Bob Law, John Litchfield, Sepp Ruschp, Bill Lash, Junior Bounous, Phil Clark, Jr., and Willy Schaeffler. An informal group called the National Council of Ski Instructors was formed as a result of this meeting. The purpose of the group was to study national certification problems.

Bill Lash, President of the Intermountain Ski Instructors Association, wrote in the summer of 1952 a twenty-seven-page report on the development of the certification of ski instructors in the United States. The evolution toward a national affiliation of certified instructors was discussed. The report was distributed throughout the NSA and it served to educate and create interest. In the summer of 1952, there were only 355 Certified and Associate Ski Instructors in the United States.

The first attempt to organize instructors nationally was in 1953 when Tommi Tyndall's National Council of Ski Instructors was formally proposed. The Lash report served as a basis, and a new certification plan was submitted to the NSA convention in May in New York City. A committee was formed composed of Kerr Sparks, Roland Palmedo, Wayne Fox, and Paul Smith. A plan for a national pin was made by Sparks. However, the committee had no operating funds, and the 1953 plan was never achieved.

The Far West Ski Instructors Association published the first effective manual for instructors in 1954, and Otto Steiner of the Far West was appointed chairman of the NSA Certification Committee. On his committee were: Bill Lash, Kerr Sparks, Jay Johnson, Hal Kihlman, Toni Matt, and Willy Schaeffler.

By 1955, the Central Amateur Ski Association attempted to certify instructors. The Northern Rocky Mountain Division had only two instructors and no plan. National plans were dormant.

Chairman Steiner in 1956 called a NSA certification meeting in Sun Valley. He had a "desire" for unification. In attendance at the Sun Valley meeting were: Willy Schaeffler, Bill Lash, Junior Bounous, Hal Kihlman, and Don Clark. There was no eastern or central representative. A proposal was sent as a result of this meeting to the NSA Aspen Convention to recognize a national council of ski instructors. It was tabled.

The United States Central Certification Plan became a reality with Jimmy Johnston as chairman in 1955. Dr. Chuck Hibbard of the Northern Rocky Mountain had a plan for certification by 1957. Willy Schaeffler was chairman pro tem of the NSA Committee in 1957, while Otto Steiner represented the United States at the IV International Ski School Congress at Storlien, Sweden. Johnston's weight was to be largely felt on the national level for many years to come.

In April, 1957, the NSA Certification Committee had met in Arapahoe Basin. They asked to be recognized as an independent organization of ski instructors. The proposal was written by Junior Bounous, Willy Schaeffler, George Engel, and Jimmy Johnston. It was presented at the Mt. Hood NSA convention and the proposal died.

The year 1958 was probably the most significant for national ski teaching development and history. It was at Alta that Chuck Hibbard, Bill Lash, Junior Bounous, Paul Valar, Ed Heath, Willy Schaeffler, Kerr Sparks, Joe Harlacher, Jimmy Johnston, Alf Engen, and George Engel, Jr., met for the first full meeting of the NSA Certification Committee. It was at this meeting that East and

West were finally able to discuss internal organization, technique, method, and certification problems.

In 1959, Paul Valar reported on the V International Ski School Congress in Poland at a National Ski School meeting in Arapahoe. Certification was discussed by many examiners across the country. This meeting was extended and in 1960 over seventy-five instructors and ski school directors met in Brighton in May at the second annual ski school meeting. An actual exam was used with twenty-one examiners (three from each of the seven divisions). The test exam proved that there was little difference among competency of division examiners. As a result of these Alta meetings, the third annual national ski school meeting was held in Whitefish, Montana, in May, 1961. Since plans to form a national organization with and by the divisions had proved fruitless, the Professional Ski Instructors of America was organized on an individual basis. Its first directors and organizers were: Bill Lash, Paul Valar, Jimmy Johnston, Max Dercum, Doug Pfeiffer, Curt Chase, and Don Rhinehart. The NSA Certification Committee was left in the hands of these organizers until November when it was disbanded, and the PSIA took over that function. The National Ski Association approved PSIA, and by December the PSIA Certification Committee held a national meeting in Brighton, Utah. The committee worked toward a national standard. At the end of 1961, there were 1,350 certified and associate instructors in the United States.

The National Ski Association in 1962 dropped its certification committee and left the responsibility to PSIA. In April, 1962, twelve ski school directors from the United States attended the VI International Ski School Congress in Italy. The United States placed a demonstration team at the Congress under the banner of PSIA. The team was praised by the European sports press, and it was at the Italy meeting that the International Ski Instructors Association was formed. The organization differed from the Congress. It was in 1962 that all seven divisions accepted request for transfer of full instructors. In October, 1962, PSIA announced the American Ski Technique. In November, 1962, PNSIA incorporated as a professional group.

Edward P. Cliff, Chief, United States Forest Service, approved PSIA as a coordinating body of certification in the United States in 1963, and the PSIA Certification Committee agreed on a national scoring system grade card, fee, etc. The PSIA *American Ski Technique* manual was published in December, 1963. This had a great influence on certification standards.

The PSIA Certification Committee in 1964 asked the divisions to adopt a standard exam to allow more candidates to take exams in several locations at different times. The PSIA and the division chief examiners recognized that the divisions need to meet the demands for new ski teachers. By the end of 1964, there were 1,221 certified instructors and 926 associate instructors, for a total of 2,184. In this year 1,118 candidates took the exams and 561 passed.

Seven divisions in 1965 tried the multiple small exam system—a uniformed score card, scoring system, and master score card. All divisions had now accepted uniform transfer applications for full instructor. At the end of 1965, there were 1,453 certified instructors and 1,102 associate instructors, for a total of 2,555 instructors in the United States. In this year, 1,237 took the exams and 570 passed. By 1966, there were 1,235 associate and 1,715 certified instructors for a total of 2,950 instructors in the United States. The number of candidates examined in that year were 1,293; the number passed were 677. This was an increase of candidates of over 77 percent in three years.

The national committee met in 1967 and again in 1968 at the Interski in Aspen. It became apparent that there was not going to be a national standard of scoring and examining or examining procedures. Some divisions wished to continue with the practices proved effective for many years; for example, the precourses used in several divisions.

The Far West Ski Instructors Association continued to examine in four techniques where most divisions examined in the American system—although this is not mandatory; it is only a standard. By the spring of 1969 (of the year 1968–69), 1,991 candidates were examined. The total number passed were 954, for a percentage passing of 47.9 percent. By 1969, there were 4,264 instructors in the United States. The Eastern Division continues to have only full-certified instructors. In 1969, George W. Savage was appointed, by President Willy Schaeffler, National Certification Chairman of the Professional Ski Instructors of America.

HANNES SCHNEIDER—GLENDESPRUNG

*Photo by C. J. Luther, 1912*

*Courtesy Herbert Schneider*

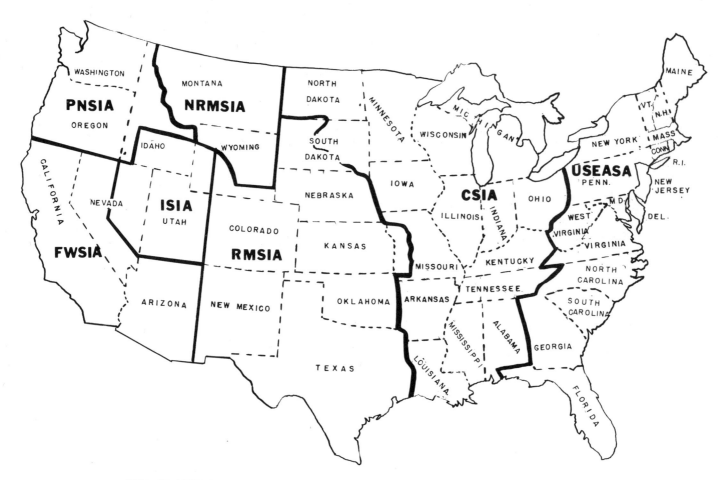

ASIA(ALASKA)

GEOGRAPHIC BOUNDARIES OF THE EIGHT SKI INSTRUCTORS ASSOCIATIONS
OR CERTIFICATION GROUPS OF THE UNITED STATES

ASIA—Alaska Ski Instructors Association
CSIA—Central Ski Instructors Association
FWSIA—Far West Ski Instructors Association
ISIA—Intermountain Ski Instructors Association
NRMSIA—Northern Rocky Mountain Ski Instructors Association

PNSIA—Pacific Northwest Ski Instructors Association
RMSIA—Rocky Mountain Ski Instructors Association
USEASA—United States Eastern Amateur Ski Association,
Certified Professional Ski Teachers Committee

# BASIC TECHNIQUE

# THE AMERICAN SKI TECHNIQUE

The American Ski Technique is based on seven basic principles—

1. Natural Positioning
2. Total Motion
3. Unweighting
4. Axial Motion
5. Edge Control
6. Weight Transfer
7. Leverage

—and is composed of three separate parts:

1. Demonstration Forms
2. Teaching Methods—(Methodology)
3. Theory—(Ski Mechanics and Biomechanics)

The separation of these components permits a definite and logical interpretation of a ski technique.

The demonstration forms, based on the seven basic principles, and the theory can be established as a standard. The American Ski Technique does not dictate style. Minor differences caused by body build, temperament, and outside influences are recognized. As long as a skier uses the same basic principles, he is skiing the same technique.

The teaching methods are the approaches used to arrive at the demonstration forms. The method allows for the needs of the in-dividual student, ski school, and instructor. They will adjust their teaching schedule to the terrain and snow condition. Any known teaching exercise or system needed to help the student may be applied. However, the school or instructor must never lose sight of the end goal: the demonstration forms.

## THE BASIC PRINCIPLES

*AXIAL MOTION:* Motion about the body axes. Rotation and counterrotation are common forms of axial motion.

*EDGE CONTROL:* The adjustment of the angle between the skis' running surface and the snow. The tilting outward of the upper body to form a bend at the hips. This position moves the hips in toward the slope in a traverse or turn. The skis will angle uphill to find the necessary lateral edge resistance.

*LEVERAGE:* The effect of the skier's weight forward or back of center of the skis. In basic technique, it is important that the skier places his center of gravity ahead of the ball of the foot. This helps maintain balance, facilitates turning, and compensates for increase in speed.

*NATURAL POSITIONING:* This considers the relation of the human anatomy to balance under normal conditions on skis. The skeleton carries the weight of the body rather than the muscles of the legs. The skier should be relaxed at all times.

*TOTAL MOTION:* Total motion implies that muscle action is a product of the entire body. Body motion should be continuous throughout the maneuver. Movements may be divided into components for descriptive purposes.

*UNWEIGHTING:* The reduction or elimination of the skier's weight on the snow.

*WEIGHT TRANSFER:* A movement of weight toward one ski.

*Class Exercises*

# SKI TERMINOLOGY

*ANGULATION:* This is the leaning away from the slope with the upper body in a traverse or toward the outside of a turn. The knees and the hips move toward the slope that controls the bite of the edges.

*BACKWARD LEAN:* A body position placing the center of gravity of the skier behind the ball of the feet.

*CAMBER:* A curve in ski contour from tip to tail.

*COUNTERMOTION:* Gradual motion around the vertical axis of the body opposite the direction of the turn to maintain natural positioning.

*COUNTERROTATION:* A quick turning motion in one part of the body resulting in a counteraction in another when resistance is markedly reduced.

*FALL-LINE:* The shortest line down a slope or the line a freely moving body would follow if influenced only by gravity. The fall-line is referenced to the skier's immediate location.

*FORCES USED IN THE CHANGE OF DIRECTION:*

(a) Deflecting force—resistance from the side; snow resistance (friction).

(b) Gravitational force (weight).

(c) Muscular force (balance).

(d) Turning force; controlled by:

    (1) Forward or backward lean (leverage).

    (2) Moving one ski at an angle to direction of travel (stemming).

    (3) Axial motion.

    (4) Transferring weight.

    (5) Edging.

*FORWARD LEAN:* A body position placing the center of gravity ahead of the ball of the feet.

*INITIATION OF TURNS:*

(a) Stemming (placing one ski at an angle to direction of descent and transferring weight).

(b) Hopping (complete unweighting and abrupt displacement of the ski tails).

(c) A forward or backward lean in a traverse (leverage).

(d) A circular motion of the body (axial motion).

(e) Stepping around.

(f) Changes in terrain.

*METHOD:* The procedure or way of teaching, the manner used in working toward a maneuver.

*OUTSIDE SKI:* The ski describing the outside arc of a turn.

*PARALLEL CHRISTIE:* A turn executed with both feet together and parallel at all times.

*PLOWING:* Simultaneous stemming of both skis.

*RISING MOTION:* Relatively slow rising, resulting in change of body position. It is not used for the purpose of unweighting; it, in fact, temporarily increases the weighting of the skis.

*ROTARY HEELTHRUST:* The displacement of the ski tails by down motion and turning of the legs.

*ROTATION:* A motion around the longitudinal axis of the body in the direction of the turn.

*SINKING MOTION:* A slowdown motion used as a preparation for an up or rising motion.

*SKI POSITION:* Relative position of one ski to the other; closed, open, plowed, stemmed, or advanced.

*STEERING ACTION:* To maneuver by

(a)  Ski position and weight transfer.

(b)  Leverage.

*STEM CHRISTIE:* A christie turn initiated by stemming one ski.

*STEMMING:* Lateral displacement of one ski tail.

*TECHNIQUE:*

(a)  The manner in which technical details are treated or used in accomplishing a desired aim.

(b)  A ski-teaching system.

*TRAVERSE:* Descent at an angle to fall-line.

*TURNING:* Changing direction on skis.

*TURNING FORCES:* Gravity and resistance.

*TYPES OF UNWEIGHTING:*

(a)  Up-unweighting—a quick extension of the body upward; an extreme lift will produce a hop.

(b)  Down-unweighting—a flexion of the body by quickly bending at the ankles, knees, hips, and waist.

(c)  Rebound-retraction—a temporary relaxation of the legs.

(d)  Use of terrain.

*UPPER SKI, LOWER SKI:* Ski position in the traverse.

# DEMONSTRATION FORMS

*STRAIGHT RUNNING:* Skis are flat on the snow and slightly apart. Weight is equally distributed; ankles, knees, and torso are slightly flexed. The body is perpendicular to the skis at all times. The elbows are flexed, hands hip-high, forward, and slightly off the body.

*STRAIGHT SNOWPLOW:* Tips of the skis are together. Tails are displaced at equal angles from the fall-line. Surfaces of the skis are at right, lateral angles to lower legs. Weight is equally distributed on both skis.

*SNOWPLOW TURN:* From the straight snowplow, angulation accompanied by slight countermotion transfers weight toward one ski which becomes the outside ski of the turn.

*TRAVERSE:* Crossing the slope; skis are together, with more weight on the lower ski. The edges are controlled by angulation. The uphill ski, hip, and shoulder are slightly advanced.

*STEM TURN:* From the traverse, the uphill ski is stemmed, eliminating the traverse position. The outside shoulder moves slightly back. Weight is gradually transferred to the stemmed ski as the upper body is angled over weighted ski. After change of direction, traverse is resumed.

*FORWARD SIDESLIP:* From the traverse, the sideslipping is started with unweighting, decreasing angulation, and releasing the edges. The maneuver is completed as traverse is resumed.

*CHRISTIE UPHILL:* From the traverse, the turn is started with unweighting and axial motion. This is followed by a sinking motion combined with angulation. The arc of the turn is completed as the skier rises to a new traverse.

49

*STEM CHRISTIE:* From the traverse, the uphill ski is stemmed with an accompanying sinking motion. With an up-forward motion the weight is transferred to the stemmed, outside ski. The inside ski is advanced and brought parallel as the skis enter the christie phase. This is followed by a sinking motion combined with angulation and a slight countermotion. The arc of the turn is completed as the skier rises to a new traverse.

*PARALLEL CHRISTIE:* From the traverse, the turn is prepared with a sinking movement. With an up-forward motion and counterrotation the weight is transferred to the outside ski. The inside ski is advanced and the edges are changed. This is followed by a sinking motion combined with angulation and a slight countermotion. The arc of the turn is completed as the skier rises to a new traverse. A check is used if the slope is steep or the snow resistance is great. The preparation of the turn can be facilitated by a displacement of the tails downhill resulting in more angulation and edging. This is accompanied by a pole-plant at the end of the down motion.

51

*PARALLEL WITH CHECK*

52

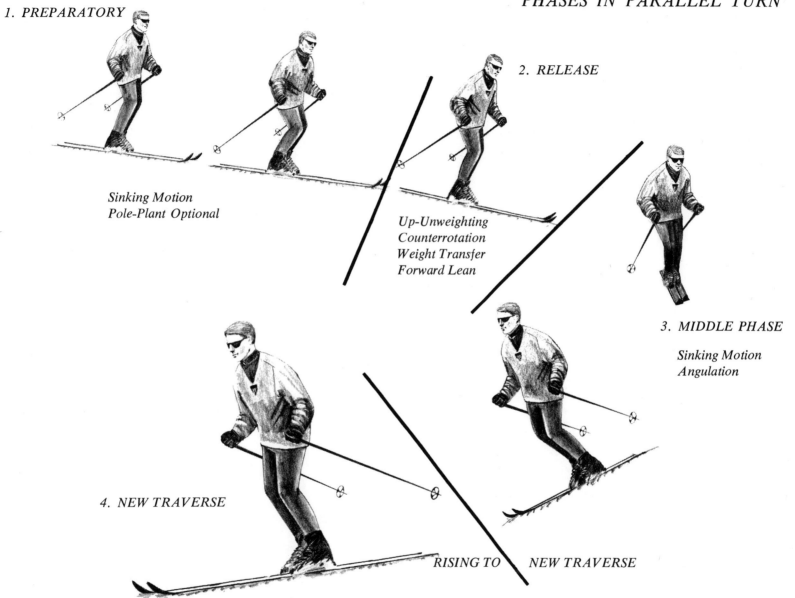

## PHASES IN PARALLEL TURN

**1. PREPARATORY**

*Sinking Motion*
*Pole-Plant Optional*

**2. RELEASE**

*Up-Unweighting*
*Counterrotation*
*Weight Transfer*
*Forward Lean*

**3. MIDDLE PHASE**

*Sinking Motion*
*Angulation*

**4. NEW TRAVERSE**

*RISING TO      NEW TRAVERSE*

**Basic Concepts: Total Motion—Natural Positions**

# PHASES IN PARALLEL WITH CHECK

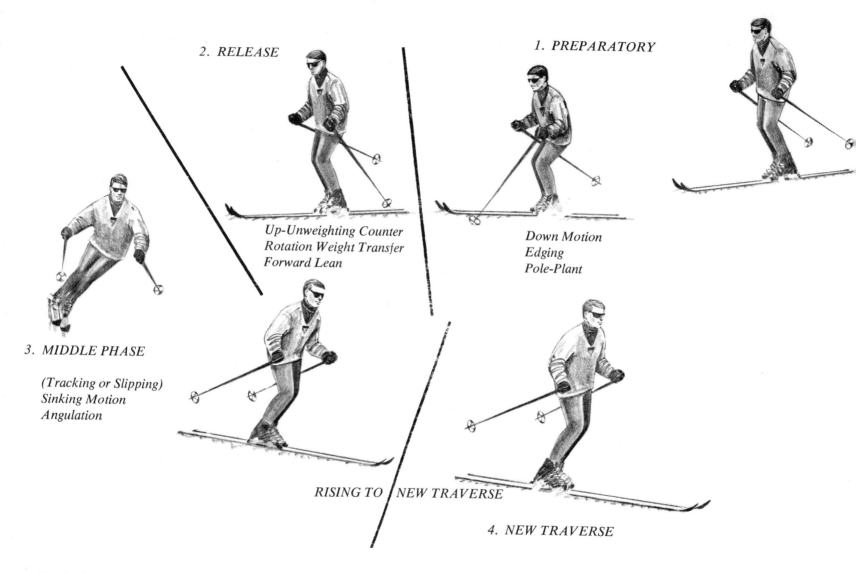

**2. RELEASE**

**1. PREPARATORY**

Up-Unweighting Counter
Rotation Weight Transfer
Forward Lean

Down Motion
Edging
Pole-Plant

**3. MIDDLE PHASE**

*(Tracking or Slipping)*
Sinking Motion
Angulation

RISING TO NEW TRAVERSE

**4. NEW TRAVERSE**

**Basic Concepts: Total Motion—Natural Positions**

*SHORT SWING* (FFD): Consecutive parallel christies without traverse. Control is maintained by angulation and edging. The pitch of the slope governs the type of turn used: for steep slopes more angulation and a pole-plant are needed for control while these movements are not mandatory on gentle slopes.

*SHORT SWING ON A TRAVERSE*

# SKI MECHANICS *by Ed Wyman*

A new skier would hardly ski expertly with only book knowledge of the theory of the mechanics of skiing. Yet for the technician—teacher or instructor—attention must be given to the kinetic and dynamic principles involved.

An instructor knowing basic ski mechanics can improve his explanation, sharpen his demonstrations, and better analyze and correct the skiing of his students.

Proper understanding and use of technical terms help establish the high professional standard in teaching skiing on a truly national and international level.

For years instructors had to rely principally on their "feel" about how they skied. It was necessary to impart this "feel" to pupils as a part of a "technique" of learning to ski. Good instructors with an art for teaching could often produce results. However, the real technician of today is now the teacher to rely upon.

A skier begins to move while standing on his skis on a slope as a result of the force of gravity (weight) overcoming friction (resistance). The product of the skier's weight component down the slope and his time in motion equals his momentum; the speed he attains depends upon the steepness of the slope, the texture of the snow, air resistance, the surface and area of the ski bottoms.

No slope is a uniformly inclined plane. Slopes change from convex to concave, and from gentle to steep. The slope has holes, bumps, and difference in snow texture. These variations cause changes in velocity. Each variation must be accompanied by a corresponding counteraction—a change in body position—or a loss of balance occurs.

Two ways exist for descending a slope: Going straight with parallel and equally weighted skis, or traversing the slope and linking the traverses by turns. The ski, of course, by natural tendency takes the most direct line down the hill—similar to a ball rolling down a hill.

A natural force that must be considered is the muscular force of the human body. Muscular force often acts to a disadvantage because of misuse by the skier. Proper ski instruction can alleviate many of these disadvantages.

Speed is controlled by the angle of traverse as a skier descends the slope. The turn is only a transition to change direction between traverses. It is important to understand that each change of direction from one traverse to another in the opposite direction at moderate speeds can happen only if the skis are unweighted—either separately, or simultaneously—because an edged and weighted ski will tend to continue in its immediate direction of travel.

Every controlled, coordinated turn on skis involves a reduction of weight, a change of edges, an exterior force, and reapplication of the skier's weight. Turns are classified into five general types:

1. Static turns (kick turn, stepping around).
2. Steered turns (stemmed turns).
3. Christie turns (counterrotation, rotation turns).
4. Jump turns (turns in which skis leave the snow).
5. Step turn running.

*LEAD CHANGE IN SKI TURNS:* The lead of the uphill ski in a traverse is in direct relation to the steepness of the slope and angle of the traverse. This will affect the amount of weight distribution between the lower and upper ski. Each change from traverse to traverse requires a weight change to the outside ski, a change of lead of the inside ski, and a change of edges. The timing of the change of weight, lead, and edges is in direct proportion to the rate of speed of the skier and his change in momentum. These are also governed by the type of turn.

Any introduction to ski mechanics should be directed toward dispelling controversy; for example, the controversy of teaching counterrotation or pure rotation turns in skiing. Both turns work on the same principle—conservation of momentum. This law has many applications in skiing. The basic law may be stated: An action in one part of a system must find an opposite reaction in another part of the system.

An experiment illustrating this law in physics would be to stand on a stool with a swivel seat and turn the shoulders abruptly in one direction. In reaction, the lower body will rotate in the opposite direction. Similarly, twisting the lower body causes an opposite reaction of the shoulders. Newton's law studied in the applied sense to skiing becomes the physical theory explaining counterrotation and rotation. *This can only be true in the applied sense when resistance against the skis has been greatly reduced or eliminated,* as is true with the swivel stool example.

In practice counterrotation and rotation appear to be opposite techniques. In theory the same principles of Newton's law are working. In rotation (classic rotation), the action of starting the turn is by movement of the shoulders and chest toward the direction of the turn. This action has no immediate effect because of lateral resistance of the snow (reaction) against the skis. Only by blocking the rotation of the upper body at the hips can this impetus be transmitted to the skis. Thus, the turning action is caused by blocking of the hips which allows the earlier momentum of the shoulders to be transmitted to the skis. Therefore, contrary to popular belief, the turning of the skis is not the reaction to the initial shoulder rotation. For example, when the shoulders' rotation is not arrested by blocking the hips, it will result in "overrotation" and upset the skier's equilibrium.

The practical differences are that counterrotation turns can be started more quickly because of the relatively lesser displacement of the center of mass of the skier in counterrotary turns. For example, in skiing ice or hard-packed snow, the body weight is more directly over the skis. This applies downward pressure on the edges enabling the skier to ride out the skid of the skis without falling. (The counterrotation possesses the advantage of having an immediate effect and is useful for high-speed fall-line turns, moguls, ice, etc. In classic rotation turns, the timing does not permit such short radius turns.) Rotation is slower and has a more gradual motion which can be advantageous in slow-speed turns on open slopes and in deep or difficult snow conditions where resistance of the snow is comparatively great.

A combination of rotation and counterrotation may sometimes be advantageous. This concept is called split-rotation. A skier in deep snow, for example, may initiate a turn with shoulder rotation and finish it with countermotion. This will utilize advantages of both forms and reduce the possibility of overrotation causing an overpowering of the end of the turn. On the other hand, the turn may be started with counterrotation and changed to shoulder rotation at the end of the turn, bringing the body square with the skis so that the next turn may be initiated by either method more easily.

In understanding Newton's theory it is possible to see that no glaring inconsistency exists between ordinary rotation and counterrotation. The same physical laws apply. Every well-coordinated movement in athletics is introduced by an opposing motion that will guarantee the development of total and harmonious movement. Furthermore, the problem of initiating the turn is important but should not be overrated. Other problems are equally important, *i.e.,* skier's biomechanics—his agility, flexibility, and promptness of reaction and feel for movement, as well as his mental attitude.

It should be kept in mind that in the accompanying diagram the center is the physics of skiing. This will not change. At the perimeter of the outer circle are found rotation and counterrotation. All forces from these should gravitate toward the center. The extreme will place the skier on a tangent to the circle, and he goes into orbit.

Theory, practice, and experience have taught that in skiing the most advantageous body position is one that will keep the center of gravity, the focus of all motion, low enough to maintain equilibrium while keeping flexibility and freedom of action. This is applied up and down, forward and backward, laterally, and in rotation and counterrotation. Every change of body position is related to the center of gravity since the total mass acts as though all of it were located at this point. A rigid body attached to a pair of skis will be unable to maintain balance.

It is because of the adaptability of the human body that one is able to change to meet all the different factors encountered during a descent. In most cases, the skier is able to place the center of mass, the focal point of his equilibrium, in a position that all these natural forces acting against each other are harmonious. Thus, the skier is able to establish a near perfect state of balance.

The study of ski mechanics is important. The day will come when classes of adults will not begin on the slope but will start in the classroom in front of a blackboard.

The study of ski mechanics and ski theory is not new. Ski theory has been the basis of many ski techniques and discussions as early as the beginning of this century. Reference has been made to use of ski mechanics to settle points of discussion in early ski books. These technical discussions were made without actually establishing any practical application. In 1931, F. Schuler, a professor of physics at a Swiss college, produced a ski technique based on ski mechanics. The book was written at the request of the Swiss Interassociation of Skiing and changed ski teaching completely in Switzerland. The publication also created many problems. The teachers from the mountains could ski well but were ill-equipped to follow the theoretical skullduggery. On the other hand, the instructors from the cities could not ski as well as the mountain boys but were better able to follow the theory approach. Over a period of years, many ski school directors realized that the

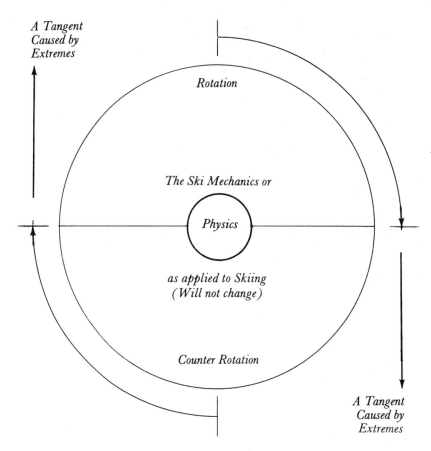

*A Tangent Caused by Extremes*

*Rotation*

*The Ski Mechanics or*

*Physics*

*as applied to Skiing (Will not change)*

*Counter Rotation*

*A Tangent Caused by Extremes*

instructor from the city was a better teacher and could explain the complex maneuvers with ease to his pupils. He had the advantage of being able to analyze the cause of the mistake in a student's skiing without confusing this cause with its most apparent outward effects. This ability led to the satisfaction of the student and led to an ever-increasing inclusion of ski mechanics in Swiss precourses and instructor examinations. Without this solid and well-established base of mechanics it is virtually impossible to come to any conclusion in a discussion about ski technique.

In order to be explicit and to be of practical value, a study of ski mechanics should only concern itself with physics as applied to skiing. The applied physics should limit its application to skiing with the major base forces at work. It should be realized that theory and practice are difficult to unite. Theory must be combined with the practical, professional know-how on the slope to be of value to the ski instructor of today. One of these factors by itself is of little value. Furthermore, theory does not take into account poor ski equipment, differences in snow conditions, or human error. In the final analysis it should be remembered that the points in learning to ski include:

1. *Understanding* (The theory of ski mechanics) by the teacher.
2. *Explanation* of the theory and/or the maneuver to the student.
3. *Demonstration* by the teacher to his class.
4. *Correction:* A recognition of errors and correction of the basic faults of the students.
5. *Practice and patience* by the students.

In addition, the objective is to teach control, safety, form, and finally speed. The ski teacher's responsibility becomes complex. Professor Kruckenhauser, head of the Austrian State Ski Teachers Course, once said that his job would indeed be simple if all his instructor candidates were college graduates. They are not and he must take all candidates to the University of Innsbruck for a three- to four-month study of physics and physiology. The allotment of time in a six-month precourse clearly demonstrates the importance given today to the theory of ski mechanics in the Alpine countries.

In 1958, Hugo Brandenberger collaborated in the publication of *Skimechanik—Methodik des Skilaufs* in Switzerland. In 1962, Brandenberger produced another edition, called *Skimechaniks*. This revised discussion of mechanics was the aftermath of the VI International Ski School Congress held in Italy in April 1962. *Skimechaniks* is a book that is a practical study of the applied laws of physics in skiing. Hugo Brandenberger is a professor of physics and mathematics and is considered one of the world's leading authorities on ski instruction and the mechanics of skiing. Professor Brandenberger has served with the Swiss Mountain Troops and has been president of the Swiss Interassociation of Skiing since 1949. He was former chief examiner and director of Instructor Training in Switzerland; he has been the head of the Swiss delegations to the International Ski School Congresses and edits all official Swiss Ski School Journals. The following excerpt from a lecture by Professor Brandenberger makes clear the intent of this portion of the manual:

Analyzing the sequence of motion in skiing we recognize different sources of energy. The sliding on an incline is mainly created by the weight of the skier. . . . The moment we change direction on skis we add resistance from the side. . . . These forces are not created by muscular activity of the skier himself but come from without and are influenced by strictly mechanical aspects such as degree of incline, amount of snow resistance, basic position of the skier and the angle of the ski edges. This is why *mechanical laws can and should be applied*. Confusions here mainly come from the fact that there always are living human bodies involved, different in size, proportions, leverages of joints, and particularly individualistic characteristics, such as reflexes of the muscular and nervous systems, allowing the skier to move his center of gravity at will, quickly and completely changing the forces from without. The skier, of course, harbors in his body considerable strength of his own which he can put to work from within, again modifying the mechanical results. This then, is the true explanation of a good skier's personal style, which is completely dictated by his personal capabilities. In order to achieve unity in ski teaching we therefore should never follow the personal style of one skier. Unity seems only desirable and possible in properly analyzing and applying the forces from without, over which the skier obviously can develop perfect control. [Trans. by Paul Valar.]

DEFINITIONS

1. *MECHANICS:* A branch of physical science dealing with motion and forces associated with material bodies, usually divided into three parts:
   *Statics:* The study and description of masses and forces in equilibrium.
   *Kinematics:* The study and description of motion without regard for the causes.
   *Dynamics:* The study and description of the causes of motion and changes therein.
2. *SCALAR:* A quantity having magnitude only.

Examples: mass, age, number of coins in a pocket, speed, etc.

3. *VECTOR:* A quantity that has both magnitude and direction.
   Examples: displacement, force, velocity, acceleration, impulse, momentum.

4. *RESULTANT:* The sum of two or more vectors. When two or more forces act in concert we must consider their combined effect.
   Examples: (1) A force of twenty pounds east and another of seven pounds west acting at the same point give rise to a resultant force of thirteen pounds east.

   (2) A velocity of thirty feet per second west added to a velocity of forty feet per second north equal a resultant velocity of fifty feet per second in a northwesterly direction.

   We will represent a vector quantity diagramatically by an arrow whose direction is that of the vector and whose length is scaled to its magnitude. The resultant of two vectors in such a representation is the diagonal of the parallelogram of which the two given vectors are adjacent sides.

5. *COMPONENTS* (of a Vector): For convenience in analysis of mechanical situations it is often useful to consider a single vector as though it were the resultant of two or more component vectors.
   Examples: (1) You push on the handle of a lawn mower which makes an angle of 45 degrees with the ground exerting thirty pounds along the axis of the handle. The useful component of this force is that which pushes the lawn mower, the horizontal component—in this case 21.3 pounds. The third vector completing this system is a 21.3 pound force directed toward the ground. (That is why the wheels make deeper marks when you push rather than pull it.)

   (2) You pull a loaded toboggan with a rope whose angle with the ground is 30 degrees, exerting a force of sixty pounds tension on the rope. This puts a vertical lifting force of thirty pounds on the front end of the toboggan and an horizontal towing force of fifty-two pounds.

6. *INERTIA:* The property of matter to persist in a state of

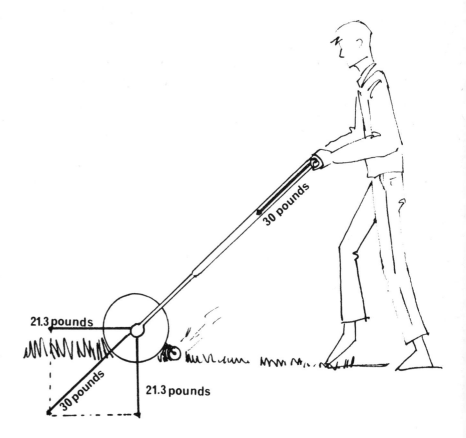

rest or uniform straight line motion. It is a qualitative aspect of matter. Inertia is a property, not a quantity. Inertia is often confused with momentum which is a vector quantity and subject to change.

A large mass like a locomotive requires a large force to set it in motion, and, conversely, a large force to stop it or turn it. A small mass like a Ping-Pong ball requires little force to alter its momentum.

7. *MASS:* The measure of the quantity of matter in a body. Often confused with weight, mass is a constant scalar measure of the reluctance of a body to alter its velocity. The English unit of mass is the slug; in the international system it is the kilogram.

The relationship between mass and weight is given by the following:

m = mass          w = weight          $m = \dfrac{g}{w}$

g = acceleration by weight
   (approx.: 32.2 ft. per second per second or 9.8 meters per second per second at sea level.)

8.  *CENTER OF MASS:* CENTER OF GRAVITY: Focus of all motion associated with a system. The point at which all of the mass or all of the weight of a body may be considered to act. (This point is not necessarily located within any particle of the body.)
    Examples: (1) c.m. of a sphere of uniform density is its geometric center.
    (2) c.m. of a rectangular box of uniform thickness of construction is the intersection of its diagonals.
    (3) c.m. of a boomerang lies outside the body.

9.  *MOTION:* The change in position (displacement) of a mass or part thereof.
    *Forms of motion:*
    1. Differences in direction: straight, curved, circular.
    2. Differences in speed: constant and accelerated. Deceleration is merely another case of acceleration: cf. tossing a body vertically.
    *Note:* To cause motion in a straight line requires only one force. In theory the velocity remains constant (inertia) after the force ceases to act; in reality a velocity not equal to zero is reduced by frictional forces.
    3. Rotation: Motion about an axis (imaginary line through the center of mass) at right angles to the plane of rotation.
    The force that creates this motion must come from outside the axis of rotation.
    *n.b.* It is clear that energy is required to create motions since the action of a force through some finite distance is what gives rise to displacement of matter—overcoming inertia —see definitions of force and energy.

10. *VELOCITY:* Time rate of change of position. The displacement divided by the time interval of positional change.
    As a practical matter we usually consider an average velocity (Units: 44 ft. per sec. = 30 mph = 13.4 meters per sec.)
    (a) Motion in a specified straight line at constant speed is called velocity.
    (b) Motion in an unspecified direction can only be described as speed.
    (c) Instantaneous velocity is always tangential to the path of the moving body at the point in time and space considered. Only in unaccelerated systems is it equal to the average velocity.
    *n.b.* Since motion along a circular path involves a continuous change in direction, this curvilinear motion is *always accelerated* motion even at constant speed, and thus requires a force to maintain it. If the force is removed or "balanced" then inertia dictates straight line motion tangential to the curve.

11. *ACCELERATION:* Time rate of change of velocity. The amount of velocity change (either magnitude, direction or both) divided by the time interval of the change.
    Dimensions: feet per second per second, miles per hour per second, meters per second per second.

12. *MOMENTUM:* Mass multiplied by velocity.
    It is clear that at rest, no matter how massive a body, it has zero momentum. Notice that momentum is a vector quantity since it is the product of a vector and a scalar.
    Dynamics is really the study of momenta.
    Consideration of this property of matter gives rise to Newton's third law of motion: To every action there is an equal and opposite reaction. In more sophisticated terms this law may be stated: In isolated systems momentum is conserved.

13. *FORCE:* (1) The time rate of change of momentum of a mass.
    (2) That which may bring about a change in velocity. (The effect of a force is called acceleration.)
    (3) A push or pull. (The same concept is contained in all three of these expressions to varying degrees of usefulness.)

*Note:* A force is partially defined by Newton's second law of motion: Acceleration is proportioned to the force causing it.

Examples of forces: Impulsive force—blow of a baseball bat.

Torsion—twisting force absorbed in the structure of a rigid body; screw.

Centripetal force—deflecting force causing a body to move in a circular path.

Sources of force available to the skier: gravitational, frictional, muscular. These are classified as mechanical forces.

14. *ENERGY:* Force multiplied by the distance it operates, or the capability of exerting a force over a distance.

Examples: (1) A ten-pound force acting over a distance of two feet does twenty foot-pounds of work = expending twenty foot-pounds energy.

(2) If the above force acts for two feet on a five-pound body at rest, the body will attain a speed of one-quarter feet per second in the direction of the force's action and bears the capability of transmitting all or part of this energy to another body.

15. *POWER:* The time rate of using energy or doing work—force times distance divided by time.

Examples: (1) If the ten-pound force in the above example (energy) must travel the two feet in one-tenth second the required power is two hundred feet-pounds/second = 0.364 horsepower.

(2) If the time interval is a full second only 0.0364 horsepower is needed.

In both cases the same energy is used, the same work is accomplished, and the same velocity is obtained.

16. *WEIGHT:* The force of gravity on a body.

In general usage this term is loosely applied. Weight is a vector quantity whose direction is always taken to be toward the center of the earth.

The term "weightlessness" refers to the condition of a body in free fall when *no other force* is acting on the body.

17. *FRICTION: THE FORCE OF FRICTION:* The force which opposes motion between the contacting surfaces of bodies.

This force acts at right angles to the force which maintains contact of the surfaces and is proportional to that force. Its direction is always such as to oppose the direction of motion (force impelling motion).

Example: A brick on a table exerts a force (weight) in contact with the table. The force of friction is equal but opposite in direction to the force required to move the brick. Two bricks will offer double that friction, either both on the table or one stacked on the other. (There is no summary relation between friction and speed.) Once motion is begun, sliding friction (force) is somewhat less than static or starting friction.

18. *COUPLE:* Two forces acting on the same body at different points from opposite directions.

It follows that their combined effect will tend to impart a rotary motion to the body.

19. *PRESSURE:* Force divided by area.

(Dimensions: pounds per square inch, newtons, per square meter.)

Examples: (1) Equal forces on each end of a thumbtack give different pressures.

(2) The larger the ski, the less pressure it will exert on the snow.

(3) Sharp edges exert greater pressure than dull edges.

20. *MOMENT:* Force multiplied by the perpendicular distance from its point of application to the pivotal point. (Dimensions: pound-feet, meter-newtons.) Layman's equivalent: Leverage.

21. *TORQUE:* The moment of a twisting force.

Example: The force (torsion) applied to the handle of a screwdriver multiplied by the radius of the handle.

22. *IMPULSE:* The applied force multiplied by the time interval of application.

In a conservative system the impulse imparted is equal to the momentum gained.

Example: Let the average force on an arrow by a bow string be twenty pounds and the time of push as the arrow is released be 0.15 seconds. The impulse is three pound-second. For a fifty gram arrow this yields a momentum of about 0.136 kilogram-meters per second (velocity: 2.72 meters per second) in the direction of the arrow's flight.

For further study the reader is referred to *Physics,* by the Physical Science Study Committee, D.C. Heath Company, Boston, Mass. (Available in several languages.) Also informative is Sears and Zemansky, *University Physics,* Addison-Wesley Publishing Company, Reading, Mass.

## ILLUSTRATIONS OF VECTOR ADDITION

The sum of two concurrent forces, $F_1$ and $F_2$, is equal to a single force, R, called their resultant, which acts at their common point.

*CASE I: Forces in the same direction*

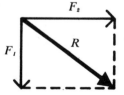

*CASE II: In opposite directions*

*CASE III: At right angles*

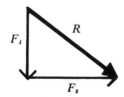

or the more convenient representation:

(For the purpose of addition, a vector may be moved parallel to itself without changing its effect on a point in common with another vector.)

*CASE IV: At oblique angles*

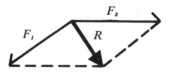   or: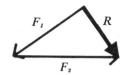

*CASE V:* For three concurrent forces: *at any angles*

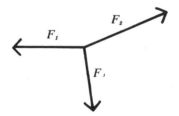

then R is found thus:

or

R may be found thus:

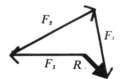

or thus:

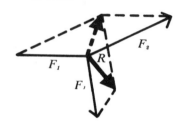

Nonconcurrent, but simultaneous:
*CASE VI*

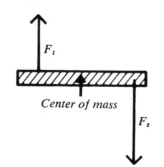

*Center of mass*

produce rotation and R

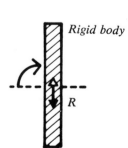

*Rigid body*

*CASE VII*

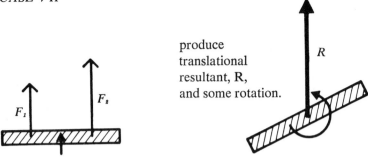

produce translational resultant, R, and some rotation.

Note that the magnitude of the sum of two vectors may be less than, equal to or greater than either component. Only for two vectors acting in the same direction at the same point is the magnitude of the sum equal to the sum of the magnitudes of the vectors.

## AN EXAMPLE OF ACCELERATION WITHOUT CHANGE IN SPEED

(Note: See definitions, page 62)

Fig. I

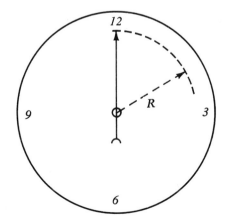

Fig. II

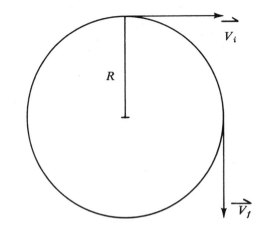

Fig. III

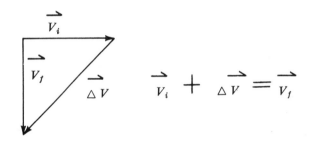

$$\vec{V_i} + \vec{\triangle V} = \vec{V_f}$$

Consider the speed of the end point of a second hand whose length is R centimeters from the center of the clock face. This quantity is given by the expression: $\dfrac{\text{pi } R}{30}$ cm./sec. which is merely the circumference of the circle swept out by the second hand divided by the time interval of the motion (60 seconds).

Its velocity at zero seconds is therefore $\dfrac{\text{pi } R \text{ cm.}}{30 \text{ sec.}}$ to the *right* (Fig. II) fifteen seconds later its velocity is $\dfrac{\text{pi } R \text{ cm.}}{30 \text{ sec.}}$ *down*. At time = 30 sec. the velocity is $\dfrac{\text{pi } R}{30}$ cm./sec. to the *left*, etc.

An acceleration is the change in velocity divided by the time interval of the change.

To calculate the change in velocity, $\triangle \vec{V}$, from time = zero to time = 15 seconds, we must consider that the velocity at the end of this interval is the RESULTANT, $\vec{V}_t$, of the initial velocity, $\vec{V}_i$, and the change in velocity due to centripetal acceleration, $\triangle \vec{V}$.

(Note: For the purpose of vector addition by diagram, a vector may be moved parallel to itself without altering its effect.)

For convenient scaling, let $\vec{V} = R$ centimeters.

From Fig. III we can see the acceleration, $\triangle \vec{V} \div 15$ sec., is directed toward the center with a magnitude of about 0.01 R cm. per sec. each second.

Notice that the speed of the second hand does not change, but its velocity does. For a 20 cm. (about 8 inches) second hand, the end point has a centripetal acceleration of about 2mm./sec./sec. (a little less than a twelfth of an inch per second per second).

## WEIGHT AND ITS DISTRIBUTION

### RESULTANT

W = weight: Each molecule of the skier and his equipment

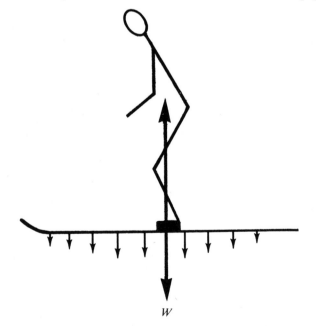

*W*

is attracted by gravity. The resultant, or full, weight is from the center of mass $\triangle$ to the center of the earth. In some body positions the c. m. may be outside the skier's body.

*n.b.* All of the diagrams on these pages are generalized schematics.

## FORCES IN STRAIGHT RUNNING

The weight of the skier divides into two components, P and N.

P = force parallel to the slope. This is the propelling force.

N = force normal (perpendicular) to the fall-line.

W = weight of skier and equipment.
$$(W = P + N)$$

R = Resistance to motion (friction).

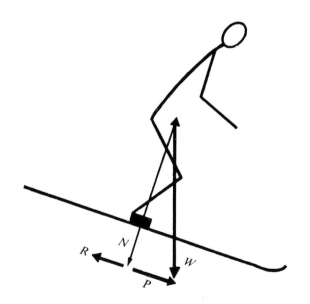

## FORCES IN TRAVERSING

Same as straight running.

P   force parallel to fall-line.

N   force perpendicular to fall-line.

W   weight: Total gravitational force.

R   Component of resistance which opposes **P**.

*Note:* Angle between N and P is always a right angle. Three-dimensional representation in the plane of the paper often distorts this angle.

*Perpendicular to fall-line*         *Oblique to fall-line*

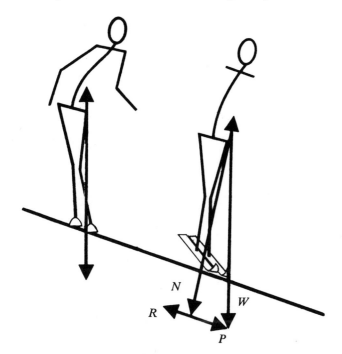

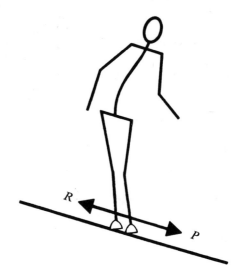

Traverse is maintained as long as resistance, R, is greater than or equal to P.

## VERTICAL SIDESLIPPING

When edges are released R becomes less than P resulting in a uniform sideslip when skier stands centrally. As edges are adjusted to make R equal to P constant speed is maintained.

*Sideslip*

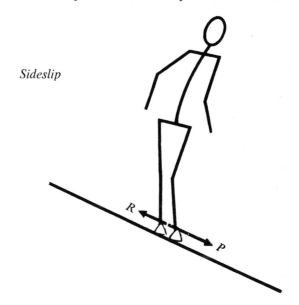

With edges released resistance is quite symmetrical from tip to tail of ski.

With R acting at or near center of ski the weight distribution is critical.

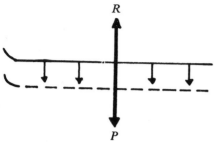

## EFFECT OF BACKWARD LEAN, EDGES RELEASED

R and P again form a couple, forcing tails toward the fall-line.

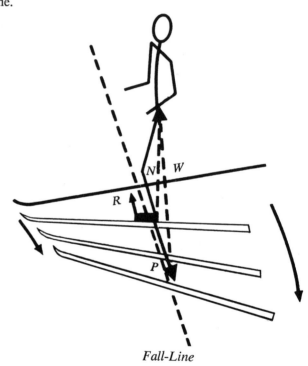

## EFFECT OF FORWARD LEAN, EDGES RELEASED

The displacement of P, forward, forms a couple with R, acting centrally, to bring the skis into the fall-line.

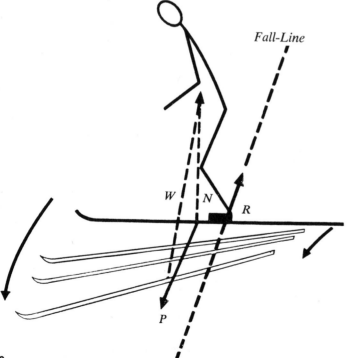

## WITH SKIS EDGED

Resistance (friction) is more dependent upon weight distribution.

### EFFECT OF FORWARD LEAN, SKIS EDGED

There is an increase in R forward of the bindings because of greater width of ski tips.

P and R form a couple that turns skis, and tails slide downhill faster than tips.

This is the guiding principle of all coordinated turns except those special forms of skiing where the skier momentarily forces one or both skis to move with muscle power.

### EFFECT OF BACKWARD LEAN, SKIS EDGED

Is similar to forward lean, skis edged; because tails are wider than binding area, the tips slide downhill faster than the tails.

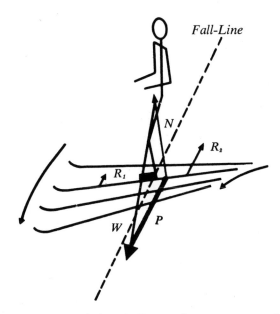

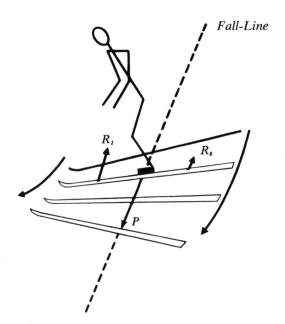

The illustration below indicates the asymmetry of resistance to lateral motion when the skis are slightly edged during forward and backward lean.

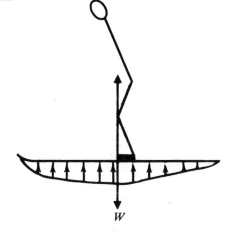

The small arrows represent some of the components of R. The body position determines the resultant of the several small frictional forces.

The leverage effect of the ski aids in these maneuvers, because even a small force acting relatively far from the pivot can equal the turning effect of a much larger force near the pivot.

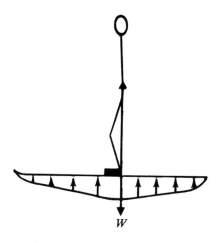

W

Summary:

As the skier's weight is applied more toward tips or tails of sideslipping skis, the more heavily weighted end is forced downhill at a greater rate by the greater gravitational component. When the skier edges the skis gently the increased friction under the weighted end more nearly balances the downhill vector, while the lighter ends slide easily over the snow in a continued sideslip. This is the basis of all steered and low speed christie turns: a greater part of the lateral resistance operates forward of the binding, letting the tails slide around in a wider arc than the tips.

### STRAIGHT SNOWPLOW

$r_1 = r_2$

$r_1 + r_2 = R$ greater than $P$: BRAKING ACTION
$r_1 + r_2 = R = P$: Speed stays the same.
$r_1 + r_2 = R$ less than $P$: Speed increases.

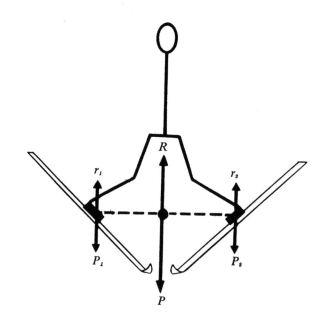

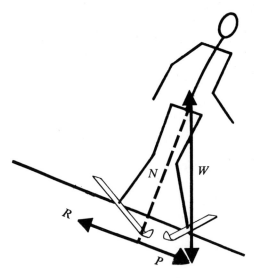

## SNOWPLOW TURN

$r_1$ less than $r_2$: TURNING ACTION

When the individual resistances, $r_1$ and $r_2$ are regulated by proper weight placement, the **P** and **R** components on the weighted ski form a turning couple which deflects the ski as it moves.

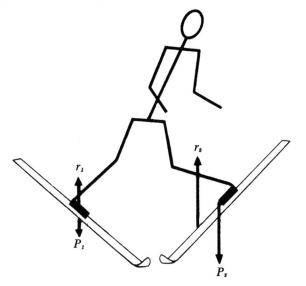

## UNSTABLE

Position makes it difficult to hold edge, reduces resistance, and produces wide skid.

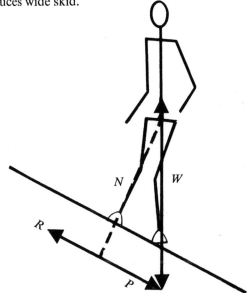

## LEANING IN (Christies)

To maintain balance in a turn, some leaning in is required since the ski bottoms (supporting surface) are inclined to the plane of the turn.

In effect what the skier is doing is bracing against a component of the centripetal force, C, which impels the turn.

An attempt to draw a balanced force vector diagram meets with failure because C is an unbalanced force. If it were balanced there would be no change of path direction.

The thrust, T, which the skier exerts against his skis is the vector sum of his weight component along his axis and a component of C. He feels this as "weight" in his legs and body.

Part of the difficulty in understanding this stems from the notion that every force has two ends. The skier's mass and the earth attract each other with equal magnitude, but we always give weight the direction of free fall. The snow and the skier push with equal vigor on the skis, but gravitational and muscular energy team up to move the skier to one side and the snow to the other. Many skiers feel that they are supplying the force for the turn rather than merely maintaining their balance and carriage over the skis. Gravitational and muscular energy team up to move the skier to one side and the snow to the other, but the real *force* that moves the skier's mass must come from outside the body.

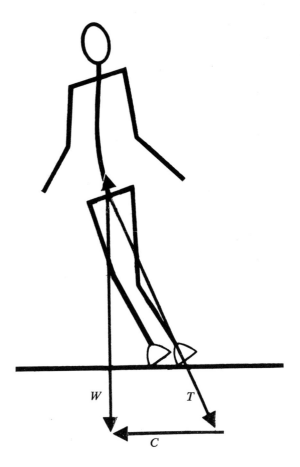

The plane of the paper is perpendicular to the plane of the running surface.

N—represents the component of the skier's weight which is perpendicular to the snow.

R—represents the resistance perpendicular to the ski bottom. This force is transmitted to the skier's center of mass through the support of his legs.

Diagram A represents straight running.

Diagram B represents a turn.

C—is the centripetal force vector which impels the turn. It is the horizontal component of the snow's resistance, R.

R1—represents the vertical component of the snow's resistance which supports the skier's weight.

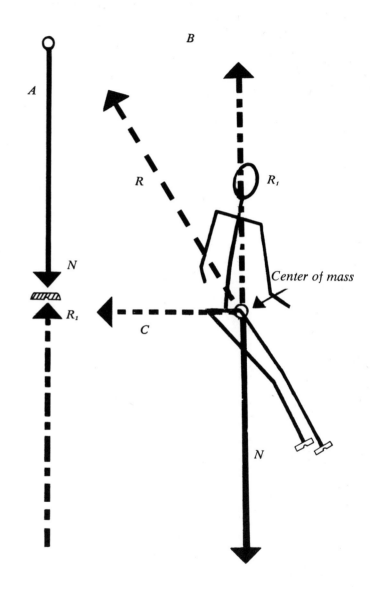

## UNWEIGHTING BY DOWN-MOTION

When a body drops down a temporary state of weightlessness is experienced while the descent is commensurate with that imparted by gravitational forces in free fall.

The same phenomenon is experienced when the feet are rapidly retracted.

Since the human body is not a rigid one, inertia of the heavier parts is an important factor in the exercise of these actions.

1. At a natural standing position, the scales show the skier's actual weight.
2. During the act of the down-motion, the scales show diminished weight.
3. At the end of the down-motion, the scales show a slight increase and then return to the true weight.

## UNWEIGHTING BY UP-MOTION

After the initial push upward this motion theoretically would continue unabated, but gravity works opposite to it and it is gradually eliminated when the skier reaches the top of his motion. Until this has happened, little pressure on the surface is possible, hence unweighted skis.

1. At the beginning of the up-motion, the scales show an increase in weight.
2. As the skier approaches the top of the up-motion, less weight is shown on the scales.
3. As the skier settles to a normal standing position, the scales show the true weight.

## STEERING ACTION

If a ski is put at an angle to the direction of travel and weighted, resistance, R, at an angle from the front develops. Working opposite to this is a component of the skier's weight, P, parallel to the fall line. These forces form a couple which deflect the ski. Inertia helps maintain speed.

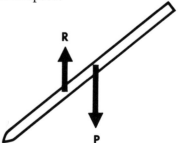

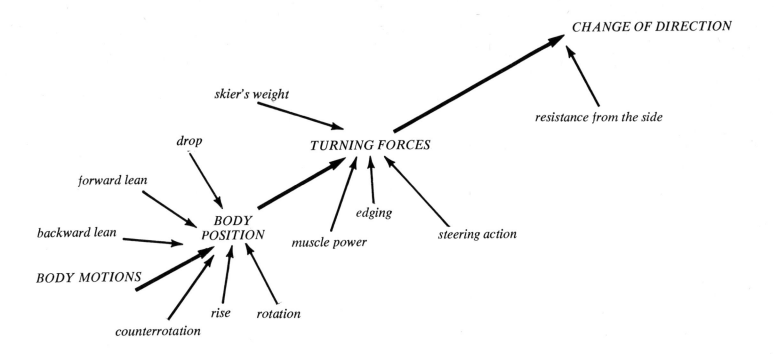

CHANGE OF DIRECTION

skier's weight

resistance from the side

drop

TURNING FORCES

forward lean

edging

BODY POSITION

backward lean

steering action

BODY MOTIONS

muscle power

rise    rotation

counterrotation

*BODY POSITIONS:* Provide the basis for coordinated motions which control *turning forces,* bringing about a *change in direction.*
*RESISTANCE FROM THE SIDE:* Develops as one or both skis are moved at an angle to the original path (release). With edge position (angulation of the body) according to snow conditions (resistance), the ski creates a deflecting force that must work throughout the entire turn.
*FORMS OF RELEASES:* Initiated by leaning forward or backward during traverse, stem, rotation, counterrotation, hop.
*TURNING "FORCES":*
1. Initiated by means of skier's *weight,* forward or backward lean from traverse or sideslip.
2. Coupled with *snow's resistance* as one or both skis move at an angle to original path.

    When these two forces have different points of contact on the ski, a turning "force" results which is called *steering action.*

3. *BODY ROTATION:* As the skier pushes off the surface he can exert a turning impetus on the skis by a motion around the long axis of the body which has to be stopped in order to have effect on the skis. (As the skis are reweighted, this increases lateral resistance to the skis from the snow which supplies the requisite turning force.)
4. *COUNTERROTATION:* A quick turning motion of the upper body while skis are unweighted results in an equal counteraction in the opposite direction in the lower part of the body. The resistance against the skis must be eliminated.

    During this action the skier's path is unaffected, only the "aim" of his skis change. The friction of the snow is necessary for a change of path other than that dictated by gravity and/or inertia.

5. *MUSCULAR FORCE:* It should be remembered that the skier exerts muscular forces to balance himself contrary to the action of the centripetal force (resistance from the side). He

feels this as added "weight." Thus the skier supplies some of the energy to accomplish the turn.

*Note:* (a) Forces that arise from the motion of a body are *frictional*. These forces differ with respect to the surfaces and matter involved, and the forces of contact; some frictional forces are practically independent of velocity.

(b) So-called inertial "forces" deriving from the condition of motion of a body are *fictional* since the real force must come from outside to alter momentum (Newton's first and second laws). The action-reaction law (Newton's third law) applies in equilibrium situations only, that is: constant momentum. Except for the action of gravity and wind resistance, this law is applicable during the unweighted phase of a turn but not during the weighted phases.

## PRACTICAL APPLICATIONS

Indebtedness is expressed to Professor Hugo Brandenberger of St. Gallen, Switzerland. It is his book, *Skimechanik—Methodik des Skilaufs,* that has been the inspiration for the following remarks.

## SKIS

Skis were invented to prevent sinking in the snow. How well they serve this purpose depends upon the contacting surface and the weight of the skier. Long skis of normal width ride high in the snow and run faster than short skis. Long skis track well—particularly if the ski is not too limber.

Resistance from the snow is the primary deflecting force in skiing. A short ski sinks deep, and the lower part of the leg drags in the snow. A short ski will rotate easily in the horizontal plane. Total lateral resistance against a long ski is greater. The two long-levers resisting a turning impetus at the middle precludes guiding long skis with feet and ankles as may be done with short skis or skates. The more rigid the ski the less it can be deformed by stresses. A straight ski has a straight track.

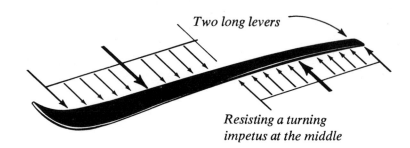

*Two long levers*

*Resisting a turning impetus at the middle*

*Ski Widths:* Ski width details have stabilized near the following ranges:

Midsection: 70-75 mm (2¾″ to 2-15/16″)
Tips: 87-92 mm (3⅜″ to 3⅝″)
Tails: 78-83 mm (3 to 3¼″)

A wide ski is difficult to hold on hard surfaces. This is because the moment of resistance is increased from the edge of the ski to the center. The actual contour, design, and stiffness of the ski is governed by the purposes of the skier. That is, recreation, competition, snow conditions, weight, and skill of the skier must be considered.

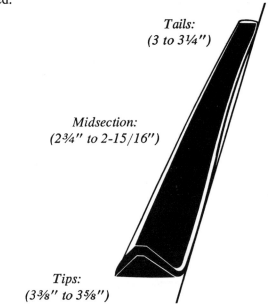

*Tails:*
*(3 to 3¼″)*

*Midsection:*
*(2¾″ to 2-15/16″)*

*Tips:*
*(3⅜″ to 3⅝″)*

*Camber:* Camber refers to the *Side Camber* (cut of the ski) and to *Bottom Camber* (convexity of ski bottom). The side camber refers to the relative dimensions of the shovel, waist, and tail of the ski. This produces a sweeping, long curve along each edge when viewed from either end of the ski. Side camber facilitates directional control and has important performance characteristics. The function of bottom camber is to maintain contact between skis and snow. Both bottom and side camber facilitate directional control and stability of the skier's descent.

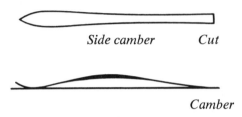

*Side camber*     *Cut*

*Camber*

In deep snow a soft ski with broad tips and tails is easily bent and will reverse the bottom camber. When a limber ski is edged, the snow it packs acts similar to a curved, banked road. A wheel that is not upright behaves in the same manner. Resistance and gravity impel the wheel toward the side of inclination. This is why barrel staves turn themselves when a skier leans into a turn at sufficient speeds.

*Flexibility*

When a ski is edged on a hard surface, the center must make contact at a point between the flat of the shovel and the tail. This reestablishes the reverse bottom camber for a turn. A limber ski tends to twist at the ends and loses the ability to guide a turn. (Fig. A.)

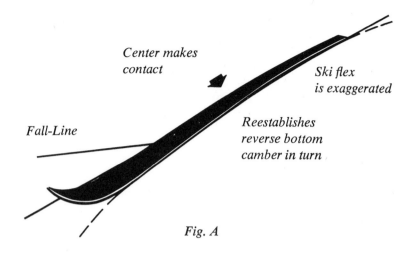

*Center makes contact*

*Fall-Line*

*Ski flex is exaggerated*

*Reestablishes reverse bottom camber in turn*

*Fig. A*

Skis of metal and/or synthetic construction have the least twist. This produces an easily turning recreational ski which will hold reasonably well on a firm surface and will flex upward at the tip and tail sufficiently in softer snow. Stability for the turn depends upon the length of edge contacting the surface.

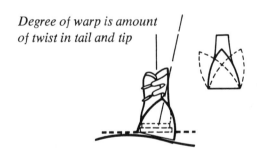

*Degree of warp is amount of twist in tail and tip*

The bottom camber helps distribute the skier's weight more evenly along the length of the ski's running surface. This avoids a concentration of the skier's weight under the feet. Theoretically, it is difficult to obtain a perfect weight distribution along the ski length, even with a very stiff ski. Therefore, all ski designs must be a compromise. The camber should form an even arc from end to end of the running surface. The arc is determined by the flexibility of the ski, total length, and weight of the skier. Most children's skis are too stiff and have little camber. Stiff skis tend to separate in turns and are awkward. A novice finds these skis hard to manage.

The groove aids straight running, tracking, and traversing. The sharper and deeper the groove, the more of a snow ridge is packed under the ski. This helps maintain direction. Jumping skis are long, stiff, and usually have three grooves. These features help the ski to run straight. By contrast, the design of the slalom ski is engineered to aid the skier in quick turning and checking of his speed. The slalom ski has one shallow groove, a relatively broad tip, narrow midsection, and comparatively straight rear half.

The bend in the tip affects the ski's running characteristics in soft snow and bumpy terrain. On a firm surface, where the skis compress very little snow, the shape of the curve is of little importance. Note the implications for soft snow skiing from a comparison of the two diagrams.

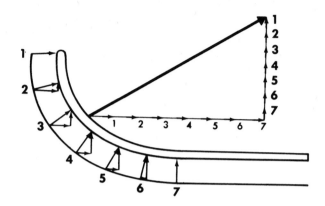

*More resistance to*
*forward motion*
*than lifting force*

The horizontal component of the resistance is the sum of the several horizontal components of the individual resistances. Likewise for the vertical component.

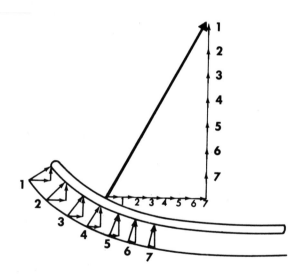

*More lift than*
*resistance to*
*forward motion*

## BINDING PLACEMENT

Binding placement is a subject of controversy. Ski design and the purpose of the skier influences binding placement. It was once popular to use the balance point of the ski as a guide for binding placement. This completely disregarded the more important consideration of the skier's weight placement. Now the total length of the ski bottom making contact with the supporting surface is considered. This is the running surface of the ski. The binding is normally placed so that the ball of the foot is over the center of the ski. Thus, the skier's center of gravity is on a perpendicular line to the middle of the ski. This is the center of the running surface when the skier stands erect. The size and design of the boot must be considered.

(a) Skier's center of gravity is on a line perpendicular from the center of the running surface.
(b) Forward positioning of the binding facilitates easier turning and high speed skiing.
(c) A mounting behind the center of the running surface is a common practice for deep snow skiing. This helps to keep the tips up and affords more leverage for long radius turns. However, some control must be given up for straight running.

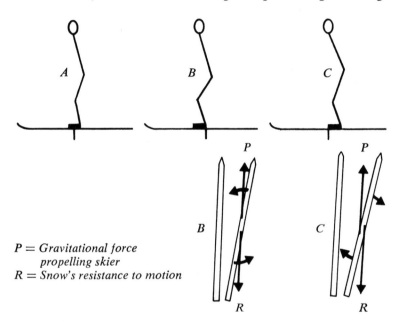

P = Gravitational force propelling skier
R = Snow's resistance to motion

This principle may be tested by towing a ski on a flat surface with string and masking tape. The tape is placed at various points to stimulate weight placement. Gravity "tows" the skis at a point below the center of mass; resistance steers them wherever they make contact with the snow.

## DOWNHILL RUNNING

The propelling force is weight. Not all this force works for the skier. The downhill component of the skier's weight (W) is desig-nated by (P). P has a magnitude which is given by the relation: $P = W$ sine $\propto$ (Alpha). W represents the total weight of the skier and his equipment. Alpha is the angle of the skis with the horizontal.

The following table gives some examples calculated for 155 pounds of skier and equipment:

*Slope Angle*

| $\propto$ | 0 | 5 | 10 | 15 | 20 | 25 | 30 | 35 | 40 | 45 | degrees |
|---|---|---|---|---|---|---|---|---|---|---|---|
| P: | | 0 | 14 | 27 | 40 | 53 | 65 | 77 | 89 | 100 | 110 pounds |
| N: | | 155 | 153 | 151 | 149 | 145 | 139 | 133 | 127 | 119 | 110 pounds |
| R: | is constant for unchanging snow, ski, and skier conditions. | | | | | | | | | | |

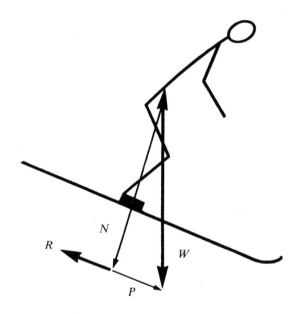

FORCES IN STRAIGHT RUNNING: The weight of the skier divides into two components (P) and (N).

P = Force parallel to the slope. This is the propelling force.
N = Force normal (perpendicular) to the fall-line.
W = Weight of skier and equipment. (W = P + N)
R = Resistance to motion (friction).

A continuous force causes a continuous acceleration. Actually, the snow's resistance opposes the propelling force. Constant speed is maintained when resistance from snow and air balance (P). These forces do not act at the same point. The skier's center of mass is near his navel. Thus, the skier must lean slightly backward for the couple effect of (P) and (R) in the vertical plane. When resistance is large, backward lean is not a conscious action. It is reflexive for balance. Ordinarily (R) is rather small, and the skier has the sensation of being in a forward position.

The skier is supported by his legs and feet. The perpendicular (N), from the skier's center of mass, must pass through the arch of the foot to the surface. This is necessary for balance and comfort. On a slope this places the plumb line (W), from the center of mass, forward of (N). The angle formed between (W) and (N) is equal to the slope angle Alpha. If the skier leans back, he literally pushes his feet out from under him.

The slope refers to the angle the skis make with the horizontal. In deep snow this angle is slightly less than the slope of the hill. Thus, "leaning back" in deep snow may not be actually leaning back. The position merely conforms to the true slope the skis follow as they compress the snow in front.

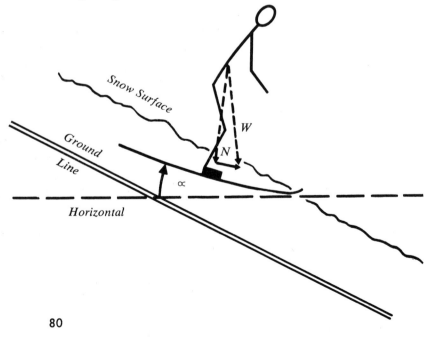

## RUNNING STRAIGHT

Running straight with skis parallel is divided into two distinct positions: *straight running* and *traverse*. Each consists of a body position and a ski position. A proper basic position is considered the most important aspect of modern skiing. Total motion means that a force is created which involves the entire body. It also implies that all joints are flexible and that the skier is able to absorb blows. These blows are from below the skier. He is also able to offset interferences from the side. Knees that are pressed far forward or corkscrew traverse positions are unnatural. This immobilizes part of the skier's body and impairs his flexibility and reaction. These extremes are poor technique. In the 1920s it was considered proper technique to ski in a low position or crouch. This disregarded the abuse of leg muscles and blocking of the hips. Physics implies that by lowering the center of mass, the base becomes relatively wider thereby increasing stability. This is a purely static consideration. It ignores the fact that a skier is not an immobile body and that physiological laws apply.

The problem of keeping a skier in balance is dynamic rather than static. The faster one skis the more vulnerable he becomes. Obstructions occur from outside the skier and fatigue from within. Changes in snow conditions and the angle of slope can alter the forces on the skier from any direction. By moving any part of his body, particularly the hips, a skier can absorb most outside interferences. Of course, the joints and muscles are used to help restore balance. He must keep his body as relaxed as possible at all times. He skis on his skeleton, that is, standing up. Only then are the skier's reactions to outside influences reflexive and automatic. A completely bent position requires change before reaction becomes feasible.

For all practical purposes, the skier must be at a right angle to his skis. It is also basic that by executing changes of position, the entire body flexes. The emphasis is placed on changes of the angle in the ankle and upper body. The upper body and lower legs form nearly equal angles with the plane of the skis.

It is evident that the greater the resistance against the surface of the ski (deep and wet snow), the more the skier must adjust his position. The modern ski binding allows the skier to stay in a more stable position. He does not have to advance one ski or lean back.

When a perpendicular line from the skier's center of mass to the slope passes behind the ball of the foot, it is backward lean. When this line passes in front of the ball of the foot, it is forward lean.

When a skier runs onto ice he must compensate for abrupt accelerations (reduced resistance) by a forward movement. (See Fig. A.) Likewise, he must compensate for an abrupt deceleration with a backward motion. In other words, he moves his center of mass when he skis into snow of high resistance. In contrast, when a skier enters a steeper slope, it differs. The decelerating force is practically unchanged. The skier has only to maintain his position relative to his skis. (See Fig. B.)

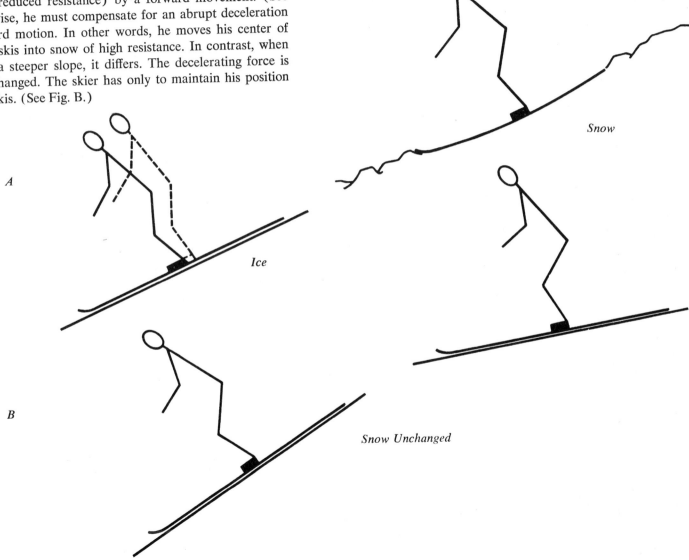

A

Ice

Snow

B

Snow Unchanged

*TRAVERSE:* In straight running (fall-line), the weight is equally distributed on both skis. When a skier crosses a slope, the upper leg must be bent more than the lower leg. This places more weight on the downhill ski leg. It allows the skier to carry most of his weight directly on the skeletal axis of his lower leg. This position is made more comfortable by advancing the uphill leg, hip, and shoulder. To obtain adequate edge control, body angulation is utilized. This keeps the center of gravity over the inside edge of the downhill ski. This position should be relaxed and natural—even on steep slopes. Assuredly, the traverse position is the most important position in skiing. Basic traversing should be practiced continually on different terrain and various snow conditions—by students and teachers.

*Note:* Weight (W) and its downhill (propelling) component (P) remain fixed in magnitude, while (R) may be increased with angulation.

*HOW ANGULATION CONTROLS EDGING:*

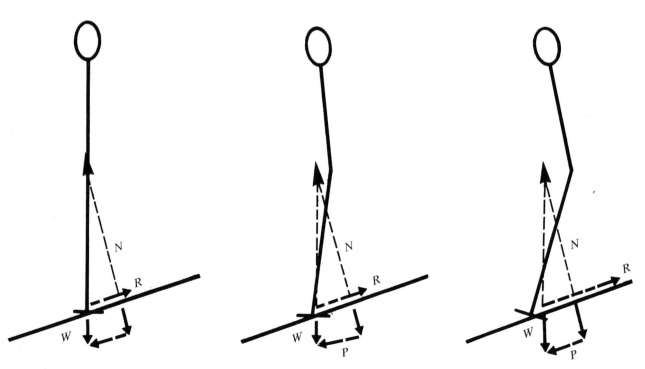

## SKI POSITION

This is the relative position of one ski to the other: closed parallel, open parallel, plowed, stemmed, scissored, advanced, telemark, raised, etc. Consider again the contrast between the hip-wide base concept for support and the form of closed skis. The contemporary position allows more mobility of the hip (center of mass). The modern binding also gives more stability than advancing one ski to overcome resistance from the front.

Ski position implies the relative planes of contact with the supporting surfaces of the snow. This leads to a consideration of edging and edge control.

*Edged Ski:*

*Flat Ski:*

*Surface*

## EDGE CONTROL

This is the control of the running surface of the ski bottoms from edge to edge with the snow surface.

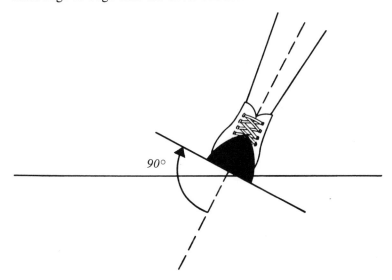

*90°*

The body position controls the amount of edging. When the lower leg is at a right, lateral-angle to the ski, it is natural edge control. The stiff sides of the boot support the ankle and assist edging. Thus, natural positioning implies that a ski is edged as soon as it is stemmed.

Edge control in a traverse or a turn may be accentuated by lateral displacement of the hips and knees. In order to be natural, the hips and knees must move according to the required angulation. Hips and knees should not move individually of each other. Hips and knees moving together with angulation keep both skis equally edged. When skis are individually edged, each ski tends to go in its own direction. Improper and uneven edging of skis is one of the most common sources of difficulty for the skier. Unnatural edge control is usually identified with unnatural body position.

The body position forward, center, or back modifies the effect of a given amount of edging of the skis. (See page 84.) The type of skis (slalom, combination, downhill, or recreational) also contributes to the specific action of the skis' edges on the surface. Hence, a general statement that is applicable to all situations is impossible. The skier must "get the feel" of his edges, by dint of practice.

*TOTAL MOTION* is the most important principle of technical perfection in all sports. It means that the entire body is involved. The skier does not attempt to ski with the feet and skis alone. The forces that affect balance and motive power focus in the center of mass. All efforts to achieve a perfect result with legwork are usually doomed to failure. The athletic skier, however, will have limited success with leg and footwork, but he pays for lack of elegance in muscular effort.

## BODY POSITION

Abrupt changes in steepness, changes on the surface from convex to concave necessitate body position adjustments relative to terrain and skis.

Assume that there is a gully (concavity) across the skier's path, or that he passes a bad transition from a steep to a flat. The skier no longer continues in a straight line. The terrain will deflect him in another direction.

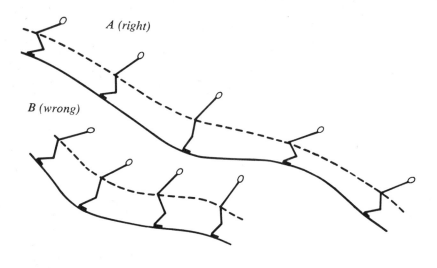

*A (right)*

*B (wrong)*

If a skier weighs 155 pounds, moving at a speed of 22.5 mph, and passes through a transition or dip with a radius of 23.6 feet, he will experience an additional force of 316 pounds. The sharper the dip and/or the greater the skier's speed, the greater the deflecting force. To reduce this force, he must slow down or change the line described by his center of mass by lowering or raising his center of mass to make it move in a more direct line.

Assume that the skier changes the radius of the line described by the center of mass from five to ten meters. The additional force of deflection experienced by the legs will be reduced by half. The skier is upright at the point of greatest force. Thus, the change of position has physiological advantages affecting balance. Most of the stress can be carried by the skeleton and not by the muscles. The extended position helps the skier reduce the leverages exerted against the body. Notice the forces on hinged sections of the body mass in Figs. (C) and (D).

The opposite occurs as the skier passes over a bump. Assume that a skier hits a bump of ten meters radius at a speed of ten meters per second. The effect on a static body is a complete offsetting of weight. If a skier goes faster or hits a sharper mogul, he loses contact with the snow. (See Fig. E.)

The difficulty can be alleviated. The skier lowers his center of gravity as he passes over the top of the bump. (See Fig. F.) He reduces the acceleration. Whenever the rate of change of velocity is 32.2 feet per second, per second, the body is subject to a force equivalent to its weight.

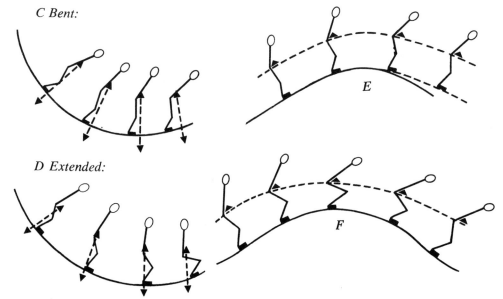

*C Bent:*

*D Extended:*

*E*

*F*

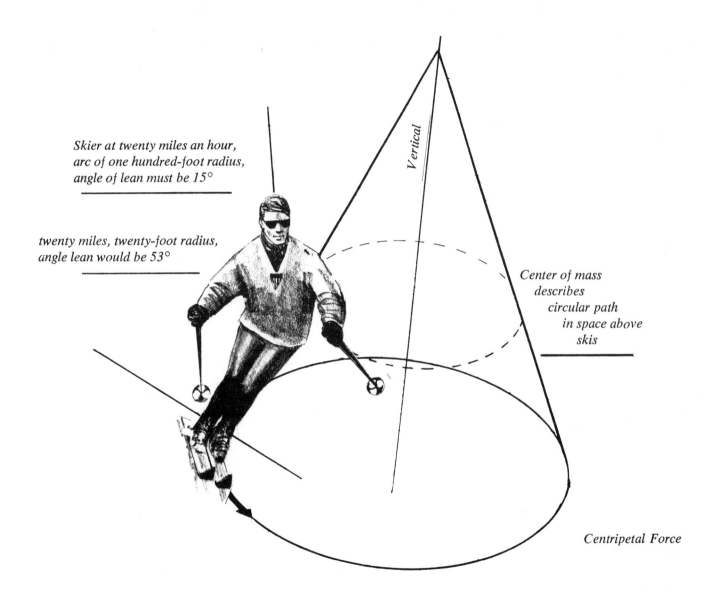

*Skier at twenty miles an hour, arc of one hundred-foot radius, angle of lean must be 15°*

*twenty miles, twenty-foot radius, angle lean would be 53°*

*Vertical*

*Center of mass describes circular path in space above skis*

*Centripetal Force*

## BRAKING

A skier slows his forward motion by moving one or both skis at an angle to the path of descent. Two methods exist: sideslip and snowplow.

*SIDESLIP:* When the skier traverses utilizing angulation, there is friction on the ski edge opposing lateral movement. Forward friction is motion. Although the total friction is less in sideslip than in traverse, there is a greater resistance vector opposing the direction of motion, and thus speed is retarded. To increase the friction, the aid of the ski must be changed. An up-motion of the body will reduce the weight on the skis; also it will move the center of mass toward the downhill side. The result is a flattening of the edges causing reduced lateral friction. In other words, the skier's center of mass should move before the skis move to accommodate the change in net force. If the mass is not moved, the skier experiences balance trouble. The weight distribution is the same in a sideslip as a traverse. To assure proper balance, the body faces in the direction of the sideslip.

*STRAIGHT SNOWPLOW:* The skis are unweighted and displaced at equal angles. This cannot be executed properly with a backward lean. There would be too much resistance on the tails causing the tips to separate. The opposite is true with a slight forward lean. The tips stay together. And the tails slide out easily to the side. The control of braking force in the snowplow is the skier's weight. To replace this with muscular effort is painful and frustrating. Proper knee position and natural edge control are essential for a continuous smooth maneuver.

A slight braking can be achieved by stemming one ski. This stemming is used as a methodical exercise for stem turn and stem christie. It refers to an unweighted, uphill ski.

## TURNING

To change direction the following conditions are needed:

(1) A skier in motion.
(2) Muscular energy.
(3) Resistance from the side.

Describing a turn on skis is difficult because: (1) two equal turns on skis are extremely unlikely and (2) each turn involves different areas of analysis. There must be a change in the path of direction. And there must be a change in orientation of the parts of the body whose path is altered.

Every turn on skis involves rotational and revolutionary energy. These are not simply related as the motions of the moon. The moon, for example, rotates once in each orbital revolution. The picture is complicated by the fact that the skier and his skis are not rigid bodies. In skiing, rotational forces are variable with respect to the timing and progress of the turn. Yet, they affect the outcome of the turning forces which accomplish the turn. To turn the skis and skier is one situation. To change his path is another.

The simple case is not entirely practical. It is applicable on a wide, smooth, moderate slope. An analogy would be coasting on skates or a bicycle. The body of the skier remains directionally faced with his instantaneous velocity, similar to the moon in its orbit. Therefore, a rigorous description of a turn on skis would be meaningless—except under controlled conditions.

The following qualitative description applies to all skiing turns—generally (a complete physical analysis of a turn is beyond this study): In a skiing turn centripetal force is needed. In an ideal turn, the skis describe a part of a circle. Resistance sets in gradually, increases, and decreases again after the traverse is resumed. Ideally there is a minimum of disturbance to the center of mass.

Centripetal force creates a need for the skier to lean toward the center of the turn. He must adjust his balance. For example, a skier has a speed of twenty miles an hour. With an arc of one-hundred-foot radius, he must lean in 15 degrees from the vertical. At twenty miles an hour, with a twenty-foot radius, the angle of lean would be 53 degrees. This implies no sideslip. The centripetal force causes a change in velocity (acceleration). If this has the same magnitude as gravity (32.2 ft./sec./sec.), the angle of lean will be 45 degrees.

The center of mass describes a circular path in the space above the skis. This path is at a lesser radius. Because the center of the arc is downhill, gravitational energy may supply the force to start the turn. However, frictional forces increase after the fall line. Therefore, muscular energy must support the body to keep the center of mass in the arc of the turn. Muscular energy can be used to hasten the initial phase of the turn. However, the skier who waits to apply frictional forces may acquire too much speed. And he will find he can't control the second half of the turn.

Consider turns into the fall-line with moderate to steep slopes. The skier's plumb line must move forward and to the inside of the path of the outside boot. This direction is downhill. In other words, the skier's center of mass moves downhill first. The skier literally beats his feet downhill. For many people, the execution of this movement has psychological barriers. Thus, this movement, necessary for balance and timing can best be learned with help of competent instruction.

Some proponents of ski technique differ; they claim the turn is started by an uphill movement of the feet. This movement would occur during the unweighting phase of a turn. At this time the skier is at the mercy of gravity and inertia; therefore he cannot actually move his feet uphill. He only momentarily retards their downhill speed. One needs the friction of a solid base to move mass uphill. In such a maneuver, the greater mass of the trunk acts as the base. The movement of the feet is against this base. A down-weighting provides the appropriate beginning for this action.

The force of gravity takes effect at the moment of edge release. Sometimes the skier remains passive. He simply applies forward lean with the edge release. Visualize that the body is moved forward at the same time the skis are flattened. The tips will be deflected down the slope. The pressure on the tails is then practically eliminated. And the skier can push, pull, or flip the skis into a new direction.

*TURNING BY MUSCULAR ACTION:* No matter the type of force used to laterally displace the skis, friction must be reduced. This is done by unweighting the skis. Both types of unweighting are used in everyday skiing. These are unweighting by a down-motion and an up-motion. In either type, the up or down is preceded by an opposite motion. The opposite motions are slow and preparatory. The up-unweighting offers more advantages for regular ski school teaching. This is because the up-unweighting is followed by a sinking motion. It allows the skier to control the distribution of the weight as it comes back to the skis. A skier who uses small bumps on the hill finds additional unweighting help.

*ROTATION:* Effective rotary motion in a body must be started from outside. That is, it must start from a solid base. The up-motion increases the pressure on the surface. This establishes the platform needed for unweighting and a rotary push. This explains why a skier finds difficulty turning on glare ice.

It is not possible to define every possibility between a rising motion and an explosive up-motion. Unweighting means a marked temporary reduction of force against the skis. At this point one can no longer exert pressure on the surface. In classic rotation turns, the rotary force has already been imparted to the body.

*COUNTERROTATION:* This is a quick turning motion of one part of the body resulting in a counteraction in another part of the body. Resistance against the ski must be virtually eliminated. An example of counterrotation is found in running. Counterrotation is a vigorous motion and not a position. Once the skis have been aimed in a new direction, resistance on the surface is needed. Resistance from the side of the ski and inertia keep the skis turning.

In short swing turns on the fall-line, counterrotary movements of the upper body are not apparent. The lower part of the body twists against the relative stable mass of the trunk. The angular momenta of the legs and trunk remain nearly equal in magnitude. If trouble in a turn is experienced, it is usually in the release stage. This is true no matter how difficult the snow conditions.

When a turn is initiated, deceleration or braking occurs. This happens as soon as the skis are in a skid at an angle to a straight path. Friction exists against the running surface. And there is resistance from the side of the skis. The resultant of all resistance acts on the skis at an angle from the front. Resistance and the skier's weight usually act at different points on the skis. The coupled effect of these forces results in a steering effect that deflects the skis as they turn. If the point of contact of these contrary vectors is identical, there is a minimum of skid or what we call a "carved turn." When these vectors act at the same point in opposite directions, the turn degenerates into a sideslip.

*STEERED TURNS:* Steered turns refers to all slow speed maneuvers. These turns are started by stemming one or both skis at an angle to the original path. Resistance from the side and weight produce the turn. With a correct, continuous weight transfer, the inside ski follows the turn passively as long as it is unweighted. A contorted ankle or body position may result in flattening the inside ski. This often results in a loss of weight to the outside ski. The skis are connected by the body making one unit. An unweighted inside ski does not create appreciable forces opposing the turn. The skier should follow the turn in a relaxed stance without body motions of consequence. The weight is the main control of the turning force. Its effect can be regulated by either forward or backward lean and proper edging.

## SUMMARY

*USE OF LEVERAGE* in ski maneuvers differs markedly with the speed. Leverage should not be confused with forward or backward positioning of the skier to maintain balance. Understanding the effective leverage in turning requires knowledge of the contributory effect of the relative degree of edging. At slow and moderate speeds forward lean facilitates a short radius turn. At higher speeds, the tails of the skis skid out of control. At racing speeds, the skier applies some back lean to reduce the skid of his ski tails and obtain the best advantage of the ski design. For the ski school student, forward lean is advantageous to turning. He has merely to move back to the center of his skis and the turn ends in a straight track.

Skis designed for different uses (recreation, slalom, downhill, etc.) behave differently in detail, but generally as stated above, except on short skis, on which leverage is outright dangerous. The type of boot and resulting freedom to apply forward and backward leverage on the skis must be considered along with the model of the ski if one is to enjoy the full benefit of his equipment.

*AXIAL MOTION:* One of the most obvious details that observers note in a skier making a turn is rotary movements about the body axis. The emphasis that some have placed upon specific axial motions (rotation, counterrotation, angulation) has been detrimental to ski teaching in some instances: (1) to change the aim of one or both skis in order to obtain a lateral resistance which will create a turn, and (2) to adjust his body position for comfortable balance and/or to obtain adequate edge control.

*EDGE CONTROL:* Only by long practice can the skier become proficient in the vital principle of edge control. The average skier does not drill himself sufficiently with edging exercises; though the young find some success with muscular effort, the more mature must revert to technical prowess. Correct body position and weight distribution are the keys to proper edge control. It goes without saying that the condition of the ski edges must be tailored to the snow conditions and that the skis must not be warped or damaged in such a way that they will not function within the intended limits of design.

*WEIGHT TRANSFER:* Confidence within the skier depends upon his stability while he is in motion. That turns can be executed on an inside ski is well known. The average skier, however, must find a means whereby he can control his skis and maintain his balance. This is most comfortably achieved by a correct and smooth transfer of the body support to the outside foot. Such action provides a margin of safety by allowing the employment of both feet when balance is threatened. In turns that occur with the feet apart, weight transfer to the outside ski is necessary to facilitate reclosing the skis.

# THE MECHANICAL PRINCIPLES
# OF SKI TECHNIQUES* *by Toni Ducia and Dr. Harald Reinl*

All ski teaching methods, including Arlberg, are basically the same: They all consider rotation or twisting in the sense of the turn a must.

They differentiate between "hip twisting," body and shoulder rotation, all accompanied by moving the outside shoulder and arm in a distinct manner. These movements are not only purely practical considerations but are considered basic to ski teaching methods.

All the previous techniques considered the body movements of the skier as the most important source of energy to turn the skis. In other words, the skier under the influence of outside forces has to change the direction of these forces by bringing muscles and joints into play. This always meant a more or less violent "twisting" of the body in the direction of the turn.

This movement is actually quite simple and primitive and corresponds to the skier's natural instinct. It is the basis of the first ski technique adopted in the Alps at the time of Zdarsky. Rotation has been used for ten years. All the ski schools under central control continue to use it today.

On the other hand, if we carefully observe the performance of today's ski experts, we realize that this twisting or rotating in

the sense of the turn has completely vanished. The skier no longer abandons the free position of the traverse. This allows him immediate reactions. He is no longer a slave to the movement that created the turn. He masters the maneuvers with amazing elegance.

As far as the ski school is concerned, how many instructors will disregard the old principles and methods? Thus, the ski school student becomes a victim of outdated theory and practices. The first one was based on old concepts that simply no longer apply. The second one disregards the advances made through international competition that brought us closer to perfection.

Actually, ski instruction has become a detrimental tradition perpetuated by famous names and ski countries. Few dare to touch it despite all the experience to the contrary. The laws of evolution seem unable to penetrate the established routine (clichés).

It is high time to come out of the shell and try to correct the discrepancies between the old theories and the new techniques. This is the goal of this work, inspired by professional experience of the authors as well as by observations made at recent ski instructors' courses. This new doctrine is already applied by a great ski school system and has produced magnificent victories for the French team in downhill and slalom.

One could say, of course, that the ski school pupil could not perform the technique used by the racer. We disagree, since it

* An introduction from *Le Ski D'Aujourd'hui,* 1935.

would imply that a ski technique should only be based on established rules and standards and not consider practical experiences.

In reality, in skiing as in other sports, the student should have only to face his own personal limits. He should not be faced with the mistakes or shortcomings of ski teaching techniques. The technique he is interested in is the one the champions demonstrate to be the most effective in competition. There is no reason to believe that a technique, providing results for the racer, would fail to do the same for the ski school student.

May we also point out that the new technique is but an exact application of mechanics influencing all downhill skiing. All movements of the skier and the skis on an incline, all changes of direction, and all possible situations can be explained theoretically. So our effort is directed in adapting practical performance to the inviolate laws of mechanics. Thus, we hope to give ski teaching, which is our main concern, new direction.

We had to find the mechanical reasons for each maneuver and establish a solid base for every necessary motion. This is how the outside forces can be completely controlled, objectively analyzed, and used to obtain the best result with the least effort.

One of the basic principles is that the skier's body should always be in a natural, unrestricted position. This assures good balance, reaction, and motion. So every muscular effort should be guided by the skier's ability to reassume a normal position.

We thus contradict most of today's ski teaching methods that emphasize rotation or twisting in the sense of the turn. Those exaggerated movements are unnecessary and based on wrong conclusions.

# SKI EXERCISES

*SNOWPLOW CHANGE-UP:* As a straight snowplow exercise, teach the snowplow change-up. From the snowplow return to a straight running. From the running position bend the knees and ankles. With an up-unweighting the tails of the skis are again displaced equally into the snowplow. Increase and decrease the degree of stemming.

*STEM CHRISTIE WITH THE POLES:* This exercise is designed to indicate the skier's arm, shoulder, and his position. It is relative to the position of the knees, ankles, and ski tips as determined by the angle of the traverse.

The ankles, knees, hips, shoulders, and poles describe parallel lines in space.

As the skier enters the new direction of travel, the plane of the hips and shoulders begin to allow for angulation in the new traverse.

This exercise is excellent for teaching body position, counterrotation, countermotion, and angulation.

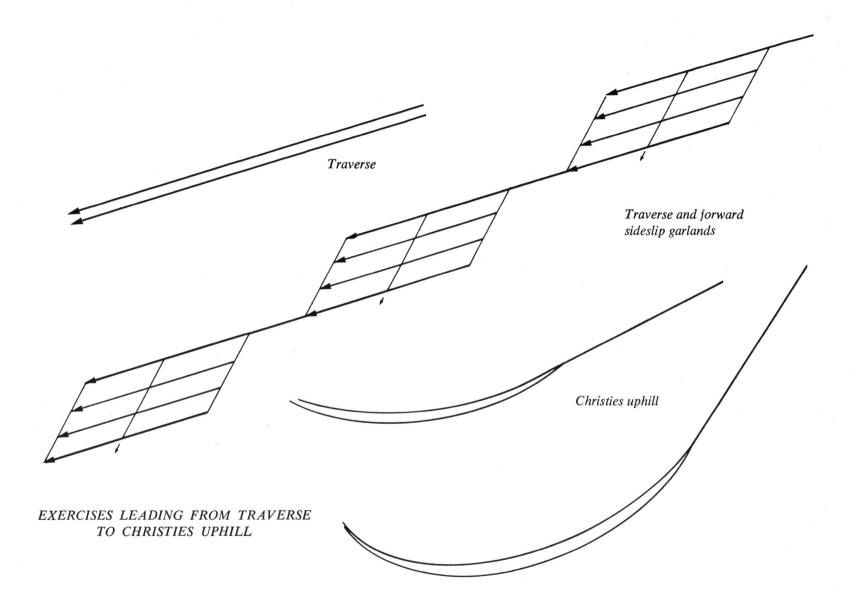

*Traverse*

*Traverse and forward
sideslip garlands*

*Christies uphill*

*EXERCISES LEADING FROM TRAVERSE
TO CHRISTIES UPHILL*

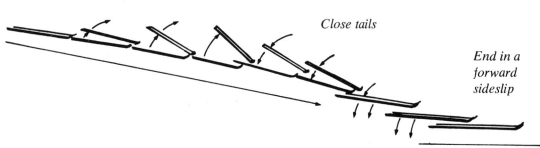

*EXERCISES LEADING TO
THE STEM CHRISTIE
PHASES*

*Close*

*Snowplow
christie
from the
fall-line*

*Open tails*

*Close tails*

*End in a
forward
sideslip*

*Ends in
christie uphill*

*Stem to the
forward sideslip*

*EXERCISES LEADING TO*
*THE STEM CHRISTIE*
*PHASES*

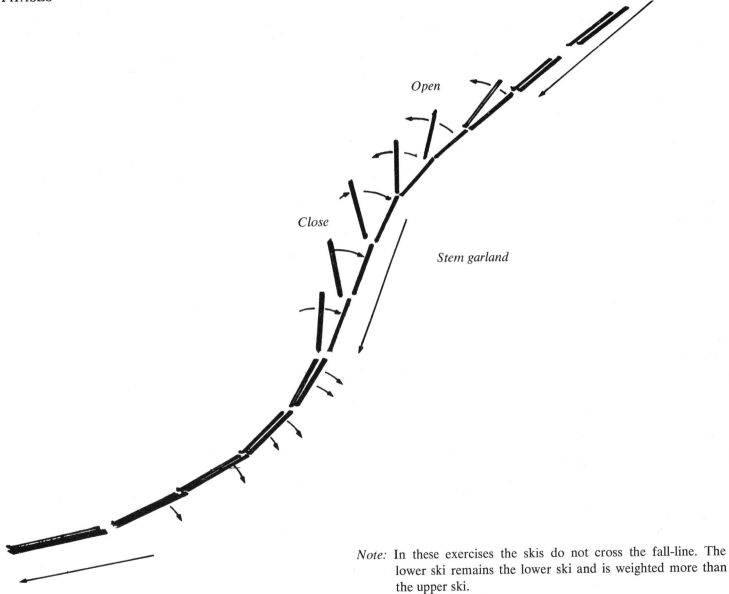

*Open*

*Close*

*Stem garland*

*Note:* In these exercises the skis do not cross the fall-line. The lower ski remains the lower ski and is weighted more than the upper ski.

*SNOWPLOW CHRISTIE:* From the snowplow, with an up-forward motion, the weight is transferred to one ski and the inside ski is brought parallel and advanced. This is followed by a sinking motion combined with angulation and slight countermotion. The skier rises to the new traverse.

*STEM CHRISTIE GARLAND:* This is a continuous exercise used as a transition between the snowplow christie and the beginning stem christie. The skier should learn to open and close the skis with fluid movements ending in a sideslip in the original direction of travel.

97

**BEGINNING STEM CHRISTIE:** This is the transition between the stem turn and the stem christie. The movements learned in the snowplow christie, stem garland, and christie uphill are utilized.

The skis are held in the stem position into the fall-line. A down motion is used followed by up-unweighting weight transfer and closing of the skis. A sinking motion and sideslip completes the turn. The skier rises to a new traverse.

Practice this turn by closing the skis progressively sooner.

*CHRISTIE FROM THE FALL-LINE:* Gradually increase the steepness of the uphill christie. This maneuver can be practiced as a stop christie by utilizing pole-plant and quick drop.

*CHECK-HOP GARLANDS:* This exercise is used to develop rhythm, unweighting, edge control, and pole-plant. The check-hop garland is a transition between the parallel and the parallel with a check. The emphasis is placed on tail displacement ending in an effective check. Practice from both directions, and then attempt parallel with a check.

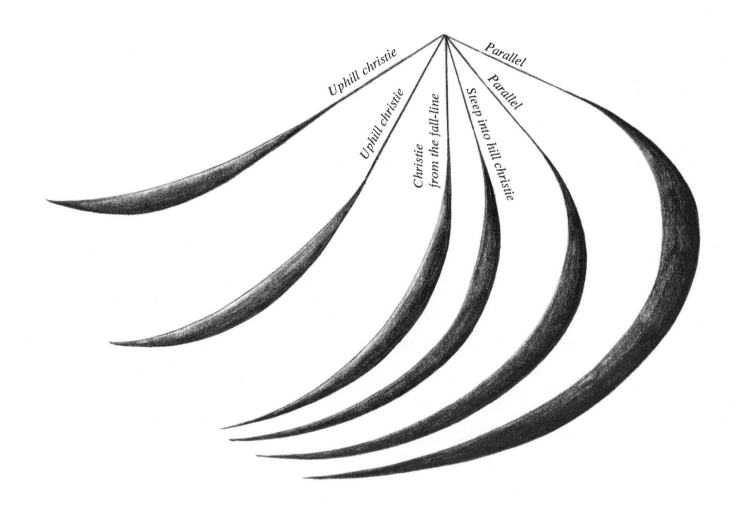

Uphill christie

Uphill christie

Parallel

Parallel

Christie from the fall-line

Steep into hill christie

*THE FAN:* This exercise shows that uphill christies can be skied at a steeper and steeper angle to allow more sideslip in the turn. From a christie from the fall-line the student progresses to complete parallel turns.

# PHYSICAL CONDITIONING

All exercise programs should be followed by at least five minutes of stretching and loosening. Physical conditioning periods should be varied from day to day and should not follow a fixed routine. Physical fitness is not something you achieve once and then forget. It is a continuous process. The main elements are agility, coordination, and relaxation.

To develop a conditioning program the following suggestions should be useful:

A daily conditioning program should include exercises that strengthen, stretch, and relax the muscles of the arms, shoulders, abdomen, back, and legs. It should also give your heart and lungs a vigorous workout.

Exercising should not reach the point of exhaustion but it is a good rule of thumb to do one or two more repetitions of an exercise than you feel you can do. There should be a continuous increase in the duration, number of repetitions, or the difficulty of your exercise program.

Your program must include variety. After strenuous exercise RELAX—do an easier exercise or a few breathing exercises.

## WARM-UP AND RELAXATION EXERCISES

1. *Body Stretching.* Stand on tiptoes while reaching up with one hand. Repeat with other hand.

2. *Head-Roll.* Relax arms and shoulders completely. Roll head slowly in circle.

3. *Shoulder Stand.* Lie on back. Raise feet to vertical position overhead. Brace back with hands, elbows on the floor. Hold position as long as comfortable.

4. *Shoulder Relaxer.* Stand with feet apart, arms stretched out to sides. Do small circles with fists closed until arms and shoulders get heavy. Then bend forward, head hanging between shoulders. Shake arms loose while relaxing arm and shoulder muscles.

5. *Touch Knee to Forehead.* Stand with feet together. Slowly bend forward. Grasp hands around ankles. Press forehead toward knees by one continuous slow pulling motion with the arms.

6. *Touch Toes on Floor Over Head.* Lie on back, arms along sides. Slowly lift legs over head. Touch the floor with toes while keeping knees straight. Hold position. Practice normal breathing while in this position.

7. *Headstand.* Place forearms on floor, hands overlapping or interlocking. Place head in hands. Slowly assume headstand by moving your feet toward face. Lift one leg at a time. Start out against a wall. Hold headstand as long as comfortable.

## EXERCISE FOR ABDOMEN

1. *Sit-ups* with knees bent and braced under chair or bed or held in place by another person, place arms behind neck. As you sit up do a twist by touching the right elbow to the left knee. The difficulty of this exercise can be increased by adding the weight of sandbags held behind neck.
2. *Sit-up Balance.* Lie on back, arms stretched out overhead. Swing arms up and forward—lift legs. Balance in this position. Do several repetitions.
3. Lie on back, arms to side. Raise legs to vertical position. Lower both legs to one hand while keeping other hand and shoulder on floor. Repeat several times to each hand.

## EXERCISE FOR BACK

1. Lie on stomach. Lift right leg and left arm and stretch. Repeat with left leg and right arm. Do a few repetitions.
2. Brace feet under heavy chair or bed and lift arms and chest away from floor. Lie on stomach for this exercise.
3. Lie on stomach, arms along sides. Elbows slightly bent. Lift one leg at a time. As you progress with this exercise lift both legs at the same time.

## EXERCISE FOR THE LEGS

Strength and flexibility in all parts of the lower body is imperative for top performance. The feet, ankles, knees, and thighs must be properly conditioned if they are to perform efficiently.

1. *Run alternately between sprinting and jogging.* Run taking short steps. Run lifting the knees high. Run kicking heels up to the seat. Walk on very steep and uneven terrain.
2. *Run down stairs* or mountain trails or slopes.
3. *Step on and off a bench* fifteen to twenty inches high.
4. *Hop over a bar or bench* ten to twelve inches high. Practice this with feet together, feet apart, or jumping from one foot to the next.
5. Place tires about eight feet apart and alternate them in two lines. Jump from one to the other landing just with the outside foot and then pushing off onto the next tire, etc. Also do this exercise by jumping with both feet from one tire to the next.
6. *Jump on toes.* Bounce short distance. Alternate with high jump or bounce with a tuck.
7. *Skip rope* is a good exercise for both breathing and feet and ankles.
8. *Bicycling* is good for all parts of the leg but especially the thigh.
9. *Run on a wall.* Try to take as many steps as possible.
10. *Hop up and down stairs* or bleachers on one and both legs.
11. *Bounce in low tuck position.* Lift one foot slightly and hop, then both feet, etc. Follow this exercise with jumps that extend legs.
12. *Run in sand* or through a foot of water. This can be done on a beach where running between sand and surf can be alternated.

## LEG EXERCISES THAT ARE NOT RECOMMENDED FOR SKIING

1. Run for long distances of eight to ten miles at the same slow speed.
2. Too much running or sprinting up hills and mountains.
3. Very low, deep knee bends, especially with weights.

## EXERCISE OF ARMS AND SHOULDERS

Strength and agility of the upper body are important in starts, pole-plants, and in maintaining balance. The upper body and arm movements must be strong but supple.

1. *Push-ups.*
2. *Pull-ups* while hanging from a bar.
3. *Climbing ropes.*
4. *Push away from wall.* Stand three to four feet from a wall. Fall against the wall. Bend arms and push away. Move back a few inches as this exercise strengthens the arms and shoulders until you reach your maximum distance from the wall.
5. *Hand Stand.* Follow arm and shoulder exercises with relaxing maneuvers. Swing arms in big, slow circles. Hang head between shoulders; shake arms and shoulders loose while relaxing the muscles.

# TROUBLE SPOTS

In an article in the March, 1949, issue of *Ski* magazine, John Litchfield said this about ski teaching, "As for the technique of teaching, I am a great believer in three factors—explanation, demonstration, and correction—all of which have been known to teachers for years, but which often are forgotten or lost. A short, simple explanation given in light of previously taught steps and followed by an excellent demonstration will provide the maximum benefit for the pupil. Corrections should not be too detailed to be confusing, but rather an analysis based on a series of impressions. As a single factor, demonstration cannot be over-emphasized." The last sentence is important—a good demonstration is important to ski teaching. Children learn quicker than adults and they learn by imitation. Remember, however, that the student cannot see himself ski.

Theory and practice are often hard to unite. Since most people cannot imitate the instructor exactly, and cannot readily translate into action the words of the instructor, it becomes a difficult task to describe a complex body movement.

Students are eager to learn from their teacher, and ultimately, some correction must be given to the student. People interpret verbal instructions in the light of their own personal experiences. These personal experiences are different, and as a result students display a variety of mistakes. Consequently, the instructor's ability

to recognize mistakes, to analyze their cause, and to prescribe a corrective exercise is of prime importance.

The instructor must be positive; avoid correcting in the negative. Too many instructors make corrections by saying: you are leaning back, your lower leg is stiff, your uphill ski is back, don't bend at the waist, don't sit back, etc. These phrases only point out or describe something that is not right. The task is to determine why these mistakes take place, and find the basic cause. Therefore, before a helpful correction can be made the true cause of the mistake must be accurately determined.

For this reason, this book has detailed the mechanics of skiing. It has explored biomechanics and the relationship of skiing to the human body. These are scientific approaches. Many instructors will become overtechnical and not use this information properly. Ski mechanics and biomechanics are only background tools for the good instructor—he should use these with discretion and never provide lengthy mechanical explanations to his class—they are tools for which the instructor can better understand and explain the technique.

If an instructor understands the technique, based on mechanics and basic principles, the job of error recognition and correction becomes easy. This is why the American Ski Technique is based upon seven basic principles that must be observed in the recognition, analysis, and correction of errors. Does the student lean forward? Is he using proper up-unweighting? Does he have angulation in his skiing? Does he exhibit total motion, and have an ease of natural position? Does the student apply weight transfer, etc.?

## THE CAUSES OF ERRORS

Errors and their causes to be noted by the instructor can be grouped in the following categories.

A. *Student's Equipment:* Check the equipment of all students before each class. A student's inability to ski may be directly related to improper equipment. This is particularly true with children. Their boots may be too loose, their skis too stiff with too much camber, and often children's skis are warped. Improper binding placement will make skiing difficult for anyone, beginner, or expert.

B. *Terrain:* The chapter on Terrain Selection points out the importance of proper selection. Remember that the class should be a pleasure for the teacher and student alike. Choose the proper slope for each maneuver, and in choosing terrain don't forget the cardinal rule: Safety, Fun, and Technique.

C. *Physiological:* Watch for fatigue in your students. Children become miserably cold, while adults may be comfortable. Women tire before men, ordinarily. Areas having high altitudes present problems of fatigue not found at lower elevations. A person's physical condition has direct influence upon his ability to learn to ski.

   A person's body build has an influence upon his skiing style. People with a wide pelvic structure experience difficulty in assuming angulation. A person with one leg shorter than the other is apt to traverse a hill with even ski tips in one direction, and have too much lead in the opposite direction.

D. *Psychological:* A person raised in Texas, and not familiar with the mountains will have a different outlook from the person raised in the mountains and used to heights. Similarly, a student overconcerned for his safety will make mistakes because of lack of confidence. The best example of this is a skier's tendency to lean into the hill, to sit back, and to have stiff or straight legs; this is caused by a natural reaction, trying to push or guide the ski. Skiing is unnatural; leaning forward and out is an unnatural experience; it must be learned; and it can only be learned through proper instruction and discipline by the teacher. Learning to ski must be fun, even though we discipline our students.

E. *Methodical:* Build confidence. The instructor must introduce the maneuver in easy segments; these should be mastered progressively. Often students make mistakes because they are not ready for the maneuver; the instructor moves them too fast. Remember, no one can consistently perform a good christie until he has mastered sideslipping.

F. *Technical:* The proper performance of the demonstration forms depends upon good use of basic positions. A student cannot perform a good linked turn until he learns a proper traverse. It is difficult to master the stem turn until the snowplow itself has been learned.

G. *Explanations:* Words themselves create difficulties. Students will interpret the instructor's words differently from those he intends. For example: to a student "flatten the skis" is not the same as "release the edges." A descriptive explanation like "come up and forward and decreasing your angulated position" gives the student something that he can do physically that will result in flat skis. The command "bend the knees" does not always produce forward lean—it will usually cause him to sit back—and for that matter the phrase "lean forward" does not tell the student how to lean forward.

   The problem of determining the basic cause of mistakes is complicated by the fact that any of the foregoing categories can interact on another. Observe these three basic rules:

1. Be certain that the student's equipment is properly suited to his individual needs. Make sure that bindings are properly mounted, boots fit well, and that nothing is faulty.

2. Use teaching exercises that break down a maneuver. For example: break down a demonstration form into easy-to-understand-and-learn segments. Then teach your students in the proper sequence of learning.

3. Be sure that each exercise and maneuver is taught on terrain that does not present psychological barriers. Terrain should be easy so that the maneuver can be executed properly. Of course, snow conditions must be favorable.

The prevention of errors is easier than the cure. Bad habits are hard to overcome even with an experienced teacher. The incorrect maneuver must be unlearned before the correct maneuver is properly taught. An alert instructor is always quick to prevent an error from developing into a bad habit.

ANALYZING ERRORS: Learn to distinguish between style and technique. Each person has a different body build and must adapt basic technique to his frame and equipment. A person with a long thighbone and a lower leg has to bend more than a short person at the waist and ankles in order to keep his balance. A person who has long poles will have to hold his arms higher than a person with short poles.

Look for the basic mistake; many times errors occur because of a chain of wrong movements. The experienced instructor never corrects just any mistake, but, rather, he looks for the cardinal fault that causes several other mistakes. Often the student must make several turns or runs before it can be determined which of his faults is the cardinal one.

Experienced teachers frequently study the tracks of their students to help determine what went wrong. Because a capable instructor knows how the tracks for every maneuver should look, he can learn a lot by studying key tracks, particularly those caused by certain parts of turns.

Study the student from several different angles while he is practicing. Facial expressions often give a clue to the student's confidence. A view from the side can reveal errors in lead change, sitting back, and straight ankles. A view from the back is best for analyzing a student's timing, weight distribution, and angulation. Watch particularly for errors in timing. If every movement is not performed at the proper time, a whole series of mistakes can happen. In many cases mistakes are caused by physiological factors. Students are simply not equipped with sufficient strength, coordination, sense of balance, experience with the body in forward motion, sense of timing, and endurance. The thoughtful instructor must carefully consider these factors when analyzing the problems of his student.

CORRECTING AND ELIMINATING ERRORS: Once the basic error has been discovered, the task of correction is simple. Numerous exercises exist for improving these specific trouble spots. Many of these exercises can be found in the section on Methodolgy in this book. Here are a few general rules for correction and eliminating errors.

Whenever possible, have the student practice the corrective measure while standing in place. Demonstrate the movement for the student and have the student repeat the motion until improvement is shown. In other words, the exact motion should be formed consistently by the student. After this has been accomplished, allow the student to maneuver while in motion. Often it is necessary for an instructor to use his hands to help position the student's body, hips, and shoulders into the required position. This is done while standing still.

When a student exaggerates a mistake, it is often necessary to prescribe the opposite extreme in order to produce a corrective exercise. Be cautious when this is done; it is important that the student and the class understand why and what they are being told.

When trying to eliminate bad habits, it is best to have a person practice the maneuvers at slow speed and on easy slopes. If this is not done the student feels a necessity to turn, and the obstruction involved makes it difficult for the student to concentrate on what he is supposed to do.

POINTS TO REMEMBER:

1. Detect the cardinal fault. Work on one error at a time. It is impossible for the student to concentrate on two things at once.
2. Be careful with the choice of words; make sure the student understands exactly what the instructor means. When words fail, give another good demonstration.
3. Verbal explanations are sometimes insufficient. Directions given during a turn are seldom understood because of the noise and the pupil's concentration and tension.
4. Be authoritative with words. Use key phrases and analogies. Keep a sense of humor and be discreet with the use of irony in your presentation.
5. Stress the mistakes of the pupil by imitation. This is helpful.
6. Learn to use encouragement at the right time. Be careful of constant praise. It will lose its effect.
7. A combination of humor and understanding works best for the correction of errors, since it relaxes the pupil.

8. Remember, the prime function of the teacher is to help the student's maturity in his skiing.

9. Human instincts can be trained. The teacher should develop each student within his special capabilities.

10. One learns to ski by doing, not by talking. A good demonstration is worth a thousand words, and practice makes perfect. As the coach said, "If you are going to learn to swim you've got to get wet."

## ANALYZING AND CORRECTING ERRORS
## CLASS A

*WALKING:* The basic problems in walking are sliding back and balancing. The student tries to walk instead of glide his skis. He often chooses the improper climbing angle and tries to walk uphill. He crosses his skis by trying to lift them off the snow rather than glide them. An overused or worn-out track will cause the student to improperly use his poles.

The correction is proper choice of terrain, explaining that walking is a gliding maneuver, and showing proper use of arms and poles. Provide an opportunity for plenty of practice in the walking maneuver.

*SIDESTEPPING:* The basic problems in sidestepping uphill are a lateral sliding of the skis and crossing of the tails and/or tips. The cause is improper use of the edges, attempting to take steps too large, and not moving the skis evenly. The ski and leg must be lifted from the hip and not the ankle.

Corrections: Be certain that the poles are placed behind the boots. Emphasize taking small steps and use of the poles to help the student take the weight off his skis. The ski should be edged and not flat on the surface. As in walking, emphasize rhythmical movements on a hard surface. The ski should be set down firmly.

*STEPPING AROUND:* The basic problems in stepping around are sliding forward or backward and crossing of the tips. This may be the result of improper terrain selection.

The causes can be from attempting the maneuver on an uneven or un-level unground, improper use of poles and by stepping too quickly.

The correction: Lift the skis with the hip, bend the knee and ankle forward, use the poles for support and leverage, avoid taking big steps, and practice stepping around at every opportunity.

*STRAIGHT RUNNING:* The basic problem in straight running is skis that are unstable and do not track. The student becomes stiff and sits back, and the skis literally run out from underneath the skier.

The cause of these faults is improper basic position. Bend at all three joints. Correct the balance troubles by moving the feet and poles. A student is not used to a sliding sensation. He has fear. A diligent teacher will overcome this by proper terrain selection and with emphasis on body position. Adequate practice will solve the problem.

Corrections: Use exercises through open gates, natural obstacles, and with ski poles. Run over slight bumps. Force the student to sink to go under a bridge made with the poles. Encourage the downhill running on proper terrain to be fun. Look for a natural run-out.

*STRAIGHT SNOWPLOW:* Basic problems are crossing ski tips, skiing out of control, and performing the maneuver with a one-sided snowplow, that is, sliding obliquely downhill sideways.

The causes of the problems in the straight snowplow are: sitting back, improper body position, and weight distribution; this causes overedging on one ski. A narrow snowplow will cause loss of control. Keep the tails pushed out and the skis at right angles to lower leg.

Correction for the straight snowplow: Keep the tips together. Emphasize knee and ankle bend, and make sure the student has the center of gravity ahead of the center of the skis. Establish proper body position by bending at all three joints—ankle, knee, and the hip. Keep the knees normal to avoid a knock-kneed position. Proper use of exercises at a standstill in opening and closing of the skis will pay benefits. Strive for proper weight distribution.

*RIDING ROPE TOWS, JAY BARS OR POMAS, ETC.:* The basic fault is falling to the side or back. The student is afraid and unfamiliar with the mechanical contrivances. He needs confidence. The instructor can provide the most valuable guidance at this stage of learning. The instructor must explain the details of riding uphill facilities.

To avoid grabbing the rope too fast, explain that you grasp the rope and do not grip it sharply. Be sure that the students are properly positioned before they get on the uphill facilities. Skis must be straight and together with weight slightly back. The student has to be alert. For pomas and T-bars emphasize *leaning* against the bar or seat and *not sitting down*. Be sure you contact the lift operators before bringing any beginners for their first exposure to uphill facilties. If the man loading the lift understands that this is a beginner, he will lend assistance.

When a student first rides the chair-lift, explain what he will be faced with when he arrives at the top of the lift. Make sure that everyone in the class understands this. Again, alert the operator.

## CLASS B

*SNOWPLOW TURN:* The basic problems with the snowplow turn are: no turn, skiing out of control, turning to one side only, and catching the outside edge of a ski.

These problems are caused by improper weight shift, stiff ankles, sitting back, and uneven plow. Other problems are over-edging of one or both skis, uneven weight transfer, moving the hip out over the outside turning ski, and not maintaining the proper plowing angle. Most beginning students will use a twisting of the body to produce a turn.

The correction for straight snowplow should be aimed at preventing advancing one ski. This is produced by rotating, which leads to crossing of the tips. Practice weight shift exercises. These should be done statically while standing on the flat. Keep tails pushed outward. The knees and ankles on the downhill ski must be pressed forward. Remember that angulation, though moderate, is present. Show the student how leaning toward the lower ski will provide stability.

*TRAVERSE:* The basic problems with the traverse are: gaining too much speed, separating tips, sideslipping, and crossing tails or tips. This results in losing control and loss of balance.

The causes of the faults: weight on the uphill ski, leaning into the hill, uneven edging, not enough angulation, and edging of the downhill ski. Other problems are facing uphill, sitting back, uphill ski back, and a lack of concentration. Remember, speed is controlled by the angle of the traverse. A traverse started properly has a good chance of continuing.

Corrections: First use proper starting position. Make certain

weight is on the downhill ski, knees, ankles, and hips are bent, and that the body angles out over the downhill ski. The skier faces toward the valley. Be relaxed, keep the knees together. The student should feel pressure on his ankles and knees. Teach the student a slight skating step so that he gains confidence knowing that he can always step uphill.

## CLASS C

*KICKTURN:* The basic problems with the kickturn are: inability to lift the ski, trying to lift the ski with the foot, hitting the ski poles, sliding backward, loss of balance, and getting stuck in the middle of the turn.

The causes are improper practice on level ground, no preparatory back swing, poor positioning of the skis and poles, and choosing the wrong terrain. Feet shouldn't be too far apart, and one ski placed farther advanced or back than the other.

The correction: More practice on the flat, repeat demonstration of ski and pole position, make certain that students know how to lift the ski from the hip joint, and do not try to do it with the foot and ankle.

*STEM TURN:* The basic problems in the stem turn are: inability to stem the uphill ski, no control in the turn, incompleting the turn, loss of control, and being unable to enter the turn.

Causes: improper body position, not bending forward at the ankle, knee and hip, weight on the uphill ski, stem too small, going too fast, improper weight transfer, no angulation, and a general lack of confidence. The student not facing in the proper direction at the finish of the turn will have problems.

Correction in the stem turns: Make certain a proper traverse is established. The traverse should not accelerate. The angle of the traverse is very important and may be maintained by keeping the weight on the downhill ski with the upper body angled out over the inside edge of the downhill ski. Practice a slight lifting of the tail of the uphill ski during the stemming action. Skating and stepping exercises on slightly inclined terrain are useful. Don't forget to practice opening of the uphill ski from a static position on the traverse. Similarly practice the closing of the uphill ski from a static position. The importance in using various exercises cannot be overemphasized in the stem turn.

*VERTICAL SIDESLIP:* The problems encountered with the vertical sideslip are: separating skis, sliding forward or backward, catching outside edges, skiing over the pole, and falling into the hill.

The causes of these problems are: improper body position resulting in too much weight on the uphill ski, leaning too far forward or backward, rolling the ankles outward, trying to create artificial edge control, improper holding of the ski poles.

Correction for errors are: Bend forward at all three joints. Keep the knees, ankles, and hips pressed forward. Lean out over the downhill ski. Keep the weight on the downhill ski maintaining an angulated but relaxed position with the skis pointed in the proper direction. A good exercise is to push off with both poles planted on the uphill side. Attempt to instill the feeling of up-unweighting and decreasing of the body angulation to effect release of the edges. If a student continues to have problems of skiing into or over the downhill pole, try one of the following: take the poles away from him or place both poles in the uphill hand or the lower pole under the lower arm.

*FORWARD SIDESLIP:* The basic problems are: crossing the tips or tails, poor balance, and catching a downhill edge.

Cause of these faults is improper body position, weight on the uphill ski, no uphill lead, sitting back, turning the upper body toward the slope, and leaning in and poor weight distribution.

The corrections for the forward sideslip are similar to the lateral sideslip, except that in the sideslip the student has a forward traversing motion as well as a vertical motion. This is an aid and should be used to induce the proper use of up-unweighting and the decreasing of angulation.

*CHRISTIE UPHILL:* Problems encountered: achieving no turn, overturning, or too much skidding.

The causes of these faults are: no deflection at the start of the turn, no turning impetus, no unweighting, and no definite edge release. Other causes are: sitting back, rotating the hips over the skis at the end of the turn, not continuing the body in motion, and failure to assume an outward leaning of the body or angulation at the end of the turn.

## CLASS D

*SNOWPLOW CHRISTIE:* The basic problems are: inability to get the skis together, no christie phase at the end of the turn, and crossing of the tips and tails.

The causes of these faults can be a plow that is too large or incorrect, no weight transfer during (at the start of the) upmotion, sitting back, no sinking motion at the end of the turn, and no countermotion of the upper body to compensate for the skidding in the turn.

To correct these faults the instructor should have his students practice uphill christies, forward sideslips, and a series of exercises emphasizing the closing and opening of the skis from a straight running to a snowplow position. Stepping and skating exercises from one ski to the other are useful.

*STEM CHRISTIE FROM THE FALL-LINE:* The problems of the stem christie from the fall-line are crossing of the ski tips, or turning too quickly.

Stem christie problems are caused by having the stemmed ski too far advanced, turning too quickly, and too much twisting. This is probably the result of fear and a desire to turn the ski sharply.

The correction of these faults would be the same as the correction of the snowplow christie and the christie uphill.

*BEGINNING STEM CHRISTIE:* Basic problems in the beginning stem christie are: inability to enter the skid phase and crossing of the tips.

These problems are caused by no down-up-down motion upon entering the fall-line, too wide a stem, an improper weight transfer, and a bad body position.

The correction of these faults is to practice the stem turn, uphill christie, and snowplow christies. Break the beginning stem christie into its components; practice each one attempting to correct each individual fault. Skating from one ski to the other to effect weight transfer is a basic exercise.

*STEM CHRISTIE:* Basic problems in the stem christie are poor edge release, loss of control of the turn, and improper balance. Too much speed is often acquired and the skis are commonly stemmed wider than necessary.

The causes of these faults are improper timing, overexaggerated stem, sitting back, a countermovement that is too late or pronounced, or a static basic body position.

The correction for the stem christies are to review the uphill christie, snowplow christie, stem christie from the fall-line, and the beginning stem christie. These should be broken into their components and the necessary corrections made. Stem garlands emphasizing weight control and stepping from one ski to another are essential in correcting stem christie faults.

## CLASS E

*PARALLEL FROM THE FALL-LINE:* Basic problems are: not effecting a turn, a turn that is too long, or a turn that is done too quickly causing a flip or a jerk.

The causes of these faults are having no counterrotation to initiate the turn, improper forward lean, sitting back, an exaggerated twist of the body, and lack of confidence of the student, and poor coordination.

Correction: Review all previous maneuvers. This may require reverting as far as the snowplow turn. Be careful to choose the proper terrain. Stem garlands emphasizing down-up-down motions are useful. Exercises from the traverse working on christies into the hill. Stressing angulation will be helpful.

*PARALLEL:* Problems with the parallel are: lower ski abstem, inability to release the turn, crossing of the tips, losing control, edge problems, track that is too wide, and tendency to fall to the inside.

The causes: transfer of weight to the upper ski during the down or sinking motion, sitting back resulting in insufficient unweighting and bad timing as well as loss of control, and a late lead change. Sitting back to start the turn and inadequate angulation will result in poor and unnatural edge control and ultimate poor, basic position. The weight should be mainly on one ski (down on the lower and up on the upper). Avoid equally weighted skis in any phase of the turn. Leaning into the hill before the turn causes problems. There must be a resistance from the side before the skier may lean into the turn; otherwise, the skis can literally slide out.

Correction: Review all previous parallel maneuvers. Faults in the parallel turn can be worked out through practicing the components. Emphasize a down-up-down movement during the preparation and the holding of the edge. Practice garlands and angulation exercises. The student must learn to be confident even while skiing upon one ski. Skating and weight shifting exercises from lower to upper ski are essential. Lifted ski exercises in the uphill christies on the downhill ski only are excellent preparations for these requirements.

*PARALLEL WITH A CHECK:* The problems are: no check actually exists; the skier sits back, skis open or stem resulting in balance problems and the need to jump for a release. Rotation is a common occurrence.

Causes: not enough down and leaning out on the preparation. Forward lean is necessary. Sitting back and too much weight on the uphill ski brings about these problems. A late pole-plant or sitting back during the check period will cause the skier to be slow in releasing the turn and hang onto his pole.

Correction: traverse (steep slope)—use sideslip—traverse garland, christie uphill to stop, practicing edge set and pole-plant; do the same from the fall-line. Practice check-hop garlands on easy and steep slopes with and without poles, check-hop to a single parallel turn. Emphasize slowing down of ski but not of the body. Increase edging by angulation.

## CLASS F

*SHORT SWING:* Problems encountered in short swing are: irregular motions, catching of the edges, and jerky rhythm. The student often finds himself unable to continue the short swing sequence because he skis too fast or becomes tired.

The causes: sitting back before starting the maneuver, skiing too fast from the beginning, and not enough edging caused by improper angulation. The lack of rhythm and timing make a student insecure. Continuous motion is necessary. Poor unweighting, poor pole timing, and balance will cause problems. Improper edge set, sitting back, and inadequate coordination will create a multitude of the foregoing problems.

The correction for short swing is a complete review of all previous maneuvers as far back as a straight snowplow. The use of hopping exercise with the poles on gentle slopes is suggested. In this manner rhythm, pole timing, and coordination can be slowly worked into the curriculum. Unweighting must be emphasized and should be exaggerated at first on shallow slopes, working up to steeper slopes and a more smooth, easy flowing of motions. Insist on speed control.

# THE SCHOOL AND THE INSTRUCTOR

The exercises and maneuvers used to teach a person to ski comprise the methodology of the American technique. They are not to be confused with demonstration forms.

A great variety of exercises are used by ski schools. Methods of teaching remain flexible; however, certain basic approaches have been proved through years of use.

Different teaching approaches are accepted and allowed. A rational and reliable buildup of exercises prevents discouragement. Suitable exercises make learning to ski easy and enjoyable.

Enough time is allowed for the student to become accustomed to his skis, the snow, and surroundings. Walking and gliding on the level make the novice familiar with his skis and prevent "defensive" positions.

Beginning is easy and slow. Maneuvers for which there has been no previous preparation are not demanded. A good teacher will be able to see the problems through the eyes of the student, and he will understand the fears and shortcomings of the students.

The choice of proper terrain is important. It can mean the difference between the student's success and failure. A change of exercises and terrain situations keeps the student keenly interested. There are different means and expressions to achieve the same goals.

Experimentation in teaching methods is instinctive to the ski instructor. Changes in approach must be subjected to experimentation by knowledgeable professionals in a controlled situation. Many ski schools will use a top instructor and select a group of students and explore the merits of a ski teaching method. *This is not change in technique.*

An example of thorough experimentation in new approaches to teaching is the Graduated Length Method. In this method the beginner starts on a ski shorter than standard and gradually progresses to the standard length. The five-foot ski has been in use by Karl Koller in the Kitzbuhl Ski School since 1952. In the sixties, Cliff Taylor developed the "shortie." In 1968, Martin Puchtler of West Germany reported on an extensive experimental course in the Graduated Length Method. In the United States, Karl Pfeiffer, former director at Killington, Vermont, is a strong proponent of the graduated method through experience as a top professional. This thorough investigation by qualified people lends credibility to the approach.

## THE INSTRUCTOR

The ski teacher will be able to demonstrate to perfection and at slow speeds. To adults, he will explain all maneuvers. Often he will overdemonstrate to his student an error in the skier's performance. Each member of a ski class is treated as an individual.

Skiing is improved mostly by practice. The instructor will be the "motor" of the class and keep the show going. He will be able to use the theoretical principles of skiing in order to analyze mistakes and emphasize corrective exercises.

The ski instructor will gain the confidence of the class through appearance, demonstrations, and explanations. The overly aggressive student will be cautioned; the timid student will be encouraged.

Instructors increase their knowledge through reading and discussion and their technical ability through continuous training.

*CLASS HANDLING:* The instructor will introduce himself; establish personal contact. The students' skis, clothing, boots, and protective equipment will be checked. Instruction will be given about the general area, lifts, tickets, etc.

The conduction of the class will be informal, friendly, and natural; skiing is meant to be fun.

Teaching skiing involves understanding, patience, and practice.

## EXERCISES FROM FALL LINE

A class may be lined up in several ways according to the exercise, size of the group, terrain, and snow conditions. Some examples:

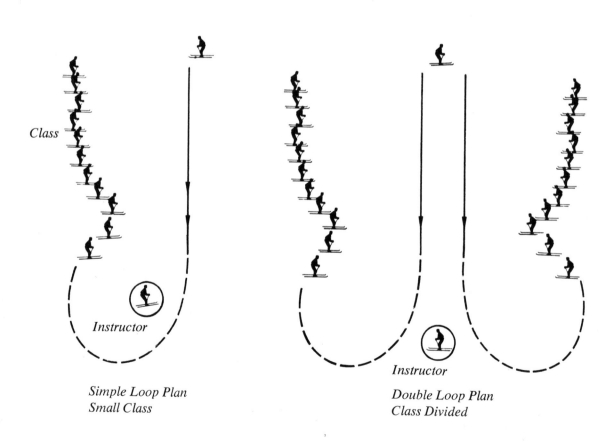

*Simple Loop Plan*
*Small Class*

*Double Loop Plan*
*Class Divided*

*EXERCISES FROM TRAVERSE UPHILL: Figure-eight plan*

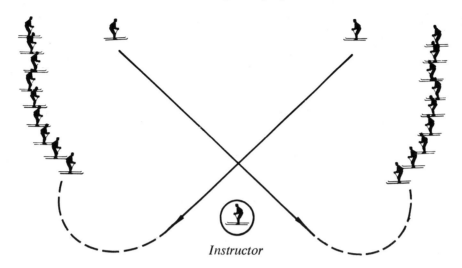

*Instructor*

The instructor will provide the basis of understanding by the following:

(a) Explanation of the maneuver, outlining its usefulness.

(b) Demonstration of the maneuver.

(c) Correction of the students' rendition of the maneuver.

The class will be lined up away from traffic.

Weather will be considered as it relates to the students' comfort.

Strict discipline will be kept for class safety.

The class will maintain a proper distance from one another while skiing.

The instructor will talk loudly and clearly.

The instructor will demonstrate often.

The instructor will normally demonstrate toward his class and face the class as he gives explanations. Normally the instructor will make the first demonstration for the class, carefully choosing the terrain, angle of traverse, etc. If a student doesn't understand a second demonstration would be made.

## SKI SCHOOL

Ski schools were organized to teach skiing. The ski school class system when properly applied is the best means of teaching and learning skiing. Each ski school student is the object of personal attention and is treated as a special guest of the ski area. He is given advice as to conditions, etc., by a polite and helpful staff. The successful ski area operation, of which the ski school is an important link, depends on the teamwork of everybody involved. Skiers appreciate a good organization: lessons should start on time; the instructor should be prompt and dependable.

Instructors do not discuss the performance of an individual, or ridicule an individual. Instructors are informed of new developments in theoretical approaches and ski teaching through training sessions to coordinate technical, methodical, and efficient procedures.

The main points emphasized in ski school are safety, enjoyment, and learning (in this order).

The following is the general procedure practiced by the ski instructor and ski school:
(1) The entire maneuver is introduced giving its practical application.
(2) The most important phase of the maneuver is demonstrated.
(3) Individuals practice that part of the maneuver, first while standing in place, then when moving on the slope.
(4) Other portions of the maneuver are practiced.
(5) The entire maneuver is practiced.
(6) Errors are corrected.

*TEACHING SCHEDULE:* The following is merely an outline of ski school methodology. Every known exercise may be used in striving to have students master maneuvers, provided such exercises comply with the basic principles.

## CLASS A

*PRELIMINARIES:* Demonstrate the correct way to carry skis. Walk class to the beginners' area. Line up the group; have them put on their skis. Inspect skis, bindings, boots, poles. Teach how to hold ski poles. Exercise at a standstill to become familiar with the skis: Lift up one foot, then the other; move tip of lifted ski up and down, turn lifted ski to the left and right; hop, supported by poles; hop with arm swing; step sideways, then back; step around by moving the tails; step around by moving the tips; step backward. Use walking steps; teach sitting down and getting up.

*WALKING:* Move the entire class with and without poles. The skis stay on the snow, the poles are slanted backward and planted close to boots. Form the class into a big loop; vary the pace. As an introduction to gliding, teach walking on downgrade with and without poles.

*SIDESTEP:* To be executed first on the level, then up and down on a gentle slope. Combine sidestep and walking to get the diagonal sidestep.

*STRAIGHT RUNNING:* Practice this position at a standstill, ski tips even. Use a gentle slope with a natural runout, and vary body position (high, low.) Use hopping, stepping, and elementary skating step. Lift end of one ski; use a double pole push occasionally.

*HERRINGBONE:* Teach basic position at a standstill, then on the flat. Use a distinct weight transfer, alternating from one ski to the other, moving the unweighted ski first without emphasis on poles, then with their use.

*STRAIGHT SNOWPLOW:* Teach first at a standstill; then use a hop to a snowplow while at a standstill until the plowing angles become identical. Other exercise: Start in a snowplow position, then slide to a straight running position. Emphasize knee action: snowplow change-up (snowplow–straight run–snowplow), decreasing and increasing stemming angle (rhythmical displacement of tails), increasing and decreasing amount of edging; snowplow to a stop, hands hip-high, poles straight back.

## CLASS B

*REVIEW:* Walking, Climbing, Running, Straight Snowplow.

*KICKTURN:* Swing one ski back and forth, with and without planting the tail of the ski in the snow; maintain lateral support with both poles. Change one pole and fold ski completely around to face tail of the other ski. Bring the second ski and pole around in one motion. Keep feet close together.

*SNOWPLOW TURN:* Practice weight transfer and slight countermotion at a standstill. From a straight snowplow in the fall-line make single turns to the left and right. Repeat, starting from the straight running position. Emphasize equal stemming angles of both skis, a natural as possible edge control, and relaxed weight transfer. Then move on to linked snowplow turns. Use ski poles or slalom flags to help develop rhythmical turns.

*TRAVERSE:* Practice position at a standstill. Explain the relationship of the ski tips, the boots, hips, and shoulders. Explain the use of angulation for edge control. Start on a gentle slope without obstacles or moguls. Some exercises: lift tail end of upper ski; use small uphill skating steps; step around knolls, or artificial obstacles, such as a glove; traverse; slight downhill hop; traverse.

## CLASS C

*REVIEW:* Kickturn, Traverse, Snowplow Turn.

*STEM TURN:* While at a standstill in the traverse position, stem the uphill ski, then replace it. Repeat this exercise several times while in motion. Be sure to practice in both directions. Make one complete turn to the left, then one to the right. Then link several. Be sure to traverse sufficiently between turns. Strive for a smooth, continuous weight transfer, and a smooth, gradual loss of the stem position toward the end of each turn.

*SIDESLIPPING:* While at a standstill and using ski poles for support, teach release of edges. Then teach diagonal sideslipping; slow traverse, up-motion with edge release, sideslip, re-edge and continue the traverse. Some other exercises: sideslip garlands, vertical sideslip, forward-back sideslip.

*UPHILL CHRISTIE:* Initially, teach as an extension of diagonal sideslipping using additional forward lean. Then while at a standstill in a traverse position, use a sideways-hop downhill in combination with counterrotation. Repeat, eliminating the hop. Be sure to practice both left and right. Teach garlands. Vary the steepness of approach.

## CLASS D

*REVIEW:* Sideslip, Stem Turn, Uphill Christie.

*SNOWPLOW CHRISTIE:* From a snowplow position in the fall-line with equal weight distribution, prepare for turn with a sinking motion. Use up-unweighting and axial motion to simultaneously close the skis and initiate an uphill christie. Weight transfer, angulation, and countermotion combine to complete the turn. Practice left and right.

*STEM CHRISTIE GARLAND:* While traversing, stem, make slight turn toward fall-line; then make snowplow christie in same direction as the original traverse. Repeat in both directions as often as possible. Vary the degree of the turn, as well as the speed.

*BEGINNING STEM CHRISTIE:* Similar to a stem turn except that more speed is required. The skis are closed progressively sooner after leaving the fall-line, and the turn is completed with a curving sideslip. Emphasis must now be placed on motion and unweighting.

*STEM CHRISTIE:* More speed is required than for a stem turn. Thus, a stem christie is started from a steeper angle of traverse. The uphill ski is stemmed in combination with a sinking motion and is immediately followed by unweighting. The skis are brought together before the fall-line is reached. Weight transfer, change of lead, angulation, and countermotion proceed smoothly once the turn has been triggered. The down-motion and angulation of the body, as the turn progresses off the fall-line, combine to displace the tails of the skis. The arc of the turn is completed as the skier rises to a new traverse.

## CLASS E

*REVIEW:* Sideslip, Uphill Christie.

*CHRISTIE FROM THE FALL LINE:* Begin with an uphill christie, gradually increasing the angle of attack until the turn is started from the fall-line. The use of a large knoll makes this exercise much easier. Emphasis must be placed on a smooth and ample up-unweighting. This is a favorable time to introduce the use of the pole-plant; the use of the hop-approach is also most helpful.

*PARALLEL CHRISTIE:* The hop-approach on gentle slopes, both with and without the use of the pole plant, is effective. Single parallel christies, practiced alternately to the left and right, around large knolls, are also recommended. The student must be able to sideslip in both directions, with good control of the edges, in order to master a parallel christie. Insist on the proper traverse between turns.

Most important are exercises to develop edge control, and especially change of edges, such as: parallel garlands with a hop, with and without pole-plant.

*PARALLEL CHRISTIE WITH CHECK:* Use check-hop garlands, with pole-plant. Then attempt single turns to the left, then to the right, preceded by a check. Then link the turns, insisting on a proper traverse between turns.

## CLASS F

*REVIEW:* Parallel Christies, with and without check; build up the confidence of students, especially with regard to speed and fall-line skiing.

*SHORT SWING:* Practice hop exercises in the fall-line on gentle slopes, and hop-garlands on a traverse on steep slopes. Develop proper rhythm and timing of pole-plant. Strive for good rhythm and smooth linking of turns, so that the end of one turn blends into the beginning of the next.

Practice slopes should become steeper gradually. Strive to eliminate the hop in favor of a smooth minimum amount of down-up-down motion. At first turns may be quite rounded, but in time the length of the arc of the turn should be gradually decreased.

Student must have sufficient confidence to schuss the practice slope. In the beginning, exaggerate the unweighting movements. Guard against overturning of the skis when the turn is initiated. Gradually polish the movements by eliminating all unnecessary motion.

## CHILDREN'S SKIING

Special attention and consideration are devoted to children's classes. Instructors who understand and enjoy children use imagination and a variety of approaches to maintain the children's interest. Since children learn by imitation, perfect demonstrations by the instructor are a must; however, perfection is not expected in the student.

Children's classes need as much preparation as any other ski school activity. Ski schools find that the children must be grouped by age in order to effectively learn: four and under; five and six; seven through nine; nine and over. Each age group has its own abilities and problems, and each age group creates a different situation for the ski school and instructor. In the younger category it is essential to make it "fun and games" or the child will lose interest quickly. Comfortable, warm clothing and properly fitted equipment are an essential part of the successful handling of the skiing child.

Ski schools having success in the teaching of children have used the same basic methods for years. A guide would be:

*Under five years old:* games; Mother Goose cutouts; easily negotiated obstacles on very shallow slopes; close personal attention from the instructor; proximity to shelter (many schools prefer not using ski poles in this age group). Suggested class maximum—six students.

*Five and six years old:* games (cutouts, etc.); some competition; can handle easy lift facilities; the boots should give sufficient support so that edging is effective; skis should be light and flexible and no taller than the child; close personal attention; proximity to shelter. Suggested class maximum—six students, and as Julie Fiorini says, "tender loving care."

*Seven, eight, and nine years old:* hand, eye, and muscular coordination will generally be developed sufficiently so that this age

group can rapidly use the lift facilities; the correct equipment becomes more essential; release bindings become vital. Use competition and more "sophisticated" games; fox and hounds, follow the leader, etc. What are actually technical exercises can be worked in as "tricks." Students will advance quickly— need an energetic instructor. Remember, having fun is more important to the child than learning a particular maneuver.

*Over nine years old:* basic teaching methods can be used but the fun aspect must still be retained.

JUNIOR RACING receives impetus from the child's early exposure to competition in the ski school class. Most ski schools, ski clubs, and national amateur ski associations have racing programs beginning with the Mighty Mites (ages six to eight) through the junior expert. School skiing programs operated through educational institutions are developing rapidly in some areas of the United States. Our junior ski programs, whether recreational or competitive, are producing an extremely high level of technical competence in the young skier, which in full circle is giving the United States a quality of recreational and professional skier never before attainable.

Racing programs could be compared to Little League baseball or football. These ski programs have been in existence for many years even though the coaching has not been developed to a technically high degree. The youngster has an urge to compete and belong. He feels a certain amount of accomplishment in this participation. From these programs they can decide to go further into racing or just skiing for pleasure and recreation.

The following are comments from instructors who have been involved in teaching children.

"As a parent you can help him in his first steps on skis; however, few parents have the patience, detachment, or technical skills to teach their children."—Barbara Jane Thornes

"Not only do children readily take instruction from a complete stranger much more easily than from a parent (who is his natural born enemy), but the spirit of competition among a group of similar age children is a lure they will rise to every time."—Betty Bell

"Young children have a tremendous sense of self-preservation. There is no problem in a day-long session with the young children. They prove they have capabilities far beyond what is expected by the parent. But then, on skis we all lose our hang-ups!"—Julie Fiorini

"I would say that the most important thing is that they enjoy skiing. Go easy, be fun, and don't expect too much. It is harder for a parent to teach his own child—'Mother is so stupid, daddy is so bossy, and it is all their fault that the snow is so slippery.' "—Sally Neidlanger McLane

"Skiing harnesses the natural 'derring-do' that children possess and directs it in the formation of such good qualities as courage, self-reliance, judgment, and initiative."—Conrad Brown

"You have got to make skiing fun like a game or the children just won't play."—Tomm Murstad

"Children of three and older believe in their hearts that they can learn to fly. They have done so in their dreams. On skis they have a chance to prove it."—Glen Springer-Miller

# TERRAIN

When Professor Stefan Kruckenhauser first looked at Sun Valley's famed Dollar Mountain, he said, "I'd like to put that little mountain in my pocket and take it home to St. Anton. It is the most beautiful thing for ski teaching I have ever seen." That's quite a compliment.

Dollar Mountain has the perfect ski school terrain. Free from trees, it has bowls that are excellent for practicing stem turns and stem christies; turning is very easy. A flat runout on the bottom is good for traverses and uphill christies. Dollar is kept in excellent condition by good slope grooming.

Proper terrain planning is important to the area operator. The ski school can take the load off lifts during peak periods. Classes can use other, less-used areas to practice. Ski schools can even help maintain the terrain by skiing different trails. Skiers not in ski school ski the same trails all the time. Good terrain selection is the link between the technique and methods. The instructor must use his teaching methods experience to adapt to the existing conditions.

Ski areas differ. Terrain within an area is variable, and snow conditions are never constant. This is why a teaching system must allow for diversification of teaching methods. All hazards should be considered. A slope usable one day may be impossible the next. Furthermore, the attitudes and abilities of the students must be considered with changes in terrain and weather.

Some teaching systems are placed in fixed sequence for the instructor, and the methodology is planned in prescribed exercises. This type of teaching takes away the initiative of the ski school and the individual instructor. More seriously, it leads to mistakes in judgment. Rather than use his own judgment, the instructor relies upon the prescribed plan. Many times the maneuver is virtually impossible under certain circumstances.

Inexperienced instructors often fail to gain the benefits of existing terrains within their respective area. A teacher should plan the descent of his class as a coach or racer would plot a course. He should figure the exercises and variations that can be used on a particular day.

The instructor should fix in his mind a typical trip with a class utilizing the various changes in the terrain. Round knolls, valleys, and open slopes should be considered to a particular exercise. Teach sideslipping, uphill christie, and garland exercises on the traverses. Gentle slopes are excellent for practicing edge control exercises, snowplows, or slow speed parallel christies.

The criterion for adequate terrain selection is good judgment. Experience is the best teacher, and as often as possible the ski school should meet and discuss various means of descending a slope adaptable to various snow conditions. These means should conform with the International Class system, A through F.

*Downhill Running:* The contour of the slope for straight running, ideally, should have a flat starting place with a flat runout. The grade should be slight with little elevation. The end of the runout should turn up. The beginning hill should be well groomed. If possible avoid hard snow or ice.

*Downhill Running* with a rounded, steeper slope—requires a counter slope. Instill the principle of forward lean as the slope steepness increases.

Fall-away slope requires forward lean at all three joints, ankle, knee, and hip. The slope is steep and short with a gradual transition to a flat and a counter slope. Try the steep to flat transition (dotted line), this will necessitate flexing of the three joints by requiring a down-up-down movement—relaxed and natural positions.

This shows ideal terrain, excellent for accentuating forward lean and flexing of all three joints. This slope requires a forward, up-movement on the counter slope and forward, down-movement on top of the roll. The gradient of the terrain must be chosen with care. Consider the ability of the student. This terrain is good for encouraging the down-up-down movement, reaction, and total motion.

*Snowplow:* A flat starting place is advantageous. The slope should be very gentle with an easy transition to the out-run. Packed, soft snow is ideal. The snowplow position can be practiced on the flat.

The snowplow turn slope should have the gradient as the straight snowplow—except it should be longer. Beware of hard snow.

## SNOWPLOW TURN

The same gentle gradient for the straight snowplow can be used. But this slope should be longer. Bowls or gullies are best adapted to snowplow learning. Bowls help the student learn naturally. As the student progresses, increase the gradient. The side slope on the bowls or gullies helps the student's weight transfer.

## TRAVERSE

The proper traverse terrain is essential. If it is not steep enough the student cannot begin the traverse. A slope with too much gradient may make the pupil slope-shy, and he may ski too close to the fall-line and lose control. A gentle slope with bowls and gullies is ideal. The diagram shows that the student is able to maintain his traverse in a constant speed (see A). By keeping the tips pointed uphill he can slow his speed (see B). It is easy to progress from less steep traverses to steeper traverses (C) and (D). This terrain helps to learn angulation. For example, the (C) figure shows how one can ski from the bottom of the gully to a traverse. The transition will require the use of angulation.

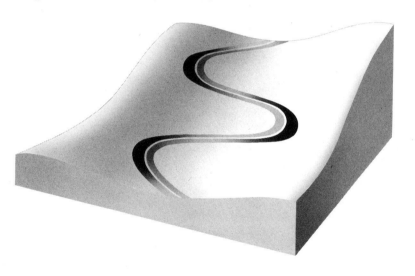

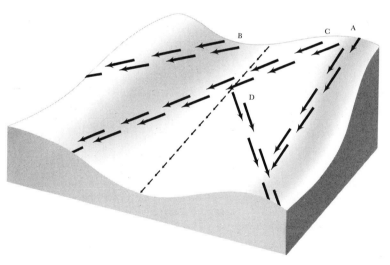

## TRAVERSING THROUGH GULLIES AND OVER RIDGES

This illustration shows how traversing should be practiced over a ridge, through a gully and over a ridge. The picture indicates how the weight is changed from one ski to another between traverses (A). The edges and lead are changed too. The reverse slope on the bowls slows the skier and forces the weight, edge, and lead change. During the transition the weight is evenly distributed with no angulation (B).

This terrain results in several changes of traverses. Remember, edging is created as a result of body angulation. Thus, the body must lean out from side to side as the skier changes from one traverse to another.

## STEM TURNS

These turns should be taught on an easy slope with good snow. Sloping bowls or gullies are best.

Turns should be made of short and long radius and with short and long traverses—depending on the *slope*. Choose terrain such that the student can easily regain the angulated traverse after each turn.

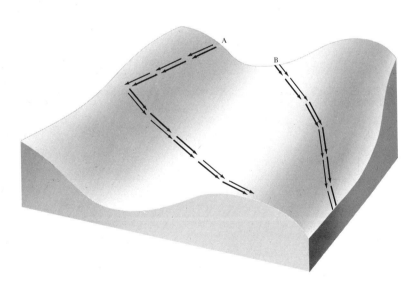

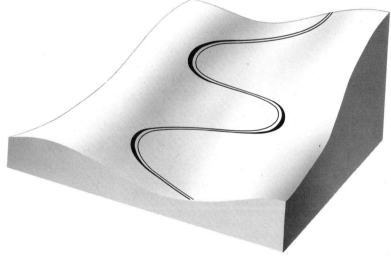

## FORWARD SIDESLIPPING

The object of the forward sideslip is to effect an edge release from the traverse. The terrain is of extreme important consideration. The gradient must be steep enough to allow the skis to release when the angulation is eliminated. But a slope that is too steep may cause the student fear and resulting of loss of control.

A gully with rather steep incline on the side is good for traversing and sideslipping exercises. Since this slope is steeper, it will require proper weighting of the lower ski. The key is not to begin the forward slip too early and too fast. If there is too much speed, the student can step uphill. If he is too slow, he can step downhill.

Slipping over a small ridge at the top of a gully or side of a trail provides easy learning. This is because the skier is literally standing over the centers of the skis with little weight on the tips and tails. This requires good balance (natural positioning), relaxation, and flexing at all three joints.

## CHRISTIES UPHILL OVER A KNOLL

To learn christies uphill attempt to find terrain that is convex, has round knolls, and large moguls. Note in (A) that the maneuver is chosen for the terrain. One can work around the knoll as in (B).

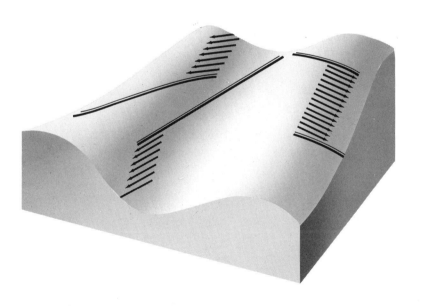

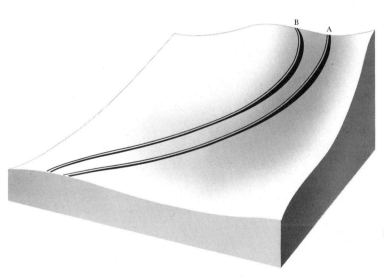

## LINKED STEM CHRISTIES ON A RIDGE

One of the thrills can be the stem christie, performed in a bowl or over a ridge (as shown). The rhythm and gracefulness is a product of the terrain. The stem christie on moderate steep terrain in good snow can be a basic bulwark in learning more advanced skiing. At this level of learning, the experienced teacher will seek terrain that will bring out all the qualities of the seven basic principles. Go through each basic principle, one by one, in this terrain with the stem christie. It will do wonders for improving the skiing and developing confidence.

# AVALANCHES* by M. Schild

*Editors' Note: This section has not been revised. The article is one of the few published as an introduction to avalanches and directed toward the instructor. The Editors do not hope to present a course in avalanches. When Mr. Schild was asked to review the article for revision, he recommended no change.*

For the ski instructor, avalanches are a professional risk. It is imperative for him to be able to recognize and judge this danger and to be well versed in how to protect a group of skiers and himself. Also, he has to know how to give first aid assistance and exactly what to do in proper sequence if an avalanche does strike.

Here are some facts about avalanches:

(a) The number of fatal avalanche accidents is rising steadily. In Switzerland over the last ten years, 72 percent of skiers caught in avalanches died.

(b) The investigations showed that, in more than 90 percent of the accidents, the victims or their friends started the avalanches. This would indicate that if the conditions had been properly evaluated most of these tragedies could have been avoided.

(c) The increase in avalanche accidents of groups accompanied

*Article published November, 1962, Swiss National Avalanche Research Center.*

by mountain guides or instructors tends to undermine the confidence in the professional; this trend will be reversed by better and continuous training.

*TRENDS:* Snow is an unpredictable matter and avalanche danger often changes quickly, due to many influences. These changes, sometimes of completely local nature, are difficult to detect from without as they are a result of internal structural changes of the snow crystals, or a result of a poor distribution of new masses of snow on the old layers. Generally, too much attention is focused on the pitch of the terrain. Besides the incline of the mountains and slopes, we have to recognize what is underneath the snow, the exposure to the sun, the relative humidity, the prevailing wind, and the altitude. So-called avalanche slopes can be made safe for the better part of a ski season.

*HOW AVALANCHES FORM:* A "loose snow avalanche" can form after a fresh snow fall on a steep slope, or in the spring, when the surface layers are soaked from melting snow. Such a slide starts at a point and is shaped like a drop, and in general is of little consequence to the skier. The dangerous avalanche to the skier is the so-called "snow-board" or slab. As indicated by its name, it consists of layers of wind-compacted snow that breaks off from the rest of the slope or mountain in sheets or boards. The following factors influence its formation:

(a) *Layers of snow:*

Invisible to us, inside the masses of snow, there is a constant change of snow crystals that can upset the mechanical structure of the layers. A slight compression can reduce elasticity. Low temperatures at the beginning of a season can loosen the thin cover or "freeze" out the base, leading to a poor foundation. Hard lids, caused by rain, wind, or sunshine and layers of heavy "frost," can be called dangerous "grease jobs" when covered with fresh or, particularly, with wind-driven snow in large quantities. The cohesion between the layers and the firmness of each layer are more influential in creating avalanche danger than the total mass of snow.

(b) *Fresh snow:*

Most avalanches form during or right after fresh snow falls. This is explained by the additional weight (approximately 220 pounds per cubic yard) added to the existing cover and the resulting overloading of the slopes. Most of the time the fresh snow departs alone, before it can settle on the old layers. If it stays on, it usually will bind well, but can at the same time create dangerous tensions in the old layers, particularly on convex slopes. This condition can linger for weeks and is a regular trap for the inexperienced skier. Any storm that deposits one foot of snow or more can lead to these conditions.

(c) *Wind:*

The wind is responsible for most snow-board avalanches. When loose, fresh snow is blown about when it falls, or soon afterward, it collects and packs on slopes in the "windshade" with mechanically disturbed snow-crystals as an unevenly distributed mass. The dangers are now numerous; some slopes are loaded with several times the actual precipitation, often referred to as "snowshields." The main weight is in the middle of such slopes, and the "anchors" on the surrounding ridges are thin and unreliable. Furthermore, wind-drifted snow cracks or breaks easy; it is not very cohesive. The wind leaves bare ridges and exposes rocks that often lure the unwary skier to enter overloaded areas in the belief that there is little cover underfoot.

(d) *Temperatures:*

Changes in temperature greatly influence transformation of snow crystals and changes in avalanche conditions; unfortunately it is not feasible to apply a definite formula. A continuous cold spell can keep powder snow dangerous for days; a quick cold snap after warm weather can eliminate avalanche danger altogether. Slowly rising temperatures make the snow settle and the layers bind well; a quick warm spell or rain usually means trouble as the surface snow gains in weight and loses cohesion at the same time. In the spring, the danger usually starts after sun and heat soften the surface, which becomes unreliable to ski on. The danger then often is acute.

*PRECAUTIONS:* How to prevent avalanche accidents and ways to survive, if you get caught:

(a) *Conditions:*

If you are not absolutely sure of the prevailing snow conditions in an area, ask the local ski patrol or professional.

(b) *Choice of terrain:*

This has to be made according to conditions. Don't traverse dangerous slopes; if you have to, cross as high as possible. A vertical ascent always is safer and allows you to take advantage of natural protection, such as trees, boulders, ledges, and small terraces in the terrain. In case of doubt, carry your skis up or down a bare ridge. If you have to cross a bad slope while climbing, take off the skins and ski across a downhill traverse; the dangerous cover thus will have to carry your weight for a shorter time.

(c) *Spacing:*

In dangerous conditions, the intervals between skiers should be such that never more than one person can possibly be hit should a slide be triggered. These intervals have to be strictly kept up to the last man.

(d) *Avalanche cord:*

A colored cord, about fifty to a hundred feet long should be used in dangerous conditions by at least the leader, or, better still, the entire group. This has proven definitely to be effective, often leading to quick discovery and rescue of the victim.

(e) *Conduct:*

Every skier should know exactly what to do when an avalanche strikes and he should plan his descent out of the sliding zone before entering the danger area. If this appears impossible, the bindings should be loosened, straps undone, and the loops of the poles taken off the wrist.

(f) *Lookout:*

A group, before entering a danger zone, should post a lookout where good visibility exists over the entire danger area.

(g) *Experience:*

Experience tells us that technically good skiers have a far better chance of survival. Intermediate skiers should be kept away from steep slopes in questionable conditions.

*MEANS OF SELF-PRESERVATION:* It is understood that getting covered by an avalanche is always dangerous. Not only can you suffocate, you can also die of shock. It is imperative that you keep a cool head and never question your getting rescued quickly. Besides the possibility of skiing out of danger, skiers are often able to cling to a small tree, a rock or a ledge, or to ram a ski, a pole, or an arm into the lower layers and let the avalanche go over. If you are washed away and have been able to rid yourself of skis, poles, and rucksack, make swimming motions with arms and legs, and press arms in front of chest and fists in front of your face before the avalanche comes to a standstill. Be sure to keep your mouth closed.

*RESCUE:* The conduct of the group skiing with the avalanche victim determines his chances for survival. One of the most important moves is the exact marking of the spot where the skier disappeared for the last time. This can reduce by acres the search area for would-be rescuers. From the marker down, look first for visible or acoustic signs of the victim. If this proves fruitless, dispatch one, or better, two, of the good skiers to go for help. Make sure they have correct information, if possible in writing, as to: location, time of accident, why, and how many involved, and what measures already have been taken at the scene. If support by plane or 'copter is feasible, advise on landing possibilities. If only one

survivor remains, he should make sure to free any of the victims that are readily accessible. The markers left behind are very important and should be substantial enough that even a strong wind cannot blow them away, or move them.

The group remaining on the accident scene should make every effort to mobilize every skier in the area and continue relentlessly to search for traces. This has to be done systematically and the most experienced should take command. By tearing the loops off the ski poles, they can be used like avalanche rods. Form a line across the area to be searched and ram the poles in the snow after every step in front of each boot. The chances of finding somebody buried at the depth thus reached is a rewarding 70 percent. Mark the area already searched and do not let anybody soil the avalanche surface with refuse of any kind, especially if an avalanche dog can be expected on the scene. Foot tracks and pole holes do not influence a dog's nose in the slightest. Cigarette butts, paper, or urine definitely will.

When the rescue team arrives, their leader takes charge.

*The Editors suggest that the instructor consider further avalanche study. Some of the best and most current works are as follows:*

*Agriculture Handbook No. 94, Snow Avalanches.* Forest Service, U.S. Department of Agriculture, Revised Edition, Washington: U.S. Government Printing Office, 1961.

Brower, David R. *Manual of Ski Mountaineering.* San Francisco: Sierra Club, Third Edition, 1962.

Fraser, Colin. *The Avalanche Enigma.* London: John Murray, 1966.

A Chapelle, Ed. *The ABC of Avalanche Safety.* Boulder, Colorado: Highlander Publishing Co., 1961.

Mountaineers, Inc. *Mountaineering—The Freedom of the Hills.* Seattle: Third Edition, 1965.

*Interested instructors and instructors associations should arrange to see the film* Avalanche Control *produced and distributed by the Forest Service, U.S. Department of Agriculture. Copies may be obtained by contacting the nearest regional office of the U.S. Forest Service.*

HANNES SCHNEIDER—JUMPING
Photo by C. J. Luther, 1910-11
Courtesy Herbert Schneider

# FOR SAFER AND MORE ENJOYABLE SKIING

I. *SKI COURTESY:* Golden rules for skiers—be aware of others.

1. Carry your skis vertically over your shoulder so others are not hit by your equipment.
2. Wait your turn in the lift line; line cutting is reserved for ski school classes and working ski patrolmen.
3. Do not walk on ski slopes without skis. The hole left by a boot may cause a skier to fall. If you must walk, do so at the edge of the slope.
4. Follow posted instructions at the ski area. Ask the lift operator, ski patrol, or ski instructor if you don't understand.
5. Fill your sitzmarks (the dent in the snow caused by your fall). Tramp the snow with your skis to smooth the area. A hole will not be left to cause a fall for another skier.
6. Ski in control. Be able to stop when necessary and be ready to avoid other skiers. LEARN BY TAKING LESSONS FROM A CERTIFIED SKI INSTRUCTOR.
7. Wear ski retaining devices to avoid loose skis (two-point, fixation, safety straps or a type of ski stop). Shout a warning to those below when a ski is loose. A runaway ski is extremely dangerous and can cause serious injury.
8. Give way to the beginner. His control may not be as good as yours.
9. Don't swing or bounce chairs. Don't "snap" poma-lift platters, T-bars, or ropes. This may cause other skiers to fall off or may result in lift failure.
10. Cooperate with the Ski Patrol. They will assist you and give you information about the ski area.
    *Courtesy will make skiing more enjoyable—HAVE FUN—tell your friend about skiing.*

II. *SKIING CONDUCT:* Rules of the slope for skier traffic.

1. Ski in control. Be able to stop when necessary and avoid other skiers.
2. Leave the ski lift, unloading platform promptly to make room for skiers behind you.
3. Check skier traffic before starting. Look uphill for oncoming skiers before descending.
4. When overtaking another skier, the overtaker shall avoid the skier below or beyond him. He may not see you.
5. Let the skier know on which side you are passing. State audibly "on your right" or "passing left," etc.
6. A moving skier avoids a stationary skier and passes at a safe distance.
7. Stop at the side of trails or at visible locations that

will not impede nor block the normal passage of other skiers.

8. Skiers entering a main slope from a side or intersecting trail shall yield to skiers already on the slope.
9. Skiers approaching each other on opposite traverses shall pass to the right to avoid collision.
10. When arriving at the bottom of the slope, do not stand in the flat runout at the end of the trail. You may be in the way of other skiers moving very fast.
    *Remember the inexperienced skiers—Don't crowd them —Give beginners the benefit of the doubt—BE COURTEOUS.*

III. *SKI SAFETY:* How you and your friends can enjoy safe skiing.
1. Be physically fit. Get a good night's sleep.
2. Eat a good breakfast. Stop for lunch. When skiing, as when driving, don't drink alcoholic beverages.
3. Drive safely to and from the ski area.
4. Dress for the weather; wear nonbreakable sunglasses or goggles; use sunburn cream even on cloudy days; check for frostbite on cold days.
5. Use proper equipment; check it often.
6. Use properly adjusted release bindings with a ski retaining device.
7. Follow posted instructions at ski lifts and on slopes.
8. Learn the meaning of the uniform trail signs: green-square—easiest; yellow-triangle—more difficult; blue-circular—most difficult. Consult a ski area map for slope difficulty.
9. Be aware of danger spots. Look for the red-diamond-shaped sign. It means EXTRA CAUTION.
10. Obey trail closure signs. A fluorescent orange octagonal sign means AVALANCHE CLOSURE.
11. Ski within your ability. Improve by taking lessons from a CERTIFIED SKI INSTRUCTOR. Ski in control; don't be a schuss boomer.
12. Loose clothing and long hair are hazards on rope tows and ski lifts.
13. When riding any lift, carry ski poles by the shafts with the points back. Don't have straps around your wrists. Take straps off wrists when skiing in trees or bushes. The jerk caused when the ski pole basket becomes caught may dislocate a shoulder.
14. Keep ski tips up when riding chair lifts.
15. Avoid deep snow until you've learned how to ski in ski school.
16. When ski touring away from the ski area, check out and check back in with the Ski Patrol or other responsible individuals. It may be worth your life.
17. Ski with companions when skiing remote runs or areas. Four or more is recommended. If an accident occurs, one stays with the victim, two go for help.
18. When an accident occurs, cross a pair of skis upright in the snow ABOVE the victim. Be sure to report the EXACT location of the accident to the Ski Patrol or lift operator. At least one person should stay with the injured person until the Ski Patrol arrives.
19. Stop skiing when you are tired or when visibility is poor. Allow sufficient time to complete your last run before the Ski Patrol "sweeps" the slopes.
20. Ski defensively; be aware of other skiers; be ready at all times to react to the unpredictable movements of beginners.
    *BE COURTEOUS—BE SAFE—SKI IN CONTROL— HAVE FUN!*

LIST OF SAFETY TIPS AVAILABLE FROM NSPS OFFICE
*Ten Safety Tips* (Recommended by USSA & NSPS)—SPI-ST63-1.
*Ten Tips for Happier Skiing* (From the NSPS)—SPI-ST63-1A.
*23 Ski-Do's*—SPI-ST64-2.
*Safety Tips for the Skier from the National Ski Patrol System*—SPI-ST64-3.
*Ski Courtesy: Golden Rules for Skiers—Be Aware of Others.* —SPI-ST66-4.
*Skiing Conduct: Rules of the Slope for Skier Traffic*—SPI-ST66-5.

*Ski Safety: How You and Your Friends Can Enjoy Safe Skiing*—SPI-ST66-6.

*Ski Wise (Color Pamphlet Containing Information Every Skier Should know. Cost—2 cents each.)*

*Posters:* Set of 12 3-color, 16″ x 22″ posters with ten basic ski safety tips. Cost—$2.00 per set.

### LIST OF FILMS AVAILABLE FROM NSPS OFFICE
(At no charge)

*Avalanche*—fifteen min. Sound-color. 16 mm.

*Ski Sense*—thirty min. Sound-color. 16 mm.

*Patrol Ski Proficiency Test*—fifteen min. Sound-color. 16 mm.

*Avalanche Control*—forty min. Sound-color. 16 mm.

*Be Safe—Ski Wise*—four and one-half min. Sound-color. 16mm.

*The Story of the National Ski Patrol*—thirty min. Sound-color. 16mm. (Order directly from your local Schlitz distributor only; NSPS office does not have copies available.)

*Slides—Avalanche*—thirty min. 35mm. Color with accompanying lecture-type script.

*Safety Tips for Happier Skiing*—ten minutes. 35 mm. Color.

International Class sign. Classes A through F

## NATIONAL SKIER'S COURTESY CODE

1. All skiers shall ski under control. Control shall mean in such a manner that a skier can avoid other skiers or objects.

2. When skiing downhill and overtaking another skier, the overtaking skier shall avoid the skier below him.

3. Skiers approaching each other on opposite traverses pass to the right.

4. Skiers shall not stop in a location which will obstruct a trail or stop where they are not visible from above or impede the normal passage of other skiers when loading or unloading.

5. A skier entering a trail or slope from a side or intersecting trail shall first check for approaching downhill skiers.

6. A standing skier shall check for approaching downhill skiers before starting.

7. When walking or climbing in a ski area, skis should be worn and the climber or walker shall keep to the side of the trail or slope.

8. All skiers shall wear safety straps or other devices to prevent runaway skis.

9. Skiers shall keep off closed trails and posted areas and shall observe all traffic signs and other regulations as prescribed by the ski area.

Be sure to see this brilliantly photographed twenty-minute color film on the National Skier's Courtesy Code. The 16 mm movie, filmed in three of America's great ski areas, features plenty of fine skiing, some humorous sequences of "how not to ski," plus a fun-to-take quiz that will test your courtesy as a skier. Produced as a skier service by Humble Oil & Refining Company, *Rules of the Slopes* enjoys the enthusiastic endorsement of the U.S. Ski Association, National Ski Patrol System, National Ski Areas Association, and Professional Ski Instructors of America.

To arrange for a showing of *Rules of the Slopes*, simply contact the nearest divisional office of the U.S. Ski Association or National Ski Patrol System. Send a postcard giving the name of your ski club, the name and address of your club secretary, date requested for film showing, and expected attendance. Showings also may be scheduled by writing to Humble Film Libraries, 1212 Avenue of the Americas, New York, New York 10036.

# ADVANCED SKIING

*On Becoming An Expert Skier*
*Basic Principles*
*Exercises*
*Maneuvers*
*Powder Snow Skiing*
*Skiing on Ice*

# ON BECOMING AN EXPERT SKIER

Since the earlier editions of the Official American Ski Technique were published in the 1960s many important changes have taken place in international skiing. These changes have been a result of intensive study of racing efficiencies, and have helped revolutionize the application of ski technique. They have not, however, changed the basic technique of ski teaching. Advanced skiing opens new vistas and fills the gap between basic technique and racing.

Advanced skiing should not change normal teaching progression of basic ski technique or of the ski school classes. It must be remembered that at the end of the fifties (in 1958) the advanced technique was short swing or wedeln. Not many people could ski the system, and a good short-swing instructor was often an exception. The public was rarely seen skiing wedeln correctly. A study of films of those days makes one realize how much better the American skier is today. Sophistication of equipment, technique, etc., have led to this improvement.

Confusion exists today among the skiing public over basic technique and advanced skiing as it did in the late fifties. At that time, quality of the skier was considered high, but it doesn't compare with today, and where will it be tomorrow?

PSIA has been under pressure to change technique often. However, PSIA's concern is for the skiing public. The instructor must live with his methods and results for years. It is not wise to change teaching methods until they are proven to be efficient, effective, and, above all, safe. Advanced technique had to be proven. It must be understood by the instructor and be teachable.

It is essential that the study plan be up-to-date in order to continue the student's interest. Young people may reach the advanced skiing stage rapidly. A basic teaching progression should be followed. Use of exercises is helpful. It must be constantly kept in mind that the teacher of advanced technique must himself be in the elite class and be able to evaluate advanced skiing students with the students' capabilities in mind.

Although we refer to advanced skiing as being beyond class "F" (highest basic technique class), we can never eliminate the basics. By the time a skier reaches the advanced skiing stage, he has developed his own style. He has the most up-to-date equipment. The fear and anxiety which one might find in the novice are gone. The skier moves comfortably, using the terrain to his advantage. He is ready to try anything. However, style is not technique. Speed is not technique. Terrain is not technique. Explore the basic characteristics of advanced skiing—those movements similiar to or different from the basic skills!

Full advantage is taken of the forces building up at the end phase of a turn to initiate the next turn. Unweighting is applied and the release executed by voluntary lateral movements. Ski-snow contact is kept as constant as possible to take advantage of the ski design. The nearly irresistible uncoiling action which results from the anticipation movement is much used. The total freely flexing body movements "escape" the terrain. The terrain is not an obstacle to the advanced skier—it is his playground.

It is not meant here to intimate that a skier must be a Killy or a Schranz to ski these maneuvers. The point is that the basic skills must exist and then be refined. Speed is not a criterion. As Otto Lang said (*Downhill Skiing,* 1946), "Speed is the thrill, but control is the art." The serpent turn which produces the precise carve gives excellent control; speed is a matter of choice when control exists. Avalement (swallowing, terrain absorbing) movements actually have the effect of modifying the terrain.

Most skiers who develop to the advanced level have found "Skiing is not exercise only, not merely a sport—it is a revelation of body and soul," as stated by Otto Lang. This is the magic that drives the skier. Thus, advanced skiing is a combining of basic skill and personal desire.

# BASIC PRINCIPLES

*UNWEIGHTING:* Subtle unweighting forces are used in advanced maneuvers. Down motion is the quickest unweighting motion and helps the skis contact with the snow. Subtle unweighting can be produced by the relaxing of the downward pressure on the skis. Terrain variations are used to assist unweighting.

*EDGE CONTROL:* In basic technique edge control is mostly effected by angulation. The skis are displaced beneath the body by various means: stemming, hopping, and counterrotation. In advanced technique edge change can be accomplished by lateral movement of the body over the skis. This movement may be started in the upper body or lower body depending upon turning circumstances.

*LEVERAGE:* In basic technique constant emphasis is placed on forward leverage (lean). This is equally important in advanced technique. The skier adjusts leverage for the most effective use of the design of the ski. However, in advanced maneuvers, back leverage (weighting the tail of the ski) is important to increasing the holding power of the ski in some instances.

Basic technique involves *natural positioning*. A high relaxed stance is emphasized in the traverse; supple flexing and extending movements are applied in turns.

*EDGE CONTROL* and initiation of turns in basic forms as well as in advanced skiing require muscular force. The advanced skier utilizes all possibilities of his anatomy. Having accomplished the basic skills, he develops a freedom of movement.

*AXIAL MOTION:* Rotary motions of both upper and lower body are used in advanced skiing. Rotation is an optional part of advanced technique. As applied to advanced skiing, rotary motions are not voluntary movements as such. They are the action of the upper and lower body working against each other.

*WEIGHT TRANSFER* becomes progressively more subtle as the skier's ability improves. Wide stance is used in the progression in basic technique. In advanced technique wide stance is used to allow the legs to act independently for lateral stability. Free leg action gives the ability to steer. There are necessarily more frequent and subtle changes in weight distribution from one ski to the other. The timing of weight shift is more varied than in basic turns. Reactions to balance adjustments must be quick and positive. The weight transfer principle applies; its application is more demanding.

PSIA expects this new and revised edition of *The Official American Ski Technique* to be a valuable contribution in teaching and learning advanced skiing maneuvers.

# EXERCISES

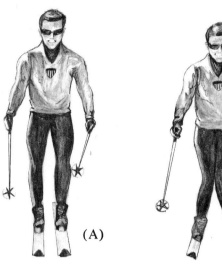  

(A)                    (B)                    (C)

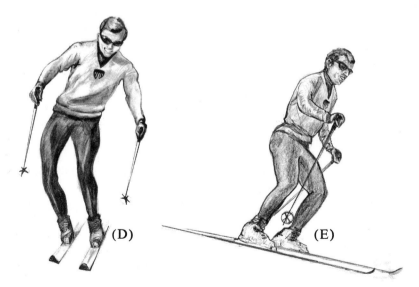 

(D)                    (E)

### REVIEW—OPEN STANCE

*EDGE CONTROL EXERCISES:*

Open stance positions will have been learned in basic methodology. Review open positions in downhill running, traverses, and in turning. The object is to prepare the skier to use each leg independently. The skier's posture is adjusted to his advantage.

(A) Straight running (open stance)—the width of the stance is determined by flat ski-snow contact, body build, snow conditions, and terrain.

(B-C) Edge control is exercised by changing from outside edges to inside edges. This maneuver should be done on gentle slopes.

(D) Traverse. The skier traverses over bumpy terrain. The entire body absorbs the changing terrain by flexion of hips, knees, ankles, and torso.

(E) Parallel (open stance)—this turn is initiated with pole-plant, up-weighting, and counterrotation.

(A)

(B)

(C)

## ADVANCED POLE-PLANT EXERCISES

The pole-plant in basic technique has been directed toward timing and unweighting. The pole-plant in advanced skiing is also used to create a pivot.

(A)    Pole-plant for timing and unweighting.

(B)    Pole-plant to stabilize the upper body while unweighting. The pole is planted toward the fall-line, deflecting the in-side shoulder and upper body into the turn. It is a pivot and partially supports the skier's weight.

(C)    Double pole-plant: This is seldom used in advanced tech-nique. The illustration is an exercise to help maintain weight forward on the skis. The skier learns to keep his upper body in the direction of the turn.

Note the relation of the pole-plant to the skis in (A), (B), and (C).

## UP-UNWEIGHTING WITH COUNTERROTATION

Although this is basic technique, it should be practiced repeatedly for advanced skiing. The purpose is to utilize the pole-plant exercise; position as shown in the second figure. Ultimately finish the turn with a stop christie (with or without pole-plant).

From a traverse, sink, plant pole, use up-forward movement, counterrotation, and transfer of weight to the outside ski. This is followed by a sinking motion and angulation. The arc of the turn is completed as the skier rises to a new traverse.

When initiating the turn with a check, the tails are displaced accompanied by pole-plant.

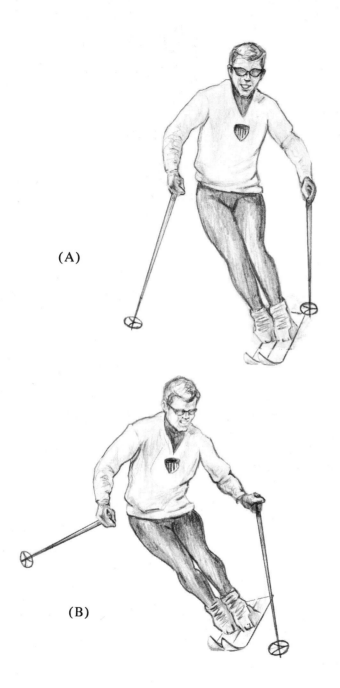

(A)

(B)

(C)

## UP-UNWEIGHTING WITH ROTATION

The turn is initiated with rotary motion of the upper body transmitted to the lower body.

## THE "HOCKEY STOP" EXERCISE

The skier begins in a slightly lower downhill running position, balanced with the hands held farther forward. Allow the skis to run until picking up speed. Pivot the skis abruptly by bending the knees quickly and weight the tails. This skier is in nearly a sitting position. The skis are literally jumped across the hill. This exercise leads to the sideslip check. The movement is the same except the skis are allowed to slip a few yards before stopping. The pressure is over the entire length of the ski, the upper body facing downhill. This exercise is applicable in advanced skiing to suddenly change direction or stop on steep terrain, or to slow down at the end of a traverse.

## STOP CHRISTIE

At the end of the turn the knees press forward. Forward motion of the skis is stopped with a down motion, displacement of the tails, edge set, and pole-plant. The displacing of the tails results in the upper body facing downhill. The skis pivot beneath the body. Practice of this exercise develops the correct rhythm and feeling for short turns and the coordination of edge set and pole-plant.

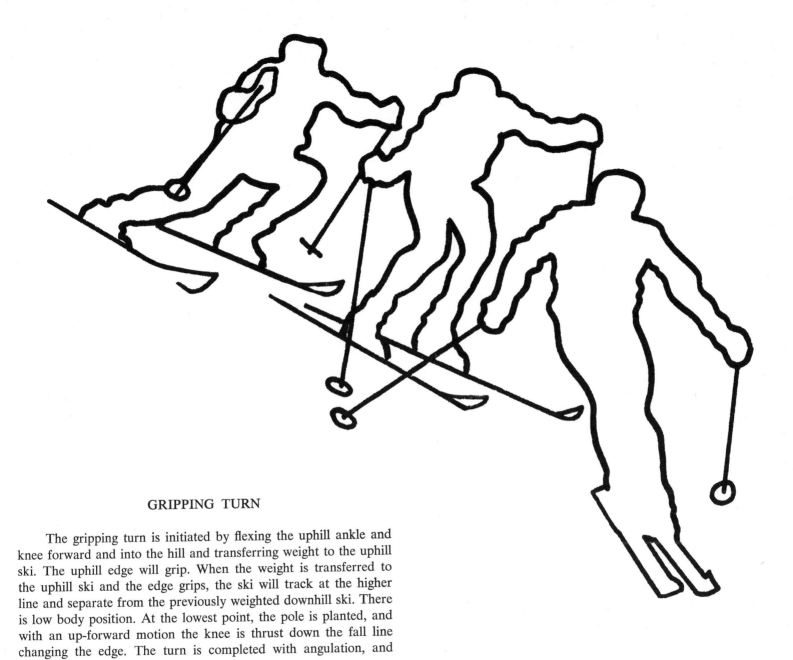

## GRIPPING TURN

The gripping turn is initiated by flexing the uphill ankle and knee forward and into the hill and transferring weight to the uphill ski. The uphill edge will grip. When the weight is transferred to the uphill ski and the edge grips, the ski will track at the higher line and separate from the previously weighted downhill ski. There is low body position. At the lowest point, the pole is planted, and with an up-forward motion the knee is thrust down the fall line changing the edge. The turn is completed with angulation, and a rise to the new traverse.

# MANEUVERS

Advanced skiing is the further expansion of ski technique. It is possible for skiers who have the physical capability and desire to go beyond class "F" (short swing). No detailed teaching plan has been presented for advanced technique. The skier at this level has the foundation of basic technique and is able to experiment. Balance and edge control are established. Learning to ski, as in all other learning, is a building process. The "check" motion learned in the parallel turn and applied in short swing and check wedeln is the building platform for expanding into new variations of the turn. The checking motion produces a body position in which the upper body faces downhill and is stabilized by the pole-plant. The vigorous down motion and edge set result in rebound and pivoting of the skis to start the turn.

The difference between the basic turn and the progressive turn begins with the attempt to retain ski-snow contact through the unweighted phase of the turn. Vertical up-unweighting is replaced with lateral movement of the body over the skis, pulling the skis into the turn. *Ski-snow contact is maintained.* Another basic difference is the pole-plant. Rather than allowing the basket to move forward toward the tip of the ski, or setting the pole in line with the heels, the pole is set obliquely downhill. Finally, the movement of anticipation is vital.

*THE SERPENT:* The serpent turn is probably the natural progression from the basic technique because of the control possible from the carving edge this maneuver creates. As in the learning of any maneuver, terrain selection is important. An intermediate bumpy slope would be best for the first attempts to learn this turn. Do not use steep terrain on which the primary concern would be safety and high control. Relaxation is the better attitude. The skier at this stage has good knowledge of the initiation of a turn. Now, however, the movement of *anticipation* becomes vital.

Anticipation is a preparatory movement in the direction of the turn. The body is "pre-sensing" the turn. There is a stretching of muscles in the upper outer torso, creating a position of readiness for the turn. This movement prior to the release of the edge creates potential turning impetus within the body in the form of muscle tension that greatly facilitates the turn because of the tendency of the upper and lower parts of the body to point in the same direction when other forces are removed.

Movements for the serpent on an intermediate bumpy slope: from the traverse, as the tips reach the top of the bump, plant the pole in the direction the upper body is facing (downhill). The pole-plant should be from twelve to eighteen inches from the skis. Without this movement the rest of the turn will not have the characteristic smoothness of the serpent. Now, allow the pole to stabilize the upper body.

Relax the back muscles and allow the upper body to drop forward and downhill through the "space" between the pole and the skis. Do not overexaggerate or the back will stiffen. Simultaneously, bend the knees and the skis will begin to be pulled into the turn as you continue stabilizing the body with the pole. A steady increase in pressure forward to the tips produces a precise carve. This pressure to the tips is reduced once you have passed the fall-line to eliminate excessive heel slip. The radius of the turn is controlled by the extension of the body in the final phases of the turn. Between turns the body should be upright, wall balanced, and supple.

On smooth intermediate slopes the serpent technique can replace the rebound (vertical motion) which results from the check and hard edge set used in basic technique. With practice the edge setting motion will be reduced to nearly zero. The skis seem to roll smoothly from one edge to the other because of the serpent movements. The dropping forward and downhill of the upper body produces an irresistible pulling of the skis into the turn. (This movement of the upper body is similar to the striking of a snake—so the name, serpent.) The skier must remember to keep the weight to the outside ski. Too much pressure on the inside ski is a common error in the serpent on smooth intermediate slopes.

Once the skier has mastered the serpent on bumpy and smooth intermediate slopes he will have little difficulty adjusting the turn to steep slopes. Rather than rebounding from the edge set, the back muscles relax and the upper body drops forward and downhill and the knees are bent—the same movements as on intermediate terrain.

*Avoid* too low a position before the turn and excessive bending at the waist before the turn. These will reduce the effect of the striking motion when it is applied.

*Remember:* Pressure to the tips is relaxed after the fall line. Pressure should be equal between the heel and the ball of the foot. Do not rebound (rise vertically) from the edge set. This too destroys the serpent movement. Do not delay the linking of the flexing of the knees with the tipping downhill and forward of the upper body. It will be hard to start the turn. Do not remain in a constant forward position—this creates slipping of the heels. The forward weighting and tipping of the body must be neutralized by the lower legs. Try to push the feet forward in the direction of the turn until some pressure is felt on the heels after the fall-line.

The vertical motions are virtually eliminated in the serpent. Be careful not to allow yourself to lose the ability to vertically act/react over the skis. Many times these quick reactions are necessary. Occasional short swing on steep slopes where the vigorous edge set and rebound are applied will retain this ability.

*AVALEMENT:* Literally, avalement is "swallowing"; it is not a turn. Avalement is another method of maintaining ski-snow contact. The retraction (folding) of the legs under the body absorbs variations in terrain. Knees retract, the legs "fold" under the torso for the purpose of ski-snow contact and balance. This movement can be applied in the turn and is vital in the bumpy traverse. Avalement absorbs pressures from the terrain.

*Remember:* The purpose is to absorb and use the terrain. Avalement maintains the center of gravity in an even path. It helps one avoid being thrown off balance in bumpy terrain by eliminating the unbalancing shock and loss of ski-snow contact. For con-

trol of speed when applying avalement in a turn, steering with the outside ski from the instant of the beginning of the turn is necessary. Without the tipping forward movement of the serpent turn, avalement in a turn would simply produce "sitting back."

*JET TURN:* A variation of the short-swing turn. The turn is initiated from an angulated sideslip. There is edge set, pole-plant, anticipation, and up-motion. The body relaxes into the up-motion, keeping ski-snow contact rather than rebounding. The pole should be planted in the direction the body is facing (downhill), rather than in line with the heels. During the control phase of the turn,

the skier is in a slightly forward position. The skis slip the turn rather than carve. Extreme angulation does not exist until the edge set and pole-plant. This stops the slide and initiates the next turn.

In the end phase of the turn the constant weight against the ski, which has been applied through the radius of the turn, creates a pressure. The relaxing of the muscles of the legs after the edge set allows the skis to run ahead. The skis momentarily "escape." The skier anticipates the radius of the next turn, and the jetting action is controlled by reapplication of the pressure of weight forward and muscle tension.

All the advanced christies have the characteristics of the stable upper body and the absorbing motions of the legs. Somewhat more reliance is placed on the pole for stabilizing the upper body than in basic technique. In the early phase of the turn, the pole can be a deflecting force.

In conclusion, the advanced skier adjusts technique to every terrain variation—at will.

# POWDER SNOW SKIING

Most of the powder snow skiing available to a skier will not present situations in which the basic technique is not adaptable and efficient. It is not until a skier confronts deep snow (over a foot of new snow) that some advanced skiing technique maneuvers will be necessary to negotiate the slope. Skiing less than a foot of powder snow affords the skier the same base as the packed slope provides, although a more "floating" feeling exists because there is no direct contact with that base. He will become aware that some adjustments in timing because of more lateral resistance from the snow against the ski will be necessary. As the skier gradually gains confidence, he will find that skiing in powder snow is even easier than skiing on hard snow.

Generally, in moderate amounts of powder snow the skier can adjust to the added lateral resistance by: weighting both skis, lowering the center of gravity; bouncing slightly with weight on both skis; planting poles rhythmically, and turning the skis left and right during the unweighted phase with little displacement. As a skier becomes more accustomed to powder snow his movements become modified and displacement of the heels can become greater.

In deeper powder snow or in wet snow the situation changes. Although in basic technique the weight is on the downhill ski, the powder skier must weight both skis. An effort should be made to keep the knees and boots together. The center of gravity should be lowered by bending the knees and weighting the heels. Pressure forward on the skis would make them dive. The down-up-unweighting motion seems particularly effective for turning in deep or wet snow. "Bouncing" unweighting when properly timed will almost bounce the skis free of the snow. This is a slow-motion bouncing. The down should be a slow and continuous sinking, and the up-motion delayed. At slower speeds, anticipation as part of the preparation of the turn will make the turn easier. As you up-unweight try to move the skis to the fall-line before weighting them. Again, as confidence is gained the skier will find it possible to reduce the bouncing motion and be able to move the skis laterally. The skis are projected forward through the arc of the turn reducing lateral resistance.

# SKIING ON ICE

"Ice"—what is it? A beginning skier might even refer to a hard-packed surface as icy; on the other hand, the racer thrives on hardpack and ice. The quality or surface of the ice depends on the water content. Ice with a very high water content *(blue ice)* is similar to that on an ice-skating rink. Few skiers are at home or comfortable in this condition. It is nearly impossible to set an edge. If the skier is faced with crossing a limited area of blue ice he should not try to perform any unnecessary movements while negotiating that part of the terrain. Rather, the skier should seek an area with more surface snow on which to initiate or finish a turn. Even the best skiers try to avoid this very slippery condition.

*Gray ice* is still very solid and slippery, but with the proper equipment this condition can afford very good skiing. This is also true in the case of *frozen granular ice,* which has the lowest water content and a crunchy surface for the edge to grip.

As with other skiing, ice skiing has been made easier for the student because of innovations in equipment. For example, the fiber glass and plastic boot materials have virtually eliminated the breakdown of the boots. New boot materials, better ski design, introduction of the cracked edge, etc., have made ice skiing easier for more skiers.

The equipment is important—stiff boots, ski edges must be sharp, etc. Generally a ski with more side camber is best for ice. However, the turning and holding capacity of modern skis make them functional on hard snow-ice conditions. Some suppleness in the ski is essential. A too-rigid ski will chatter.

Ice skiing demands economy of motion. Down-up-down movements should be subtle. Movements are all smooth and flowing. The important consideration of skiing on ice is keeping uniform pressure on the edges. Angulation is the means of keeping the balance over the downhill ski. If slipping occurs, angulation is adjusted by the skier. Another aid for continuous pressure on the edges is down-unweighting. The better skier is aware that a slight increase of pressure to the heel of the ski increases the grip of the ski. Skis are kept in contact with the snow as constantly as possible. Application of the serpent technique provides best control.

# RACING

# THE OBJECT IS SPEED

The new and revised edition of the American Ski Technique does not attempt to expound on racing or racing techniques. This is clearly a highly specialized, dynamic, rapidly changing field of skiing. Ski theory and ski instruction seem to have lagged behind the dynamic changes in ski racing. This is true, of course, because instructional methods must first be proven safe and effective for the recreational skier. In any case, the ability of the American ski public is probably as high as any nation in the world. Today's instruction in ski schools is excellent.

The dilemma often facing the ski school director or instructor is that his students often desire to learn ski techniques used by current world ski champions. This is because racing success is associated with national teaching methods and publicity. This has always been a result of modern racing in any period of ski time. In the late forties, following World War II, the gap between the recreational skier and the racer was not great. It is far larger today. This is because today's modern racer literally skis ten months of the year on snow and glaciers, and trains the other two months. The racer today benefits from the best of scientific sophistication, including technique, equipment, coaching, etc. To say the least, today's racer's physical conditioning is superb. This is why there is often less than a tenth or even a hundredth of a second between the best racers of all alpine nations. What should be understood or explained to the skiing public is that even today's top racers had to start as beginners. As children, they probably learned snow plows, stem turns, walking maneuvers, and stem christies. It is through ski experience, instruction, coaching, and training that they developed a high level of skiing. It is for this reason that ski schools should make the public aware that even racers require a basic technique. For a skier to master all of the skills of basic technique in this book is quite an accomplishment. There are only a few skiers in advanced classes in comparison with the total number of ski school students, and fewer than that will go on to racing endeavors. Ski schools, however, while providing basic essentials in elementary skills and basic skiing for large masses of skiers, will find a demand and a need for racing techniques, particularly with juniors from the nine to sixteen age group. With today's sophistication in equipment, teaching techniques, and methods, the upgrading of the instructor, and more available skiing time, the youth of today learn skiing through basic technique and advanced skiing extremely rapidly. This is why it is essential that the reader differentiate between the following classifications:

(1) Basic Technique (American Ski Technique).
(2) Advanced Skiing in all types of terrain and snow conditions.
(3) Racing.

Basic technique's primary purpose is safety. Fun is second. Technique and method become the means by which safety and fun are achieved. In basic technique, the goal is to learn as rapidly as possible and safely parallel turns and short turns. The methods used may encompass any number of exercises or systems. For example, short skis, graduated ski length method, accelerated learning programs, parallel approach by elimination of snow plow, stem turns, etc. The American technique allows for difference in methods. However, a method must have a sequence of instruction. It cannot differ enough so that it does not allow standardization in ski schools at the international level. Nevertheless, although there exists literally an international technique, there is still evidence of conflicting opinions concerning racing success in certain nations and their ski school techniques. This axiom often disregards the most important consideration in basic technique—safety. The ski instructor with basic technique is attempting to control his students. We are constantly trying to slow the student down; keep the student's skiing in control. That is why the traverse is stressed in the American technique.

In advanced skiing the object is not so much learning to maintain control, but rather learning how to ski on various terrain in different snow conditions safely. The complete opposite is true for racing. The object is speed. The coach is faced with the one goal: to ski through the course in the fastest possible method.

## THE RACING SCHOOL

The ski school should provide a basic technique foundation. This, of course, must be expanded and improved for the racing school. It should, in its evolution, include the advanced techniques, since these exercises are stepping stones to racing. They enable the coach of the racing school to build a broad base, and lead to the differentiation between the recreational and racing skier. Again, the object is skiing against the clock. This is true in all forms of competition with the exception of jumping. The instructor of racing must become highly specialized in his skills. It is preferable that he has been a competitor, because his own racing experience is often invaluable. In the final analysis, the racing instructor must take care to learn and profit from the top racing experts.

Many of today's racing schools center primarily around youngsters. These youngsters are extremely well equipped both in technique and equipment and are very talented. They rapidly progress beyond the ski school and advanced skiing level. In the transition from basic technique to racing school or coaching, the instructor finds himself in an entirely new world—a world of coaches, ski associations, its society, politics, and rules.

In the ski school operation for advanced skiers the actual entry into competition or ski racing need not be a goal. An exceptional skier will benefit from the training; it will improve his skiing, his knowledge of the sport, and enhance his pleasure.

# GUIDELINES FOR THE INSTRUCTOR *by Willy Schaeffler*

*Ski Coach, University of Denver, Denver, Colorado*

Foremost in the training of junior and inexperienced racers is to teach basic technique and fundamentals. This should be taught by professional ski instructors. Only after this groundwork should the junior be introduced to the running of gates. The running of gates is of great value to the recreational skier as well as the competitor if the gates are set by experienced people.

The relationship between the junior racer and teacher is one of building confidence. Furthermore, if the teacher is to gain confidence of the student, he should be in firm control of his program.

It is very important that the junior racer familiarizes himself with the rules and regulations of course setting before he runs the gates. Often the junior racer is pushed into running against a clock without prior knowledge of rules and technique. This happens because of influence from untrained friends or parents— the latter often not even being skiers. This type of supervision could push the racer into competition beyond his skiing or racing ability and could be very dangerous.

It is necessary to understand the Fédération International d' Ski racing rule book in order to become a racer. Also, knowing preseason exercises and understanding the need for conditioning is a must.

In training and course setting the instructor should be able to set a safe course. This is determined by terrain and the racer's ability. The instructor should keep in mind that safety, control, and perfect course preparation must come first in order to provide the fun and encouragement racing is supposed to give. It is clearly spelled out in the FIS rules, which can be obtained through the United States Ski Association, 1726 Champa Street, Suite 300, Denver, Colorado. This manual is an absolute must for the instructor. In particular, the latest development in modern downhill requires utmost adherence to these safety rules. Juniors will not become tough on poorly prepared dangerous courses. All we achieve is a great number of discouraged dropouts from the racing program.

A good course should bring the racer down a variety of terrain, bumps, schuss's, and convex and concave slopes. With the changing terrain and the proper placing of gates, racing can be fun and safe.

## TYPES OF RACES

Even though 80 percent of all programs deal primarily with the Alpine events—downhill, giant slalom, and slalom—the ski instructor should be up-to-date in the Nordic events, which are cross country, jumping and Nordic combined. See the definitions of downhill, giant slalom, and slalom as well as the Nordic events in the FIS rule book.

In regard to cross country, it should be said that the training of juniors for cross country should be started carefully. Cross country running can be a pleasure but only if the skier is in condition and properly equipped. This training should start on short, easy, and well-prepared courses. At later dates, snow permitting, the training progresses to free running in the woods. Again, preseason training can shorten the snow training time. Before any running against time is done, the young skier should learn the fundamentals of the racing technique; otherwise, he will never enjoy cross country. Touring should be part of the introduction to cross country. A very fine booklet, *Cross Country Racing,* from the Swedish Ski Association, has been translated by Sven Wiik, Ski Coach, Western State College, Gunnison, Colorado, and is available through the United States Ski Association.

One of the best detailed books on how to run a jumping program came out several years ago. It is *Jumping Hill* and is by Dave Bradley of Hanover, New Hampshire. This book can also be obtained from the United States Ski Association.

## PRESEASON CONDITIONING

Each racing program should be started with a thorough conditioning program prior to going on skis. This should include at least two afternoons or evenings a week, mixing calisthenics and running. Soccer is one of the best conditioners known for the skier. There are many different exercise plans available such as the Royal Canadian Air Force Exercise Plans for Physical Fitness. Students can follow this plan daily where there are no meetings.

The weekends should be used to enjoy long hikes. The hike should be in the mountains on terrain similar to ski terrain. These hikes should not be on trials only; take the students into rocky, wooded terrain. Lots of uphill and downhill running, jumping, and dodging rocks and trees, with quick changes of direction, adds interest and enjoyment to the conditioning program.

The purposes to keep in mind for presnow conditioning are to develop strength, endurance, speed, and flexibility.

Strength and endurance are developed with special exercises and long hikes, mixed with sprints and fast climbs.

Endurance is the building of the lungs and breathing. A person can be very strong but can tire easily if he does not have the breathing capacity. Breathing can be developed by regular exercises and repeated endurance tests.

The better conditioned a racer is prior to the start of skiing, the better is his chance for quick progress, and he lessens the possibility of getting injured in case of a spill. If his muscles, tendons, and ligaments are conditioned, he will be in a much better position to keep his balance to avoid falls and, in case he does fall, his well-conditioned body can take the beating better.

## FIRST SNOW TRAINING

This session should be directed toward review of basic ski maneuvers, and it should include finished technical forms of snowplow, stem turn, stem christie, parallel, and other turns. At the start is the time to correct and improve the racer's basic technique. As training progresses, there may be less time devoted to basics. However, never lose sight of fundamentals. Classes should be based on the seven basic principles of the *American Ski Technique.*

During teaching periods time should be spent on instruction and practice of the three basic racing forms: slalom, giant slalom, and downhill.

The giant slalom turn is a clean, narrow, shallow track that changes the direction of travel with the least possible reduction of speed. From this turn the instructor works toward the slalom with the quick, stepping-turns and toward downhill with the higher speed, longer radius turn.

During the slalom training and course running, climbing the course is necessary to prepare the course and condition the racer's legs and breathing.

Basic racing fundamentals as well as techniques are an absolute must in the first training sessions on snow at the start of the season. A racer cannot start out the new season until he has regained his confidence in his progress. No fast skiing should be done before the technical perfection is achieved.

*CLINIC ON TYPES AND RUNNING OF GATES:* For this class a dozen slalom poles will be necessary. The time will be devoted to the setting and running of single, simple gates and combinations of gates. For a sample, use a series of three open-gates and show the correct manner of running. Another example would be a hairpin gate. A hairpin can be changed many ways. Each way requires a different approach of a different type of turn. This session should be interesting in the variety of gates.

CLINIC FOR FREE SKIING AND DOWNHILL: Free skiing in a group represents fun, such as, follow the leader, and change of leaders to add variety to the class. Ski the different runs on the mountain looking for different snow conditions—include small jumps.

With free skiing, more serious work can be devoted to the practice of downhill running. Work on the different downhill running positions on a gentle outrun where speed and people are not a problem. Work on single high-speed turns showing tuck position and edge control.

CLINIC ON SHORT COMBINATIONS OF GATES: It is necessary to have thirty to forty poles to set a few combinations on a short steep hill. The slope should be well-packed with a steepness of about 30 degrees. Set ten to fifteen gates, run these a few times, and change often. Speed should be well controlled but develop a flowing pattern with an even rate of speed for the entire course. Some time should be spent in keeping gates in good running conditions. As soon as ruts show, change the gates. This is a confidence building stage, and ruts destroy confidence quickly. This practice shows how to ski through one combination after another without loss of rhythm. Never keep practice too long. Adjust it to the physical ability of the group you work with. Remember, you won't get anything out of your racers, particularly juniors, if they get mentally or physically tired.

CLINIC ON FREE SKIING AND GIANT SLALOM: Repeat fun skiing with more time spent on running bumps, jumping and prejumping. The serious time should be devoted to the perfect turn. The teacher explains the principle of the turn, watches the students practice, and has the racers follow close behind the instructor. The students try to keep up and stay in the instructor's ski tracks without short cuts. This teaches discipline and controlled skiing. The instructor should use his best pupil first behind him and the rest following according to their abilities.

CLINIC ON RUNNING A FULL COURSE UNDER RACE CONDITIONS: Full, preset runs should be set and prepared as the foregoing courses. Time should be spent on all three types of competition. Usually more time is devoted to slalom training because of the availability of terrain. It requires more time and effort to set the downhill and giant slalom courses. Unless there is a special area set aside for this practice, these activities interfere with the recreational skier, and it requires added policing. This is often the reason the junior skier has little experience in downhill running. Many areas are setting aside training areas and this practice will aid the problem. Don't ever train on a poorly prepared course anywhere. It only leads to injury and disappointment.

## TRAINING AGAINST TIME

Too often the instructors start training sessions with a stopwatch in their hand. This adds to the tension of the skiers. The racers should run against the clock before their first competition, but this should come late in the training schedule. More than one run should be taken for time; a comparison should be made of the individual's time in two runs, one trying for a smooth, technical run and the other for speed. This often shows that haste makes waste or that a smooth, steady-run is faster than the skier who goes too fast and loses the rhythm of line through the gates. There cannot be enough emphasis put on technique, and even though time is used, technical corrections should be given to the pupil with the time.

One word of caution—it is more important to keep the program with juniors stimulating, interesting, and fun rather than being overly technical and, therefore, boring.

The successful future instructor has to be an expert coach and the coach must also be an instructor. With this combination of knowledge, he can't help but be successful in whatever program he steps into.

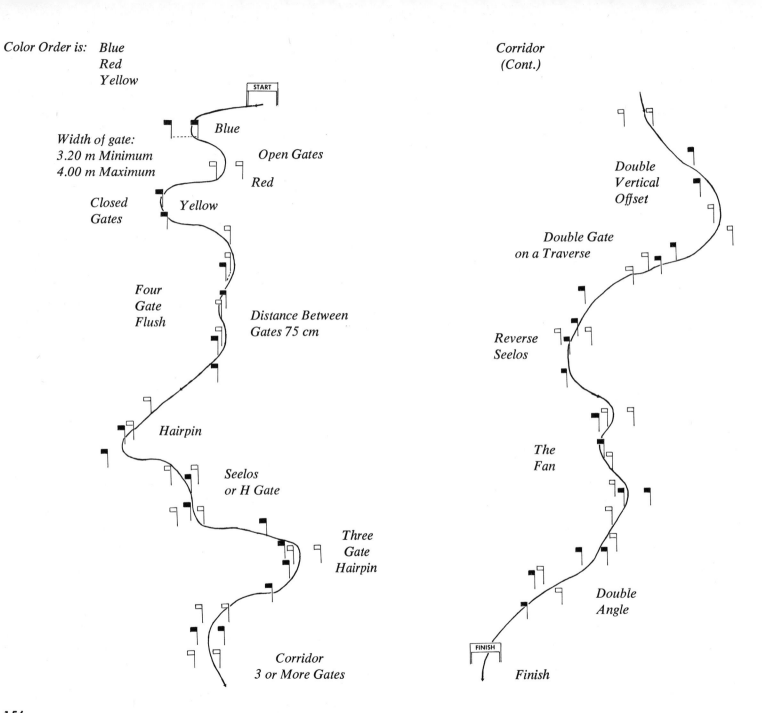

Color Order is:  Blue
                 Red
                 Yellow

START

Blue

*Width of gate:*
*3.20 m Minimum*
*4.00 m Maximum*

*Open Gates*

*Red*

*Closed*
*Gates*

*Yellow*

*Four*
*Gate*
*Flush*

*Distance Between*
*Gates 75 cm*

*Hairpin*

*Seelos*
*or H Gate*

*Three*
*Gate*
*Hairpin*

*Corridor*
*3 or More Gates*

*Corridor*
*(Cont.)*

*Double*
*Vertical*
*Offset*

*Double Gate*
*on a Traverse*

*Reverse*
*Seelos*

*The*
*Fan*

*Double*
*Angle*

FINISH

*Finish*

# RUN A BETTER RACE* *by Willy Schaeffler*

Advisor on race trail design and development for the
United States Ski Association; *SKI* Technical Editor.

## TIPS ON PLANNING A SKI MEET BY THE COUNTRY'S LEADING AUTHORITY

Each year the importance of efficient ski race management grows as the number of races increases. This winter there will be about 500 sanctioned races in the United States and 250 in Canada, to say nothing of a host of unclassified club races. The sanctioned races alone take in about twenty thousand competitors in downhill, slalom, giant slalom, cross country, jumping, and biathlon (shoot and ski). Fortunately, organizations like the United States Ski Association and the Canadian Amateur Ski Association (the groups that govern and give official status to races in North America) have established some guidelines for holding ski races. Under USSA rules, a sanctioned race is one that affects a racer's class rating—A, B, C, junior, veterans. Each division has slightly different requirements for classification. But generally a racer must attend a specified number of sanctioned races to qualify for a class card and move up to a higher rating. All the divisions use the FIS (the international governing body of ski racing) point system to rate the racers and results. As a result a competitor can travel from one division to another and race in his established class.

* *Ski Magazine*, January, 1965.

A club or group of clubs interested in sponsoring a *sanctioned* race should start planning six months to one year before the event. The first step is to select a race chairman. He is the key person in organizing and administering the race. Certainly he should be familiar with racing, but if the division officials feel that he needs assistance, they may assign a technical advisor to work with the club. There is often a charge for the advisor's time spent at meetings and the race.

Some time early in the planning, the site of the race must be selected by the sponsoring group. Because ski races are usually held on weekends when areas are most crowded, it is important to consider only those areas that have sufficient trails to be devoted exclusively to the race.

Other factors to consider in selecting the area are: availability of the trails for practice prior to the race; adequate lifts or snow vehicles to take racers uphill between runs; proper snow equipment and vehicles to prepare the course; facilities for the extra ski patrol needed for the race; and nearby housing accommodations for racers, officials, and spectators.

When a site is selected the group can apply to the competitions committee of the local USSA division for official sanctioning of the proposed race. Tournament rules, regulations, and fees vary slightly from division to division, but usually you will need to provide detailed information on the who, what, when, and where of the race.

Once the application is approved, the committee chairman can start gathering personnel to prepare and run the race. Several race officials may be appointed by the competitions committee. For instance, in the Rocky Mountain Ski Division of USSA (whose rules and regulations are drawn upon for much of this article), the referee, chief of course, course setter, chief timer, and jumping judges must be certified officials. This means that they have special training or experience for handling these jobs.

Officials drawn from the organization sponsoring the race are: chief starter, start judge, start secretary, judge of finish, and forerunners. You'll need many other people to gather equipment for the race, handle entry blanks, supervise gatekeepers, recruit course police and ski patrol. At the race itself, people will be needed to distribute number bibs, collect number bibs, record results, calculate results, operate radios and telephones and public address systems, assist starters and timers, and serve refreshments. Many of these posts will require one or more relief men, especially if it is very cold.

Subcommittees must be appointed to handle prizes, programs, publicity, housing, entertainment, and the banquet after the race. Keep in mind that more people will be needed after the race is finished to clean up the course and remove ruts and hazards, return borrowed equipment, write thank-you notes, and so on.

Prior to the race, however, one of the most critical jobs is gathering equipment. Items of equipment start with slalom poles which should be bamboo, eight or nine feet long, one-and-a-quarter inches in diameter and painted red, blue, and yellow. You should have two spare poles for every three gates set on the course. Blank express-type tags can be used to number the gates from the top of the course to the bottom. Tape the tag on the outside gate. Slalom flags should be the same color as the poles.

Other special items of equipment include: four phones or radios and spare batteries, six timing watches, officials' arm bands, pinnies or number bibs for each racer and for the fore- and post-runners. (Incidentally, arrange with the area to have some identifying insignia for racers to wear during the practice period before the race. Area management and lift operators should also be sup-

plied with a list of racers and officials who will be using lift facilities.) You'll need vegetable coloring or other water-soluble fluid to mark the slalom gate positions for the first run (blue) and changes for the second run (red). To handle poor snow conditions, such as extremely wet snow or cold sugar snow, have several hundred pounds of rock salt and ammonium chloride available. Of course, first aid equipment and toboggans should be available at three positions on a downhill course and two positions on all other courses. Each gatekeeper will need a rake or shovel to repair the course. They should also be outfitted with fluorescent-colored vests (which may be obtained at army surplus outlets) to signify their positions as gatekeepers.

Paper work and office supplies needed at the race include: entry blanks, racing order sheets, time sheets and cards, gate-keeper's cards, at least five clipboards with plastic top cover sheets, two typewriters, an adding machine, a computer, paper, pencils, carbon paper, paper clips, a stapler, mimeograph machine with stencils and paper. Signs needed are: start and finish markers, a blackboard and chalk to mark race results, a blackboard and chalk for last-minute information for racers and officials, card-board and felt-tipped markers for posting announcements.

Some of these items, such as official forms, watches, and arm bands, can be bought or rented from your division office. Others may be borrowed from other clubs or the area management.

The starting area should have a shack for officials and racers. If this isn't available, you'll need to bring a tent for this purpose. The area around the start should be level and elevated. If crowds are likely to be a problem, have extra bamboo poles and rope or snow fences to hold them back. If the area doesn't have a starting gate, use two-by-fours set two feet apart and about two-and-a-half feet above the snow.

The finish gate should be large and highly visible. Plan to construct snow chutes two or three feet high on either side of the finish to protect fallen skiers.

Between the start and finish is the weightiest problem for the officials—safety. This is where the advice of a technical advisor or experienced racer will be most valuable. The International Ski Competition Rule Book gives specific descriptions of the terrain requirements for all the races. Trail and snow preparation is spelled out thoroughly. Follow this advice closely and go beyond it by exaggerating the possibility of open or hidden dangers on the trails. Wherever an obstacle might pose a safety problem, build a snow or straw safety wall, barrier or net.

Certain safety factors of a race are, however, left to the judgment of the racing officials. For instance, the rule books say nothing about a downhill race in 35 degree below zero weather or winds up to fifty mph or fog, flat light, or poor visibility. These are problems that rest on the shoulders of the key people who run the race. They need to have the courage to cancel or stop or delay a race to remove hazards or allow time to make it safe rather than take a chance on accidents.

A course that can break up or become hazardous or rutty after only fifteen or twenty racers is inadequate. Rolling equipment, tramping, and chemicals properly used on a race course should enable it to hold up for eighty or more competitions.

Weather conditions and course preparations are particularly important in junior races. Older competitors are seasoned to the difficulties of racing. One bad experience may be enough to make a youngster drop out for good. For junior races, take extra safety precautions and keep the atmosphere happy.

One safety feature to check on the day of the race is protective headgear. All competitors in downhill and giant slalom events must wear a race helmet bearing the approval decal of the Snell Foundation. This means it has been tested for impact safety.

Announce and post unofficial results as soon as they are available. While these may be changed later, you'll make the race more exciting by giving racers and spectators some reference immediately. You'll need two or three people to work out these calculations.

Be prepared to act promptly on protests. The referee and his committee should use the FIS rules as a guide in disqualifications. Whenever there is a doubt about a dispute, allow the racer a rerun. You can make the final decision later.

Always have some kind of an award ceremony, a banquet if you have time, or presentations immediately after the race near the course or in the base lodge. Prizes may be trophies, medals, or diplomas and should not cost more than $5 to $8.

A final word on holding a better ski race. Even if you follow all of the above advice to the letter and carry out every procedure, your image will be muddied if the race doesn't START ON TIME. The time schedule below will guide a race chairman to that critical moment when he gives the signal to GO.

## CHECK LIST FOR SKI RACE PLANNING

*Six months before race:*
1. Name race committee chairman.
2. Select committee members who are potential race officials.
3. Investigate sites for race.
4. Prepare application for sanctioned race.
5. Appoint subcommittees.
6. Assign duties.

*Six weeks before race:*
1. Check equipment available.
2. Distribute press releases.

*Four weeks before race:*
1. Check arrangements with area.
2. Check progress of committees.
3. Mail entry blanks to clubs and other potential racers.

*Three weeks before race:*
1. Notify all officials and committee chairmen of time schedule and duties at the race. Be sure they contact all workers.
2. Check snow cover at race site.
3. Check equipment procurement.
4. Install wiring for phones.
5. Obtain prizes.

*Two weeks before race:*
1. Check progress of all officials.
2. Mail second press release.
3. Check arrangements for spectator control and first aid.
4. Check office supplies, race forms.

*One week before race:*
1. Arrange to pick up equipment borrowed from division headquarters or other ski clubs.
2. Transport some equipment to the area.
3. Check on press representation.

*Two days before race:*

1. Check snow report.
2. Arrange for preparation of the course with snow vehicles and/or chemicals.
3. Arrange to mark the course and the practice areas.
4. Hold a meeting to have draw for positions in the first event. Print race order sheets.
5. Check the order of time cards.

*One day before race:*

1. Hold a meeting of the racers.
2. Check course conditions.
3. Arrange for distribution on the numbers either at the draw for second and third events or on the start.

*Day of race:*

1. Recheck communications system several hours before.
2. Recheck condition of course.
3. Check classification cards and distribute numbers.
4. Check helmets for Snell okay.
5. Check on refreshments.
6. An hour and a half before race brief officials.
7. Half an hour before race, officials should be in their positions and police the course.
8. Ten minutes before race, forerunners on the start.
9. Start the race—on time.
10. Have five racers lined up and ready to go at all times. In giant slalom and downhill allow one to two minutes interval between racers. In a slalom the course should be cleared before another racer starts. In cross country, racers can start every thirty seconds.
11. Announce and post results as soon as they are available. Post disqualifications and reruns.
12. Be prepared to act promptly on protests.
13. Have bibs collected at finish.

*After the race:*

1. Check gatekeepers' cards.
2. Make final computations of results and post them.
3. Distribute press releases.
4. Clean course, collect equipment.
5. Hold banquet and awards.
6. Mail results to clubs, papers.
7. Return borrowed equipment.
8. Send thank-you notes to all who assisted.
9. Hold post-race meetings of officials to get suggestions for future races.

## INFORMATION

For a rule book on ski racing, write to your local division headquarters. *The International Ski Competition Rule Book* is available from the United States Ski Association, 1726 Champa Street, Suite 300, Denver, Colorado. *The National Collegiate Skiing Rules* can be obtained from the National Collegiate Athletic Association Bureau, Box 757, Grand Central Station, New York, New York.

**PERSONNEL ON STARTING PLATFORM ARE**
*(1) chief starter*
*(2) assistant starter*
*(3) start judge*
*(4) and (5) radio or phone men*
*(6) start recorder*
*(7R) racer in gate*
*(8R) and (9R) next two racers on deck.*

# GIANT SLALOM

The giant slalom is probably the closest to recreational skiing. It is also undoubtedly the easiest for the recreational skier to learn. A practice giant slalom is no longer than three thousand feet with a vertical drop of six hundred feet and probably twenty gates. An international competitive giant slalom would be at least six thousand feet long with a fifteen hundred foot vertical drop and up to seventy-five gates. While a practice giant slalom for the recreational skier might reach speeds of twenty-five miles per hour, an international race would average speeds from forty to fifty miles per hour. It is at this point in the sophisticated skier's repertoire that it becomes evident that speed, skiing against the clock, is the important consideration. Giant slalom creates, for most skiers, an excessive sideslip in the turn. This causes the skier to drop too far down the course and slows him down. Give the student exercises that will not make him turn too sharply. He should turn high above the gate skiing round, carved turns. The basic principles apply in racing as in basic technique and advanced skiing. A correct body position is extremely important in racing, whether it be giant slalom, slalom, or downhill. The correct body position is when the ankles, knees, and hips are bent slightly forward. The racer must be stable, in a natural position, and, above all, relaxed. Unlike basic technique, the hands are forward waist high and apart, because speed requires balance. Similarly, the skis are farther apart

than found in demonstration forms. Many of the basics are still evident. The traverse position allows the uphill ski, boot, knee, hip, and shoulder to be slightly advanced. The best racers in the world assume a position of the body square on the skis, facing the direction of travel in one plane. Edge control and angulation are present because the ankles and knees must be pressed into the hill often in a localized situation rather than a total body position.

Edge control then can be done in another manner as in advanced skiing. Therefore, the edge control becomes local with the lower body and lower leg, with the upper body acting as a stabilizer for the lower body to turn against. The upper body maintains stability for the lower, and the upper body leans in the opposite direction of the turn. The degree of angulation or edge control depends upon the terrain and snow conditions. If the terrain is steep, more edge control is needed than for gentle terrain. Ice requires a great deal more edge control (angulation) than soft snow.

Pole-plant, type of poles, pole grip design, single taper, double taper, and type of basket become extremely refined in racing techniques. The pole-plant is used to initiate or deflect a turn and is planted differently according to timing and the situation. It is essential for balance. Where and when it is planted depends upon the type of turn, steepness of terrain, radius of the turn, speed, and snow conditions. When the terrain is steep the pole is planted farther to the side. On the other hand, on gentle terrain and in racing techniques, the pole and arm are in front of the skier. This also is true when skiing the fall-line on steep terrain.

Unweighting in the basic principles applies to racing techniques, but the unweighting in racing becomes more involved as in advanced skiing with up-unweighting, down-unweighting, and down-weighting, and the retraction-extension of the legs as the skier becomes more compressed. However, because of the speed and the hard snow on the courses the unweighting movement must not be exaggerated but must be subtle and refined.

A carved turn is the racer's goal. He must be in a good position throughout the carving process, so that he may make use of the ankles, knees, and hips to absorb bumps, ruts, and changes in terrain that are forever present in the course. The racer is faced with the object of maintaining contact with the snow at all times. Whereas in basic technique the object is to maintain control, the goal of the racer is acceleration. Acceleration may be accomplished by an abrupt extension of the downhill leg at the end of a turn (a push from the downhill leg projecting the upper body forward), weight transfer from the downhill to the uphill ski, allowing the skis to "shoot" in front of the skier by retraction-reaction, and by skating steps used to accelerate through open gates.

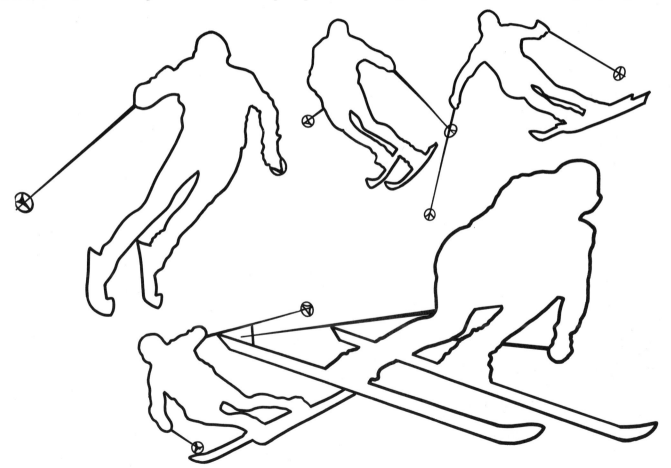

163

# SLALOM

Slalom is an excellent exercise and practice in the normal ski school function in class "F" skiing. Children love slalom. The enterprising instructor will carry a chronograph or stop watch and he may set a few simple combinations or flushes for his students to run through while pitting themselves against the clock. As soon as a student is able to short swing a little, he can begin to practice slalom. Ski school slalom races are fun and are becoming a more integral part of the basic technique. Running a flush is a good way to begin. Start with open gates, twelve to fourteen feet wide and five yards apart. Running flushes will acquaint the student with the fastest rhythm. It will help the pole-plant and develop a sharp edge set and subsequent push-off. Slalom practice is good for basic technique. Since the aim of the slalom is to control the skis, running slalom will develop control and stabilization in all snow conditions: soft snow, rutted snow, gentle slopes, steep slopes, and icy terrain.

Slalom skiing requires the feet to be more wide apart than ordinary free skiing. Weight transfer to the outside ski is primary. The hands, arms, and poles are out in front and the racer faces downhill, looking ahead at the next gate or combination of gates. Pole-plant is quick at all times and helps maintain the balance and control. Learn to ski a rutted flush. This will require a lower body position. One must practice on varied terrain and snow conditions and learn to ride the skis accordingly.

Slalom skiing on soft snow requires less edge control or angulation. Conversely, slalom skiing on hard, icy courses requires constant, extreme angulation. One does not always need excessive unweighting. The movements are very subtle. The upper body acts as a stabilizer, and the initiation of the turn is localized in the lower leg. As the advanced skier becomes more proficient in the slalom, he will find that the up-forward movement and weight transfer become less essential, and that the serpent-type techniques become more advantageous. At this level the equipment (sharp edges, good skis, stiff boots) are a major aid. Control is the goal in slalom, but acceleration is the key. The skating step becomes a common method of skiing in slalom. It is a means of initiating a turn at the end of the previous turn. This is why these exercises are stressed in the Advanced Skiing section. Skating exercises should be practiced continuously through all phases of classes "E" and "F" and advanced skiing, with both single and double pole-plant in all types of terrain: ice, soft snow, bumpy, slalom, etc.

To maintain control with acceleration, the racer must pick a line that is the shortest distance between two gates. This is where experienced, trained professional coaching or race instructing can lend to the over-all advancement of the racer. Competitive skiing is an extension of ordinary ski school, but it is entirely different. A good instructor may prove to be a poor racing coach. In organized skiing there is a dividing line between being a certified instructor and a qualified certified coach.

The line of the racer is direct. The tails of the skis must follow the same line as the tips of the skis—carve, not slip. The body, however, does not necessarily follow the same path. Depending on the speed and the radius of the turn, the body is inside of the arc described by the skis and the skis are moving outside the center of gravity.

Errors in slalom are: starting the turn late—carving must start before the fall line or the skier is forced to turn the tails outside the desired turn radius. Excessive leaning will create an undesired sliding of the tails. Other common errors are improper or inadequate pole-plant causing a bad initiation of the turn.

Possibly one of the best experiences for the neophite slalom racer is to allow him to set a small course. The FIS rule book is a good guide and should be read or studied by all advanced skiers or racers. It is essential that the course be set with the proper distance between poles and gates using the right type of combinations. The recent trend in slalom is toward gentle slopes and straight courses. In such a case, it is often wise to use the maximum distance between poles and gates. This gives the racer more room, resulting in a rhythmical course, varies the speed, and creates long, tight turns without requiring braking. The last gates of the course should be open, and it is preferable to have two or three open gates at the start of the course to enable the racer to gain rhythm. For slalom practice the course should be set on varied terrain including all types of racing conditions. The course need not be long to be effective for training purposes. Variety is the key to slalom training.

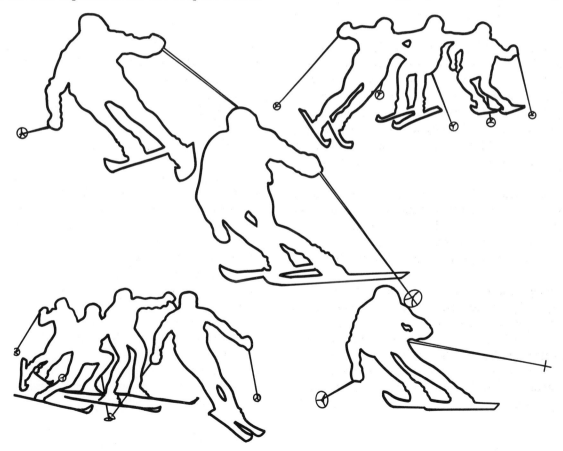

# DOWNHILL

High-speed skiing is not easy—it requires practice, skill, and a proper course. Today's ski areas with their crowded conditions do not always provide trails that can be used to practice downhill. The coach or ski school director operating a racing program may make arrangements with the area manager to close off one section of the hill. Many coaches find it advantageous to use the lifts early in the morning at seven or eight o'clock. Thus, the downhill practice can be over by ten, or by the time the skiing public arrives on the hill.

Although high-speed skiing is not easy, skiing at high speeds in a schussing position is often not as difficult as trying to make turns or snowplows at high speeds. It is best to integrate the downhill running with the other racing programs, that is, skiers should have competed in slaloms and giant slaloms before attempting downhill.

Downhill coaching must, of course, be coupled with practice. Many coaches today feel that the best successful downhill racers are those that have more miles downhill training than the other racers. Training involves skills during the practice running, and the coach or instructor familiarizes the students with when it is best to check in a schuss or to snowplow on the course, or even stop in a narrow section. Today's racer has minimized the sideslip. There are often places in downhill courses where it should

be used, however. The goal of the downhill, as in other racing, is to go from the top to the bottom of the course in the quickest possible time. Any means or techniques that can be used to achieve this is permissible.

The best training for downhill is to make practice runs on different parts of the course—the course being divided into sections. These parts of the course can be linked together for a complete nonstop run. This type of training is for the accomplished skier, and even at this point the training must be within that skier's limits of ability. The object in downhill is to reduce wind resistance against the body, allowing the skis to slide as fast as possible over the snow, and to avoid a fall during the course. Practice for downhill should include attempting to avoid obstacles while riding over bumps, ruts, etc. A skier wants to learn to hold a true fast line in a traverse. Exercises should include traversing while weighting both skis, angulated positions, weight on the downhill ski for bumpy terrain, and weight on the uphill ski where the snow might be extremely hard. Long carved turns are to be perfected; different turns of different radiuses are to be practiced. And the skier should, as in traversing, practice by weighting both skis in the turn, weighting the outside ski and then weighting the inside ski. On hard snow this may very well cause the edges to hold better on the downhill ski, but one must be careful in the use of the inside ski at high speeds. Since most downhill turns are long radius turns they should be practiced implementing the basic principles (weight transfer, forward lean, and angulation). The point is to almost entirely do away with sideslipping. These exercises should be practiced on different types of snow conditions (soft, hard, wet, etc.).

The adage of a carved turn might not always hold true because the soft snows might dictate that a flat ski would give more speed.

In downhill there are, of course, high speeds and momentum. Therefore, one does not need an aggressive unweighting; the movements are subtle. The racer by standing up out of a low position obtains better leverage. Turning in a low position or a tuck may result in the skidding of the skis. Although this low position in a turn would lower wind resistance, the sliding or skidding action would probably be ultimately much slower.

A long downhill turn may be initiated by leaning the upper body into the turn. The weight is gently shifted to the outside carving portion of the turn. Ankles and knees are used to control the arc. Hardsetting or application of the edges increases friction. This is why movements are subtle.

The short downhill turn will require more positive use of the knees and ankles. Again, movements are subtle, and the turn is a smooth arc.

The low tuck, referred to as the egg position, is the position aerodynamically for relatively flat and straight schusses. The skis are spread apart hip or shoulder width, chest down on the knees and thighs. Thighs are back and parallel to the skis, arms are close to the body, and hands tucked up near the face. On a smooth terrain poles may be tucked under the arms, and they extend along the sides of the upper thigh. The poles are parallel to the skis. The back should be held flat and the head held up for visibility.

Conditioning and training are the first order for downhill. To hold a proper tuck position the racer must continue to strengthen the muscles of the back, thighs, and neck. The neck must be strong to hold the head up to allow visibility. Arms may be dropped to the sides of the legs if more stability is needed. In the full-tuck position if the arms are dropped they should be extended in front of the body or alongside the boots to maintain stability. The poles should not drag in the snow. And it should be remembered that the wind resistance against the poles is great. Consider what happens when you hold a ski pole out of a car window going forty-five to fifty miles per hour, and note how different positions will reduce wind resistance.

The aerodynamic body position in the schuss is important. The position of the skis and how the skier adapts to the terrain all affect the skier's speed. To maintain speed on the flats the skis must be flat as possible; edges cause deceleration.

Speeds in a downhill may be increased by careful use of the terrain. Bumps, hollows, and variations can increase the speed. Knees and ankles are flexed softly to pass over bumps. The racer can unweight the ski when approaching a bump and push on the downhill side of the bump increasing speed. Dips can increase speed by the pressing of the ankles and knees at the bottom of the dip. Properly timed, this will increase momentum. The whole body is used subtly (knees, ankles, and hips) in maintaining and increasing the speed of the skier. Relaxation, of course, is a must.

The prejump is used going over bumps and dropping over steep pitches in downhill courses. It is executed by unweighting the skis before passing over the top of the high point. The skier attempts to ride these obstacles without flying out of control in the air, a condition that slows the skier down.

In the prejump the racer places his fist to the boot tops, pulling his legs up under him. The ski tips are held down so wind resistance is less. The body is kept low to reduce wind resistance. The racer again attempts to maintain good aerodynamic positions, and avoids staying in the air for long distances.

# TRAIL PREPARATION *by Professor Willy Stickler and Willy Schaeffler*

University of Denver, Denver, Colorado

The preparation of trails in this modern age is accomplished largely through the use of chemicals.

*All* chemical substances have the characteristic property of lowering the freezing point of the liquid in which they are dissolved. For water, in particular, the freezing point lowering constant equals $1.86°$ C per gram molecular weight of solute per 1,000 g. of solvent (namely water). Thus 32 g. of methyl alcohol, $CH_3Oh$, lowers the freezing point of 1,000 g. of water by $1.86°$ C (that is, the solution will freeze at $-1.86°$ C).

*Salts* of any description are more efficient for this purpose because they can dissociate into two or more individual fragments (ions), each of which has this freezing point lowering effect. Thus, sodium chloride (table salt, rock salt), NaCl, acts as sodium ion and chloride ion, lowering the freezing point by $2\times1.86°$ C for each 58.5 g. of salt. From this viewpoint alone, sodium chloride, potassium chloride, ammonium chloride, etc., should have the same effect.

Calcium chloride, $CaCl_2$, on the other hand, has a three-fold lowering capacity (that is, $3\times1.86°$ C) because of its property of giving rise to three fragments, namely, one calcium ion and two chloride monium chloride. Furthermore, *anhydrous* (water-free) calcium chloride has the ability to act as a dehydrating (water removing) agent by the following action:

$$Ca^{++} = 6H_2O \quad Ca(H_2O_6)^{++}$$

Thus, *anhydrous* calcium chloride has a dual effect: dehydrating action and freezing point lowering.

The physics of the action of salt on snow is extremely complex (in fact, it is not fully understood at the present time). An attempt is made to offer an oversimplified picture of the action in the following paragraph.

Because of the freezing point lowering effect of a salt, some snow near the salt crystals is melted and a saturated salt solution results; more snow will dissolve in this solution, making it more and more diluted. This process *raises* the freezing point of the solution again, approaching that of pure water. Through an interchange with the cold snow the solution will freeze again, possibly rendering a harder layer (because snow crystals have been changed to ice crystals).

In the absence of a clear theoretical understanding of the factors involved in the action of salts on snow, trail preparation with chemicals is at best an empirical art. Unfortunately, systematic studies have not been carried out. Some of our experiences, and those of other groups, are summarized below.

Aside from economic factors, anhydrous *calcium chloride* may be one of the best agents, both for dry powder snow at high altitudes (low moisture content) and for extremely wet conditions, when it has been reported to act within seconds and to last up to three hours.

*Rock salt* (sodium chloride), which is much cheaper, appears to give good results, also. For instance, the International Downhill trail at Crystal Mountain, Washington, two miles in length, was salted in its entirety every day for three consecutive days at temperatures of up to 65° F, which resulted within half an hour after application in a hard, perfectly even and hence safe running surface. A work force of three snowcats and three thousand pounds of rock salt was available.

If extremely dry snow conditions exist, such as one encounters in the Rocky Mountains and the Andes (Portillo), salting should be done at least twenty-four hours, but preferably forty-eight hours, before the piste is being used. The rock salt should be foot-packed into the snow. Final course preparation should involve sidestepping on skis rather than sideslipping. We have been using rock salt and calcium chloride in the Rocky Mountain areas for over a decade with very satisfactory results.

It has been reported from Mammoth, California, that *ammonium nitrate* $NH_4NO_3$, is very efficient when wet spring and summer snow conditions exist. It can be applied a short time (within thirty minutes) before the snow surface is used. Possibly its efficacious action is due to the fact that ammonium nitrate is more water-soluble than the other salts in use, and it has a greater heat of solution than its competitors. This means that it withdraws more heat from its surroundings, namely, the wet snow surface, thus cooling it more.

Application of salts should be made with a spreader or should be hand-sown. Care should be taken that not too much material is applied. Granules of rice grain size have been employed successfully, but no study is known to us that considers efficiency of action relative to particle size.

# THE BODY IN MOTION

*Biomechanics*

# BIOMECHANICS *by Richard L. Voorhees, M.D.*

The physical principles governing skiing have been the subject of considerable writing and discussion. It is possible to define and relate skiing to the principles of physics that govern movement. This is true in skiing and other sports. However, more time and effort should be devoted to the study of those factors within the human body to produce motion. It is important that the ski instructor have an understanding of how the body works if he is to properly understand his student as an individual. The physiologic mechanisms of the body govern, in a broad sense, a student's ability to perform in all athletic endeavors and certainly in skiing.

Biomechanics may then be broadly defined as a study of those factors acting within the body to produce motion. Properly it would be termed the Kinesiology of skiing. Kinesi comes from a Greek word meaning movement or motion. Kinesiology is the science that investigates and analyzes human motion.

Motion of the joints of the body is produced by muscle contraction, which coordinated through multiple joints produces motion of the entire body. The contraction of one muscle fiber acting across a joint is dependent upon the functioning of other systems in the body. For example, the nervous, circulatory, respiratory, digestive, and excretory systems are involved. Naturally any comprehensive review of these various systems in the body would be a detailed study of physiology, which is far beyond the scope of this chapter. This is not a substitute for the numerous standard and informative medical texts that are available. However, the needs of a ski teacher may be met in a simpler fashion, one aimed primarily at gaining a practical understanding of the workings of the body.

The physical laws governing matter are universal. Human body mechanics represent another illustration of these general principles. In order to understand the science of motion, it is necessary to become involved in numerous fields.

*ANATOMY:* The study of anatomy is necessary to understand the direction and application of muscle pull.

*PHYSIOLOGY:* A knowledge of the subject is basic to the understanding of muscle function. It is necessary to know that muscles constantly receive electrical and chemical stimuli from the nervous system. Increased activity of muscles increases the activities of the rest of the body. The demand for oxygen increases, more waste products must be eliminated, etc.

*PHYSICS:* A study of physics used in ski mechanics is similarly important in the area of biomechanics. This is necessary to understand the characteristics of the different types of levers in the skeletal system of the body. This provides a greater ability to analyze and evaluate individual performance in sports.

The understanding of normal motion brought about through

a study of these fields provides a basis for understanding irregular, uncoordinated, and spastic types of motion.

In summary, then, the purpose of this chapter is to understand skiing as a physical state involving the movement and position of joints, the tensions of muscles and tendons, and the orientation of the body with respect to gravity and other acceleratory forces. There must further be a conscious recognition of the orientation of the different parts of the body with respect to each other in terms of position and rates of motion. Finally, it will be shown that there is a relationship between physiologic laws and the seven basic principles of the American ski technique.

## ANATOMY OF THE LOWER EXTREMITY

The prime concern in the lower extremities is the design of the joints in relation to:

1. The different types of motion of which they are capable.
2. The binding effects of ligaments as they bridge the joints.
3. The directions of muscle pull.

At times instructors have developed pet teaching phrases such as "knee crank," "foot swivel," etc. These phrases may be descriptive and impart a certain feel to the student. However, it should be realized that they are structurally not consistent with joint and muscle action.

In general, the types of motion found in joints in the body are as follows:

*Flexion:* This is a type of motion in which the contributing segments move toward each other.

*Extension:* This represents motion back to the original starting position after a flexion activity. Motion continuing beyond the normal extended position is said to be hyperextended.

*Abduction:* This is motion away from the central axis of the body.

*Adduction:* This is motion toward the center line of the body.

*Circumduction:* This is rotation about the long axis of the contributing member.

The principal joints used in skiing may be described in these terms:

*HIP JOINT:* This is a ball and socket joint. The ball portion is the proximal end of the large bone of the thigh, the femur, which fits into a cuplike socket in the hip. The anatomical structure of the joint is exactly as described and is capable of an indefinite number of axes and planes of motion. Any limitations in the degree of motion are usually due to the surrounding capsule or ligaments.

Flexion range 115 to 125 degrees; extension is slight, that is, 5 to 10 degrees. Abduction range 45 to 50 degrees. Adduction is back to the point of contact with the other leg. Circumduction or rotation may be said to be complete.

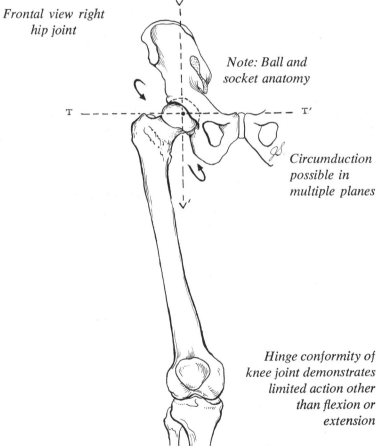

*Frontal view right hip joint*

*Note: Ball and socket anatomy*

*Circumduction possible in multiple planes*

*Hinge conformity of knee joint demonstrates limited action other than flexion or extension*

*T-T'   Transverse axis for flexion and extension*
*V-V   Vertical axis for rotation of femur*

*KNEE JOINT:* This is a hinged joint. The knoblike protuberances at the lower end of the femur (thigh bone) fit into the plateau-type receptacles of the tibia (lower leg). Flexion range 120 to 150 degrees, that is to the point where it is checked by the contact of the opposing muscle masses. Extension is complete. Maximum rotation of the knee joint is 25 degrees. This degree of rotation occurs, however, only when the knee is flexed nearly 90 degrees and beyond. A racer may use this much extreme knee flexion in his downhill positions; however, the student skier would not be placed in this extreme position. The marked mechanical disadvantage to the main extensor muscles of the thigh is too great. These muscles are generally weak in beginning skiers. A thigh position with the knees slightly flexed permits the main weight to be carried on the skeletal axis rather than by muscle power. Furthermore, the muscles that produce rotation, when the knee joint is flexed 90 degrees, are not strong muscles for this type of action. For this reason, the expression "knee crank" is a misnomer. The instructor looks at the arc described by the knee and assumes that this means the action is actually taking place in the knee joint. The true focus of motion in this instance is primarily in the hip joint.

*ANKLE JOINT:* This is also a hinge-type of joint. A mortise is formed by the small bone on the outside of the leg—the fibula and the larger bone, the tibia, on the inner surface. Together they present bony prominences which extend over the top bone of the ankle joint which is called the talus. The mortise of the ankle joint largely prevents lateral movement and rotation at this juncture. Flexion is 30 to 35 degrees and extension is 40 to 45 degrees. This is best understood by careful examination of the accompanying drawings.

Skiing is primarily maintaining a standing posture while in motion. Therefore, the normal stance should be understood. In the erect posture the body weight is transmitted through the ankle joint to the foot. The inner one-third of the foot is primarily concerned with propulsion through the longitudinal axis of the great toe. The outer two-thirds of the foot serves chiefly for balance. In the erect balanced stance the weight is largely carried by the heel and the ball of the great toe. The drawing showing the ligamentous attachments of the ankle joint and the directions of muscle pull indicates problems in skiing connected with this joint.

It may be seen that there are no muscles that would produce a flat rotation of the foot in the horizontal plane. Because of direction of the muscle pull, side to side motion is accompanied by some vertical up and down displacement of the foot. In analyzing foot rotation, consider first the fact that the foot does not rotate in a flat plane to any appreciable degree; and second, the

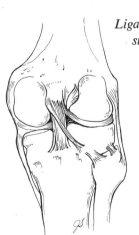
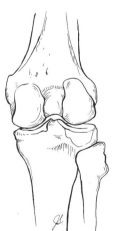

*Ligaments and articulating surfaces of right knee joint from behind*

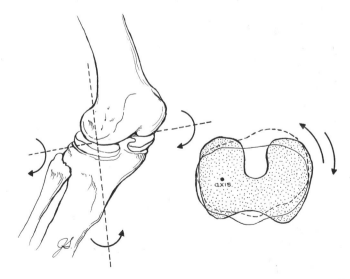

muscles involved are probably not strong enough to rotate the foot through the act of the ski-levers opposed by the resistance of the snow. Skiing is accomplished along an arc with resistance along the entire ski and not on a piano stool where swiveling is possible.

*PRINCIPLES OF MUSCLE ACTION:* A limited concept of muscle action is essential to the understanding of body mechanics. The muscles of the body are arranged in antagonistic pairs; as one set contracts, the opposing set bridging the same joint relaxes. For example, the extensors of the knee cannot produce lower leg extension unless the opposing muscles (the hamstrings) relax. Similarly, the muscles of the back may be used to fix the hip bones permitting the muscles bridging the hip joint to produce

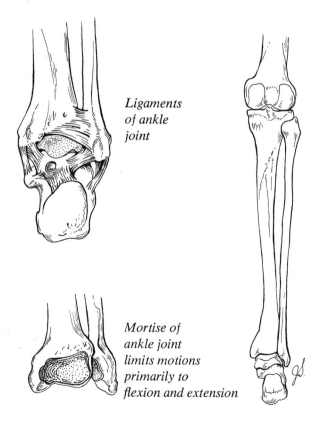

*Motions of the ankle joint and large muscles responsible*

*Ligaments of ankle joint*

*Back view right lower leg*

*Mortise of ankle joint limits motions primarily to flexion and extension*

motion of the thigh. Muscles only pull; they never push. Muscles generally bridge one joint but may bridge two in some instances. Motion of joints requires coordinate action of many different muscles and muscle groups. The coordination-cooperation between these muscle groups is dependent upon nerve impulses received and sorted within the central nervous system.

The functional unit of a muscle is a motor nerve and the group of muscle fibers that it supplies. The muscle itself is made up of many motor units. The nerve stimulus to the muscle is a succession of rapidly repeated electrical impulses to the motor unit. If the motor units act simultaneously, a strong contraction results. If they react out of rhythm, the strength of the contraction is weaker. One motor unit cannot change the strength of its contraction. An increase or decrease in the strength of the over-all muscle contraction is dependent upon the number of motor units contracting. It equally depends on the rhythm in which they contract. The muscle fibers are in a continuous state of contraction and alternate relaxation—a phenomenon called muscle tonus.

176

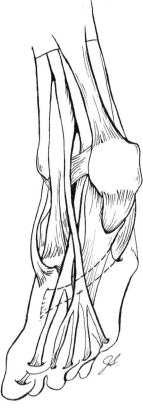

*Muscle attachments—sole of foot. The direction of pull indicates that motion occurs in two planes simultaneously*

In addition to the mechanical factors concerning muscle action, the biochemical changes within the muscle should be considered. Such changes are exceedingly complex and are the subject of extensive medical research. Eventually, a knowledge of biochemistry will provide students of sports medicine with a scientific basis for training athletes. However, such details are certainly beyond the scope of this book.

A brief review of certain aspects is essential. Oxygen is brought to the muscles by the available blood supply. The waste products of muscle action are lactic and carbon dioxide. The carbon dioxide is neutralized by the buffer systems of the blood and removed through expiration via the lungs. Lactic acid builds up in the area of muscle contraction. In proper concentration lactic acid increases muscle irritability and improves the strength of muscle contraction. If the concentration becomes too great, fatigue results. This happens in a stair-step fashion and is known as the Treppe phenomenon of muscle contraction. The strength of the muscle contraction becomes stronger although the intensity of the stimulation remains constant. This plus the increased heat developed help to avoid injury. These things constitute the warm-up period.

It should be realized that each individual has a different warm-up period and the standard of one performer cannot be inflicted upon the other. If the accumulation of lactic acid continues, states of muscle fatigue occur. This produces an inability of the muscle to relax and eventually muscle cramp results.

Muscles cannot move in a coordinated fashion unless directed from the higher centers of the brain. However, before the brain centers can direct the muscles, they must have certain informer sources of the body's current activities. That is, the following must be known: (1) the degree of joint flexion or extension; (2) the relationship of the extremities to each other; and (3) the degree and speed of muscle contraction. In addition, the orientation of the body with respect to the pull of gravity or other acceleratory forces must be considered. These informer sources are located in the inner ear, the eyes, muscles and joints, pressure pads in the soles of the feet, and in the skin. Stimuli from these sensing structures are transferred to the brain, processed and referred back down to the muscles to produce appropriate contractions.

Muscle tonus is increased under certain circumstances. For example, states of excitement and position of readiness. An increased state of tonus will increase the rapidity with which the muscle may react to an incoming stimulus. This is similar to one car towing another. If the rope between the two cars is already taut, no time is required to take up the slack. The proper degree of tonus aids in the strength of muscle contraction by producing a more coordinated and effective reaction. Consequently, less energy is involved in accomplishing the action. On the other hand, confusion in the mind of the performer may greatly reduce the efficiency of the muscle contraction. This is brought about by an imperfect relaxation of the antagonous muscle group which provides resistance to the contraction of the desired muscles.

Muscle sense or proprioception stems from nerve receptors within the joints and muscles which indicate the degree and speed of joint motion. These receptors also indicate the state of muscle contraction. The acuity of position sense varies from person to person. The teacher certainly welcomes the student who is highly developed in this respect. Well-coordinated individuals sense the proper strength of muscle contraction and the proper rate of speed that a muscle must contract. In addition, these individuals perceive the degree of joint motion and the rate of motion accurately.

The eyes function in maintenance of balance and equilibrium by the visual detection of the erect stance. Slight, straight-line, or rotational movements of the body instantly shift the visual images on the retina of the eye. This information is relayed to higher equilibrium centers. It is coordinated with other body motions. The eyes are particularly valuable in skiing. They constitute an early warning system. They provide definite advantages over the other more slowly reacting portions of the balance and equilibrium system.

In skiing the body may assume positions of readiness for transitions in steepness of the slope, bumps, and other variances that might produce a fall if not visualized ahead of time.

THE BALANCE ORGAN OF THE EAR: The portion of the ear in which the organ of balance is located is called the inner ear. This consists of a bony labyrinth made up of three canals semicircular in shape and arranged in planes perpendicular to each other. These bony canals contain fluid and each has a delicate membrane-type inner duct which follows the pattern of the bony canal. This is similar to an inner tube in a tire. The three inner canals have dilated ends and contain specialized nerve structures for the maintenance of balance. The semicircular canals open as a labyrinth of winding ducts into a central area termed the vestibule. In a fashion similar to the semicircular canals, the vestibule contains specialized nerve tissue in a structure called the utricle. The utricle is designed to pick up changes in straight-line motion. This consists of motion from side to side, forward or backward, and sudden gravitational changes. This is in contrast to the tissue in the semicircular canals which detects spinning or rotational-type movements.

The microstructure of the utricle is shown in the diagram on page 182. It should be noted that the utricle contains fine hairs on which are stones—that is, deposits of calcium—that are heavier than the surrounding medium. A sudden forward motion leaves the stone behind the rest of the body because of its greater inertia. A nerve impulse is immediately relayed to higher levels of the brain indicating a change in motion has taken place. This same type of action will occur with regard to changes in gravitational pull. For example, when a skier goes over a sharp bump at high speed, the body would in effect drop away from the tiny stones in the utricle. A resultant nerve impulse is initiated so that the skier is made aware of the change. In the instance of going downhill with the weight back, the stones would be relatively back in relation to the immediate surrounding fluid. This information is sent by nerve relays to higher portions of the brain making the individual feel as though he were falling backward. This causes immediate compensatory muscle action to reposition the center of gravity forward into a more balanced posture.

In downhill running, the action of the body to prevent falling backward is mediated by the body leaning forward. This produces a forward shift of the calcium deposits in the ear to a point equaling the original tendency to fall backward because of the acceleration. A sense of equilibrium would then be detected by the associated balance organs in the body and any further shift forward would be stopped. As long as the forward motion remains constant and the body is in balance with proper forward lean, the student will not fall.

As the speed is increased, further adjustments in posture are brought about by reflexes initiated by the air acting against pressure receptors in the skin. These reflexes go to the brain and correlate with the ear and other centers of balance and muscle action. The experienced skier has a more accurate sensation of speed. He knows by experience that his center of gravity must be displaced forward as the linear acceleration increases. It should be kept in mind that the utricle has its deficiencies. For example, it will not pick up changes of head position with respect to gravity of less than 24 degrees. For this reason, the body must rely on the early warning system of the eyes to prepare for sudden changes. Excellent proof of this is manifested in skiing in flat light or in fog when the visual aids are greatly reduced. The skier becomes similar to the pilot who can no longer fly by "the seat of his pants." The high speed of modern aircraft necessitates quicker reaction time than one would get on the basis of utricular reflexes alone.

Reflex action in the semicircular canals is initiated when the body is rotated about an axis at a certain rate of speed. The amount of acceleration required to stimulate the semicircular canals varies from 0.02 of a degree per second, per second to 2 degrees per second, per second. This averages 1 degree per second, per second. In other words when one begins to rotate, his velocity of rotation must be as much as 1 degree per second by the end of the first second, 2 degrees per second by the end of the second second, etc., in order for him to barely detect that he is rotating. It is for this reason that the people in Seattle's space needle do not feel a sense of rotation; nor does an astronaut in orbit when rotation is two-thirds of a degree per second.

The speed of rotation is important in skiing because with an initial sharp turn the action will be detected by the semicircular canal. The body will be advised to make appropriate adjustments for the turn. However, after the first few seconds, the nerve firing in the semicircular canal stops and the skier continues the turn without a turning sensation. Skiing in fog is an impressive example. A parallel may be drawn with the airplane pilot who enters a turn slowly with his rotational acceleration less than 2 degrees per second. He may not perceive the fact that he is in a turn until problems develop.

*OTHER FACTORS INFLUENCING EQUILIBRIUM:* The balance apparatus of the ear detects the orientation movements of the head so that one is able to ascertain his position in space. However, the brain also receives information depicting the orientation of the head with respect to the body and different parts of the body with respect to each other. Our regular muscle sense apparatus, previously described, is supplemented by reflex mechanisms labeled "neck righting reflexes" and "body righting reflexes." These are the reflexes that permit a cat to turn over automatically and land on its feet when dropped in an inverted position. Neck righting and body righting reflexes represent deeply ingrained reflex mechanisms that have a bearing on the coordinate activities of balance. Similarly, the reflex actions in standing and walking have been long established; that is, since infancy. It is felt that whenever possible the ski teacher should direct his teaching efforts along these already entrenched reflex paths. This offers a situation similar to rehabilitating a partially paralyzed extremity. Contracting muscles elsewhere in the body strengthen the contraction of the injured member. For example, in the downhill running position one should assume the feeling of a forward stance on the balls of the feet. This is closely allied with our basic standing posture governed by reflexes which have been operative since childhood. A beginning skier learning angulation may be positioned with greater angulation than necessary. On the other hand, angulation is necessary as higher speed turns are performed. The angulation is taught at the beginning to condition the body to the feel of this position. The acquired discipline will be rewarding as the student approaches the problems coincident with higher speed skiing. It is felt that the progression in the American Ski Technique is based on sound physiologic mechanisms. The relationship of the seven basic principles of the American Ski Technique to body mechanics will not be illustrated.

*NATURAL POSITIONING:* The use of natural body positions is based on the need for economy of motion. This is true in skiing and other sports. The difference between a champion performer and one of less caliber is often the greater economy found in smoothly coordinated and well directed muscular activities. An upright stance in skiing means that the weight bearing of the body lies as close to the skeletal axis as possible. This insures that the body weight is carried primarily by the skeleton, preserving the energy and muscles as much as possible for movement. The muscles remain free to maintain balance.

Body support is quite critical at the hip joint. Here the ligaments relieve muscles of much of the work of supporting the body. The ligaments of the pelvis are located so that the direction of gravitational pull is slightly ahead of the axis of the hip joints. Gravity tends to extend the hips into the ligaments causing the stress to be borne by these relatively inert sructures. In the knee and the ankle joints, the line of gravitational pull runs slightly in front of the midposition of the knee and well in front of the ankle joint. The tension of ligaments rather than muscles under stress primarily maintains the weight of the body against gravity in these areas. Furthermore, the strength of a muscle in reacting to a command is enhanced by being in a more relaxed position. In the upright stance, the skier uses his postural muscles primarily to maintain equilibrium rather than to support the body against gravity. This places the muscles in a position to react more rapidly in combating the changes in balance. The downhill racer is specifically taught to assume aerodynamically efficient positions. These are highly costly for energy utilization. A recreational skier, on the other hand, must be taught to avoid stiff and tense positions and to use his muscles with a minimum of energy expenditure. The use of established body postural mechanisms in teaching helps to eliminate confusion in the mind of the performer. It helps to avoid wasted energy from incoordinate activities.

*UNWEIGHTING:* The advantages of up-unweighting versus down-unweighting are quite detailed in the other portions of this book. For biomechanic and student purposes, preparatory down motion to set the lower ski also sets the large extensor muscles of the thigh. This increases the strength of contraction by increasing the state of tonus and readiness. The beginning skier who is generally weak in this muscle group needs this advantage to the greatest degree. The subsequent up motion is used to effect unweighting and is a natural consequence of the initial down motion. It is physiologically sound. This is comparable to a similar type of contraction in the quadraceps muscles as a gymnast prepares to do a back flip. The initial down motion increases the strength of the subsequent extension of the thigh muscles as he propels upward in the flip.

*WEIGHT TRANSFER:* The body motions in weight transfer may be subtle insofar as the degree of shift is concerned. They may be virtually undetectable. The importance of weight transfer is therefore sometimes neglected. It should be realized that the amount of weight transfer varies with the speed of the skier, the steepness of the slope, snow conditions, and the turn radius. The basic principle applies without quantitative aspect.

*TOTAL MOTION:* This is one of the most applicable of all the basic principles; yet it is difficult to define except by example. The physiological application of total motion is equally as broad. It may be considered as starting from the time we think about skiing, through the actual physical application of these thoughts. This applies to a beginner considering the aspects of a snowplow turn as well as to the racer contemplating a high-speed turn.

Physical warm-up activities prepare the body for action by increasing the strength of muscle contraction due to increased local temperature within the muscles and increased oxygen availability. The increased strength of muscle contraction is facilitated by the Treppe phenomenon. This is associated with the increased stimulating concentrations of lactic acid. The process of total motion continues as we start down the mountain. The acceleration of the traverse aids in the performance of the first turn and adds more in the performance of the subsequent turns. At this stage a muscular rhythm has been established which has a conditioning effect on the pattern of the coordinate, neuromuscular activities within the body. This is manifested in the natural continuation of the down-up-down motion throughout a series of turns. As the skier rhythmically unweights, counterrotation becomes an effective turning force. It is at such time that the true dynamic effect of counterrotary movements are applicable. The principle of total and continuous motion is embraced in the complete involvement of the skier's psychological and physiological performance.

*AXIAL MOTION:* Counterrotary movements as used in turning skis have several sound moorings in body physiology. The concept embraces the center of the body mass acting as a focal point for turns. This facilitates the performance of short radius turns such as a short swing, accomplished by the least displacement of the center of body mass. Contrast this with rotation turns. In such turns the outside turning arm and hip are propelled in the direction of the turn at a greater speed than the turning ski. Consider for a moment the weight of the outer half of the body rotating in the direction of the turn, which often produces overturning with loss of balance. This is particularly true if increased resistance such as ruts, soft snow, etc., is met. The weight of the skier should be carried down through the foot to an effective edge set. Weight should not be carried high away from the axial forces of the body, for this produces an unstable position. It is felt that counterrotary movements maintained close to the center of gravity permit faster reaction time in maintaining balance.

Rotary forces are applicable in advanced skiing and racing. They are powerful turning forces and must be controlled to be effectively transmitted to the ski. Greater muscular strength, co-ordination, and balance are necessary to use both turning forces effectively. The advanced skier and racer, therefore, make greater use of these forces.

*LEVERAGE:* A forward leaning position is necessary to maintain balance as the skier accelerates down the slope. The natural position of balance in standing and walking is with the weight slightly forward of the hip joints. The pressure receptors in the soles of the feet are accustomed and conditioned to bearing the weight on the ball of the foot. Forward lean utilizes these already established conditioned reflex patterns for maintenance of balance. Forward lean also applies to skiing deep snow. The compressive effect of the soft snow on the tip of the ski virtually decreases the steepness of the slope.

Leverage may also be applied by backward lean, used in advanced techniques. Muscular force is necessary to recover from a backward leaning position to a balanced downhill running position.

*EDGE CONTROL:* Angulation is used in traverses or turns to maintain edge control by body position. The skis must be edged in the snow in order to hold. The upper body tilts over the downhill ski in order to keep the center of weight over the holding edge. The primary strength in edging comes from motions in the hip joint. Ankle motion is slight because of immobile boots. There are fine motions of the ankles due to the muscles bridging the joints but the strength of holding an edged position is based primarily on the degree of body angulation. This is true in higher speed turns where the propelling forces tend to "project the skier off the mountain." This must be counteracted by a more angulated position. The courage to assume such a position at high speeds requires well-conditioned reflexes. An angulated position at low speeds is a conditioning process necessary to create proper positions for higher speeds.

This chapter is a survey of mechanisms within the body in relation to skiing. A medical text could be written on the physiologic involvements and the orthopedic applications in such a complex activity. However, it is felt that this would be far beyond our avowed purpose, which is to enable the teacher to better understand his pupil.

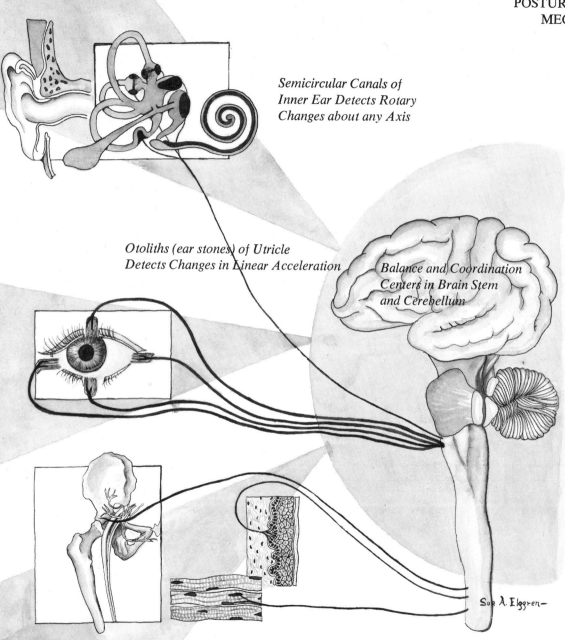

*Semicircular Canals of
Inner Ear Detects Rotary
Changes about any Axis*

*Otoliths (ear stones) of Utricle
Detects Changes in Linear Acceleration*

*Balance and Coordination
Centers in Brain Stem
and Cerebellum*

Sue A. Elggren—

*Kinesthetic Senses, Muscles, Tendons,
Joints, Pressure Receptors in Skin*

# EQUIPMENT

*Understanding Ski Design*
*How to Choose a Good Pair of Skis*
*Equipment Today*

# UNDERSTANDING SKI DESIGN

The following is a comprehensive analysis of the various materials used in high quality skis, their method of application, their advantages and disadvantages, and their ultimate performance in the final product. To avoid misinterpretation, let us first agree on general terminology regarding materials and skiing terms.

## TYPICAL SKI TERMS

1. *CAMBER*—The arched shape on the bottom of a ski necessary to distribute weight along the length of the ski. This avoids a concentration of weight directly under the feet. The amount of camber is a function of stiffness, stiffness distribution, and the reaction of the material used on various types of surfaces. Generally, a harder ski should have less camber.
2. *ELASTIC CURVE*—The type of curve formed by the ski when it is bent past its flat position.
3. *VIBRATION*—A fluttering, trembling, quivering motion of the ski. Vibration frequency occurs at relatively high speeds over hard, uneven terrain.
4. *DAMPING*—The quality of the ski to absorb shocks and vibration.
5. *TORSIONAL STIFFNESS*—The resistance to bending forces applied relative to the horizontal axis of the ski (twisting).
6. *UNWINDING*—The capacity to recover from a twisted or torsionally deflected position at maximum speed.
7. *PLASTIC SANDWICH SKI*—A ski having a wooden core with two plastic skins.
8. *METAL SANDWICH SKI*—A ski having a wooden core with two metal skins.
9. *ALL FIBER-GLASS SKI*—a ski manufactured of fiber glass entirely (with the exception of steel edges, polyethylene base, thermoplastic top sheet, top edges, heel caps, toe caps).
10. *MECHANICAL PROPERTIES*—Tensile strength, compressive strength, interlaminar shear strength, bond strength, etc.
11. *PHYSICAL PROPERTIES*—Bending, twisting, deflecting, weight, etc.

In general, each manufacturer aspires to produce a ski that will have four basic characteristics:
(1) The ski should turn easily.
(2) The ski should hold well on ice.
(3) The ski should perform well in deep snow.
(4) The ski should have good damping qualities or high-speed stability.

The ability to turn easily is directly related to the flexibility of the ski. Generally, a soft ski will turn easier than a stiff ski. Properties such as bottom camber and side camber play a role. But all things being equal, it is the stiffness and its distribution that make a ski that is easy to turn.

A ski that holds well on ice is a stiff ski, right? Not necessarily—holding is a function of torsional stiffness, and it has very little to do with longitudinal stiffness. Again, it must be mentioned that bottom camber and side camber play a role. But in a ski fabricated to the normal accepted standards of the industry, it is torsional stiffness that dictates the amount of ice-holding power in any ski. This is a very delicate point, however, and it is wrong to assume that a ski should not deflect torsionally at all. A certain amount of deflection is required because the edge must adapt to the steepness of angle of the surface. Only if the steel edge can be deflected to the best angle of attack (at 45 degrees to the neutral axis of the ski) can it work at peak efficiency. There is one more imporant quality that a ski must have in order to hold on ice—the speed at which this torsionally deflected beam unwinds. Since icy slopes are never smooth and without bumps, the ski must react quickly and adapt to changes in terrain.

A ski's ability to perform well in deep powder is a function of proper flex, its distribution resulting in an elastic curve. In this type of skiing condition side camber and bottom camber lose most of their importance. A deep snow ski must first of all have a very soft tip. When flexed, the ski must "break" right in the curve of the shovel. This allows the ski to "float" on the snow. Secondly, the ski must be soft longitudinally to allow flattening of the camber with a minimum effort. With the swimming tip and the flattened camber the ski is now in a slight reverse bend and will glide over deep soft snow with ease, always providing lift to keep the skis from sinking too far below the surface.

Damping or stability is perhaps most important to the intermediate and advanced skier. The beginner will never ski fast enough to make use of this quality. Nevertheless, a ski that is stable and absorbs shocks well for the expert is also an advantage for any skier simply because it is a well-designed product. Speed is a relative phenomenon. What is "slow" for the racer may be "fast" for the beginner. Good damping qualities are present in wood and some plastics. In thermoset materials one can find excellent damping qualities if the glass fiber orientation is random—such as in the core of some plastic skis. Metal, for instance, is at a slight disadvantage in this department. Metal promotes and entertains vibration because of its high modulus of elasticity. Good stability

or damping have a very close relative in what the writer terms "memory of the material." This can best be explained by saying that in the all fiber-glass skis the glass fiber and the resin-supporting structure are molded into a certain shape. This shape is the material's natural position, and whenever deflected it wants to go back into this shape as quickly as possible. The result is that at any given moment there is a maximum amount of ski (and edge) giving excellent stability and tracking.

It appears that in most of the above characteristics side camber is always playing a certain role. It is perhaps the subject least understood by the industry today and the views held by experts vary. The reason is simple. The effects of other physical and mechanical properties such as stiffness, bending, fatigue, etc., can readily be measured. But the effects of side camber can be judged only on the slope. One has to trust the expert skier to tell which type of side camber is best for a certain type of skiing. The human element is introduced, and human legs can hardly be compared with the accuracy of strain gauges and other measuring devices. As a result, there are virtually no two skis on the market today with the same cut.

The following illustrates the functions of side camber as applied in various types of skis:

DOWNHILL SKI: This type of ski is designed for high speed. Emphasis is placed on good tracking as opposed to turning. A downhill ski is seldom called upon to execute short turns. The turns are long and sweeping. This type of ski has a minimum amount of side camber. The widest point is at the front, before the upturn of the shovel; the smallest dimension is just behind the center of gravity; and the heel dimension is approximately in between. The heel is not as wide as other types of skis. This relatively narrow heel cuts down drag and helps to make a fast ski. Also, the shovel part of the ski should be soft and the radius slow and long. A soft, long shovel prevents digging and helps to absorb bumps and ridges in the terrain.

SLALOM SKI: A slalom ski is slightly narrower than other skis and has more side camber. The widest part at the front and at the back of the ski should be close to the extreme ends of the gliding surface. This is to obtain benefit of the length of the ski. The ski is always turning. In a turn the ski is put on edge and the front and back bite into the surface. It can be seen that the larger the ratio between front, heel, and middle the more effective the steering. There is a limit to side camber in a ski. The three dimensions have to be carefully balanced or a ski will overturn.

*GIANT SLALOM SKI:* This ski is a compromise between downhill and slalom. The amount of side camber is about halfway in between the two extremes. Recreational skis are in most cases GS models to allow relatively easy turning and relatively high speeds.

The above outlines what the ski designer uses as the fundamental design criterion. There are many other details to consider such as appearance, top edge protection, binding screw holding capacity, heel and toe cap design, cost, etc. etc.

Examine the four basic types of skis, construction, advantages and disadvantages.

*WOODEN SKIS (NOT LAMINATED):* Until the end of World War II, the solid one-piece ash or hickory ski was the most popular ski. The only significant differences were in the edge material, or no top edges at all. Hidden steel edges were unknown and a fancy pair of skis featured the wide screwed-on sectional edge still found on some cheaper skis. Most ski manufacturers did not place importance on side camber, camber, flexibility, etc., mainly because skiing was at its early stage of development and hard-packed slopes were unknown. These ski were dimensionally very unstable and absorbed water like a sponge. By today's standards they would be quite unsatisfactory.

*LAMINATED WOODEN SKIS:* After the war, laminated skis began to appear frequently and became popular. For the first time an attempt was being made to orient the fibers in order to gain some control over the mechanical properties of the ski. These skis were better than the one-piece skis.

Soon the first plastic bottom surfaces began to appear, the first hidden edges were seen, and top edges became standard. The ski industry was now off to a revolution in ski design brought on by the rapid growth of the market.

Then the industry approached the modern era of ski design. Experts investigated the effects of side camber, camber flexibility, stiffness distribution, etc. The old craft of making skis evolved to the point where engineering principles were applied, material research accelerated, and soon some strange new skis were on the market. The wooden ski had gone through its cycle and could not be improved upon much more.

*THE MODERN METAL SKI:* The metal sandwich ski generally uses a laminated wooden core and two aluminum skins. In a structure such as a ski, it is the material farthest away from the neutral axis of the ski that does most of the work. It is exactly the same principle that applies to a steel I-beam. In other words, the aluminum on a metal ski is doing all the work when this ski is subject to stresses. However, when this ski is flexed extremely hard the glue line between metal and core is subject to high stresses.

The glue is stronger than the wood, and the surface of the wood absorbs the punishment in the form of sheer loads. As a result, the bond between metal and wood breaks the wooden fibers one by one, and the ski frequently loses camber and life. The average skier may never know what is happening. He knows that the ski is not holding on ice any more. He may blame himself and think that he must be doing something wrong. Not so, it is merely that the ski has tired glue lines. The wooden fibers of the core are either torn or loose and allow the two stress skins to move slightly back and forth when flexed.

The damping capacity of a metal ski can still be improved. Attempts have been made to solve this problem on high-performance skis by using a rubber membrane between two sheets of aluminum. Thus, a sandwich is used instead of a single skin for the top or bottom of the ski. This has been effective but has not provided the solution. A further problem is the wooden core. Wood is dimensionally not stable and absorbs water. No matter how well the core is laminated, it will inevitably keep on working. It expands, shrinks, twists, and rots. Water seeps into the ski through binding attachment holes and often results in delamination of the top skin in the binding area. Despite a lot of disadvantages some metal skis are good products and are here to stay. However, there are better materials and better methods available, and in the near future there will be changes.

*PLASTIC SANDWICH SKI:* This ski is basically the same as a metal ski except that the two skins are made of reinforced plastic instead of high-tensile aluminum. Perhaps the most distinct advantages are that reinforced plastic is easier to bond than metal; also the damping qualities of reinforced plastic are somewhat better than metal, thus offering a ski that skis better. Again a wooden core is used; and when the ski is flexed hard, the wood surface fibers loosen and partially break due to fatigue. The ski loses life and camber.

*FIBER-GLASS WRAPPED WOODEN CORE:* This ski is a big improvement over the sandwich ski because it has a larger plastic content. Water absorption is less and the dimensional stability is improved. The problem in this ski is production control. The ski is wrapped with fiber glass and resin and then placed into heated metal molds. Pressure is applied. The resin is now dropping in viscosity and, combined with the high pressure in the mold, the wooden core is difficult to locate. As a result, these skis vary from molding to molding. Side-wall thicknesses are not the same and shrinkage varies. The use of this process results in the fact that there are literally no two skis alike. Another problem is that binding screws are often pulled out because the top skin is connected to the bottom skin with relatively soft wood. This wood, depending on how the fibers have grown in the tree and how fast the tree itself has grown, often has not sufficiently interlaminar shear strength to withstand the tremendous tensional loads applied.

*ALL PLASTIC SKI:* In this ski, inflated polyethylene tubes instead of a wooden core are wrapped with pre-impregnated glass. This package is molded in a metal mold achieving a hollow core design. It is hard to control the location of these tubes under heat and pressure. They tend to float producing uneven laminate thickness and glass content within the laminate. Such a ski will eventually warp. It is a messy and time-consuming way to make skis. This process is not best for high-volume production. However, the ski is very good and its handling characteristics were well accepted.

Ski manufacturers agree that fiber glass is an ideal material for the construction of skis and offers a multitude of advantages both in the manufacturing process and the final product.

# HOW TO CHOOSE A GOOD PAIR OF SKIS

Picking a good pair of skis is an art; it requires a keen eye, patience, and numerous pairs of skis in the desirable size. Skis differ and there are no two pair of skis in the world that will ski exactly alike. This is due to the materials used in manufacturing. There are five things to look for in selecting a perfect pair of skis: edge match, straight line, matched flex pattern, freedom from kinks, and bottom configuration.

*EDGE MATCH*—Place the skis together, bottom to bottom, clamp them snuggly with a small C-clamp at the center of the running surface. Make sure the tip and tails align with each other; then look carefully along the edges of the skis. There should be complete contact along the entire edge with no gaps visible. Check both sides in this manner.

*STRAIGHT LINE*—Look along the skis from the tip or tail (clamped). The edges should be in contact and form a perfectly straight line.

*MATCHED FLEX PATTERN*—Hold the ski with one hand at the shovel running surface, the other at the center of the running surface; flex the ski about twelve inches and hold it in that position. Observe the flex pattern of the entire ski and make a mental picture of it. Do the same with the other ski, and make sure they match.

*KINKS*—To check for kinks along the bottom edge, hold the ski about shoulder height with both hands at the tip, the tail resting on the floor pointed away from you. Place your right or left foot at the center of the running surface and flatten out the bottom camber. Observe the line of the ski from the tip. Is it smooth and free from kinks? Now apply more pressure and observe the even curve of the bottom line.

*BOTTOM CONFIGURATION*—When the skis are held bottom to bottom the edges should be in contact at tip and tail. When looking between the skis you should be able to see light (concave bottom). If the skis have a convex bottom it will be necessary to remove some of the plastic base with a scraper. Concave bottoms require bottom filing. Below is a drawing of how the ski should be.

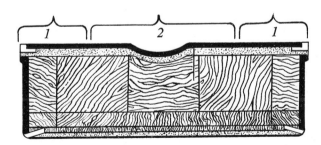

Area 1 should be perfectly flat with edges, and area 1 on opposite side of the groove.

Area 2 should be slightly concave so that you can just see light under the straight edge. The edges must always be flush with the running surface.

## FILING YOUR SKIS

If the edges are higher than the running surface, it is necessary to bottom file your skis. The same is true if the running surface is higher than the edges. It may be quicker to use a sharp paint scraper to remove the kofix. Be very careful not to remove too much as it is very thin on most skis.

*BOTTOM OR FLAT FILING PROCEDURE:* Clamp the ski firmly in a vice, bottom up, tip and tail section supported. Use a second cut mill bastard file; I prefer a Nicholson 12 inch. Always begin at the shovel and work your way toward the tail with slow, long, smooth strokes. Be careful to hold the file in the center with the thumb and first two fingers of each hand. This will help exert the pressure in the correct place on the ski and will prevent any bowing of the file which would create a convex bottom. File about one-third of the ski at a time, checking your progress with the straight edge. It might help to draw lines across the bottom of the ski with a felt tip marker; this will act as a dye and assist you in observing where the file is cutting. During this procedure it is a good idea to wear a thin pair of old leather gloves to protect the hands against cuts and blisters.

*EDGE FILING:* Place the ski on its side and clamp it securely in the vice. Always start at the shovel and work your way toward the tail. Hold the file so that it is cutting away from the bottom, toward the top of the ski. Make sure you are maintaining a 90-degree edge. Keep the file square; a file guide (available in most hardware stores) may come in handy at first. After completing all edges, lightly brush over them with a piece of #500 wet-dry silicone paper, removing the microscopic burrs. Dull the shovel and tail section on both edges about two inches from each end to prevent the edges from catching and climbing uphill.

## BINDING PLACEMENT

The proper placement of the toe piece on the ski is very important. Generally the ball of the foot is placed directly above the center of the running surface. (The running surface is determined by placing the skis bottom to bottom, clamping them, measuring the edge contact length and dividing it in half). As previously stated, this is a general rule; some skiers mount ahead or behind this point.

Slalom skis—mount ball of foot 1 cm. ahead of center of running surface.

G. S. of RSL.—mount ball of foot directly above center of running surface.

Downhill—mount ball of foot 1 cm. behind center of running surface.

Combi—done the same as the G. S.

## REPAIRING STRIPPED SCREW HOLES

Clean out the hole as well as possible. Mix equal portions of Duro Epoxi metal* (available at most hardware stores in small tubes) and force the putty into the hole. Carefully replace the binding, turn the screws in so they are all the way down, but not tight. Let it dry for a few hours in a warm area (above 70 degrees). After the material is dry, tighten the screw firmly.

* While any good metal epoxy repair may be used, this brand has proven most satisfactory.

# EQUIPMENT TODAY

*SKIS:* Choosing a ski can be confusing. It would be difficult for the beginner without assistance. Likewise, it could produce a dilemma for the advanced skier. There are about fifty different brands of metal skis, over sixty fiber-glass skis, and probably one hundred wood skis. The instructor will be called upon by parents or students to help choose the right ski considering design, material, construction, price, and need. The beginner doesn't need the most expensive skis, and the average man with a family skiing can't afford them. Choosing children's skis is very important. Some are too stiff or have too much camber. Wood skis are a common and less expensive model of children's skis.

The choice of ski will vary depending upon the purpose for which it is intended: recreational or competition, ice or powder. One cannot even say that there is a set rule for choosing the length of the ski. The skier's physical capabilities, weight, skiing skill, and experience are all factors in the decision. Therefore, the ski instructor or reputable ski shop can be of vital assistance to the skier.

The advent of the short ski, generally four- and five-foot lengths, make it possible for many to ski who would not otherwise consider the sport. The ski is not only shorter but of lighter construction. Even the elderly or less energetic can enjoy skiing immediately without becoming discouraged on these "easy riders." In some ski schools the short ski is incorporated into the teaching system.

*BINDINGS:* To help insure the reliability of the ski binding, a three-part equation must be considered: basically good design and manufacturing, proper mounting and adjustment, and continued maintenance. Until recently, 80 percent of the "safety" bindings on the market were not reliably safe. The remaining 20 percent of the bindings available accounted for something like 90 percent of the total number sold. With care on the part of the person mounting the bindings and the skier himself, the chance for injury as a result of a malfunction is cut immensely. Manufacturers have greatly improved their bindings, but that is not the entire story.

Remember—*binding safety is a three-part equation.* The binding must be designed soundly and precision manufactured. It must be mounted and adjusted carefully and correctly. The skier must follow through with maintenance and periodic readjustment. Any weakness in the equation, and the "safety" margin of even the best product vanishes.

Many ski shops sell only merchandise that is of top quality, top reputation, and top dollar value. They provide competent mechanics to mount the bindings. They thoroughly test the bindings after mounting. (The cost of a release binding—$15 to $50; mounting may cost up to $15.)

Perhaps a perfect binding has not yet been invented; perhaps it never will be. It must hold your boot firmly through all maneuvers: edging the ski from side to side, turning it forcefully, and rocking back and forth. This same binding should release your boot when you fall. It is obvious that the forces involved will be quite varied. The individual factor must also be considered: How heavy are you? How strong? How well do you ski? These factors have been taken into detailed consideration in design.

When a binding is properly designed to provide release under virtually all situations and the binding is correctly mounted and properly adjusted, interferences restricting ideal performance may still happen. Leather-soled boots soak up water and swell. The swelling can throw off the original correct setting. If ski boots are allowed to "curl," friction against the welt-holding flange of the toe unit can build up to offset what was a correct setting. Skis carried on the car top are subjected to spray from salted highways. Release mechanisms of the bindings should be protected by having periodic lubrication or even by being encased in plastic bags while attached to a ski rack. Wear and tear of the parts can change the binding setting after a few weeks of hard use. So many release bindings are on the market (no less than seventy, plus twenty for children), it is impossible to ski on and know the qualities of each. Your local ski shop will carry a few top lines with which you can become familiar. The owner or operator of the shop can be of assistance. Remember, the three main factors for reliability in a release binding: (1) sound design and manufacturing, (2) mounting and adjustment, and (3) maintenance.

*BOOTS:* Boots are as important as having good skis. Modern skiing would be virtually impossible without the recent developments in boot design. Experts believe that many of the techniques have developed only as fast as boots have permitted.

The boots must prevent the foot from sliding, twisting, or lifting simultaneously. They must stiffen and strengthen the ankles laterally while allowing the ankle to be flexed forward freely and comfortably. You should be able to wiggle your toes easily even though you may not have much room at the toe of the boot. You need to be conscious of the boot touching your instep, but it should not press. Remember, force your foot to the back of the boot before closing to adjust to the built-in forward lean.

Manufacturers have been experimenting with boots that can adapt to the shape of the foot. There is a plastic that molds itself to the foot in five minutes. There is a boot that has padding installed at the store to fit your foot. There is a boot that has a separate padded interboot that is laced, then encased with a rigid outer boot.

There are over eighty different boots on the market from which to choose, and over fifty children's boots. Each pair of feet represents an individual problem and each skier represents a different complex of needs, skills, and desires. The best advice—just make sure they fit.

*POLES:* Every piece of equipment counts and poles are no exception. Even to a recreational skier, the weight, swing weight, length, and strength to the pole are important. There are some objective ways to choose a pole that is right for you.

*Length:* Manufacturers recommend that a pole be no more than 77 percent of your height although many expert skiers prefer that it be somewhat shorter.

*Weight:* A fifty-four inch pole might weigh anywhere from ten ounces to over a pound. Over-all weight is less important than the balance of swing weight. The weight at the tip is what contributes most to fatigue; therefore, swing the pole to feel its balance.

*Handle:* Top-quality poles use vinyl. Most handles are notched or have finger grips or are tilted or shaped to make it easier to plant the pole far enough ahead while skiing. Most of these considerations come down to a matter of personal preference.

All in all, there is a variety of good quality merchandise available today. Ask your instructor or consult a competent ski shop.

# BIBLIOGRAPHY

Advisory Committee on the teaching of the French Skiing Method. *Handbook For The Teaching Of The French Skiing Method*. Grenoble: Boissy and Colomb, 1966 (translation by Betty Palmedo).

*Agriculture Handbook No. 94, Snow Avalanches*. Forest Service, U.S. Department of Agriculture, Revised Edition, Washington: U.S. Government Printing Office, 1961.

Albouy, Robert. *The Allais Technique*. Seattle: Craftman Press, Inc., 1950.

Allais, Emile, Gignoux, Paul, Blanchon, Georges. *Ski Français*. Grenoble: B. Arthaud 1937. (French.)

———. *How To Ski By French Method*. Paris: Editions Fleche Publishers 1947. (English.)

American National Red Cross. *First Aid*. Fourth Edition. Garden City, New York: Double Day & Company, Inc., 1957.

Amstutz, Walter. *Skiing From A-Z*. London: Oxford University Press, 1939.

Atwater, Monty. *Avalanche Hunters*. Philadelphia: Macrae Smith Co., 1968. 288 pages.

Auran, John Henery and the Editors of *Ski* Magazine. *America's Ski Book*. New York: Scribner's and Sons, 1966.

Beattie, Bob, and Casewit, Curtis. *Learn To Ski*. New York: Bantam Books, 1967. 148 pages.

———. *My Ten Secrets of Skiing*. New York: The Viking Press, 1968. 50 pages.

Bilgeri Georg. *Der Alpine Skilauf*. Muncheon: 1911. Second Edition.

Bourdon, Robert. *Modern Skiing*. Philadelphia: J. B. Lippincott, 1953.

———. *The New Way To Ski*. New York: Universal Publishing and Distributing Corp., 1961. 89 pages.

Bowen, Ezra, *The Book Of American Skiing*. Philadelphia: J. B. Lippincott, 1963. 320 pages.

Bracken, W. R. *Skiing, Its Technique*. London: Borough Press, 1937.

Bradley, Miller and Merrill. *Expert Skiing*. New York: Holt, Rhinehart & Winston, 1960. 224 pages.

Brady, Michael. *Nordic Touring and Cross Country Skiing*. Olso: Dreyers Forlag (distributed by Arthur Vanous Co., Hackensac, N.J.), 1969. 70 pages.

Brandenberger, H. and A. Lauchi. *Skimechanik—Methodik des Skilaufs*. Ra-Verlag, Rapperswil, 1958. (German.)

Brower, David R. *Manual Of Ski Mountaineering*. San Francisco: Sierra Club, 1962. Third Edition. 224 pages.

Brown, Conrad. *Skiing For Beginners*. New York: Charles Scribner's Sons, 1951.

*Canadian Ski School Manual*. Canada: The Canadian Ski Instructors Alliance, 1969. 56 pages. (French and English.)

Carpenter, "Jerry." *Skiing In California*. Fearon Publishing Co., 1957. 120 pages.

Casewit, Curtis W. *Ski Fever*. New York: Hawthorn Books, Inc., 1965.

————. *Ski Racing: Advice By The Experts*. New York: Arco Books, 1963. 280 pages.

Caulfield, Vivian. *How To Ski*. London: Nisbet & Co., Ltd., 1911.

————. *Skiing Turns*. London: Nisbet & Co., Ltd., 1922. Second Edition, 1924. 280 pages.

Day, Frank. *If You Can Walk You Can Ski*. New York: The Crowell-Collier Press, 1962. 126 pages.

Dole, Minot. *Adventures In Skiing*. New York: Franklin Watts, Inc., 1965.

Ducia, Toni, and Reinl, Dr. Harald. *Ski d'aujourd'hui*. Paris: Skiklub de Paris, 1934.

Dudley, Charles M. *60 Centuries Of Skiing*. Vermont: Stephen Daye Press, 1935. 208 pages.

d'Egville, Alan. *Skiing—Basic Techniques For The Beginners*. London: William Heineman, Ltd., 1947. 50 drawings.

————. *Slalom*. London: Butler and Tanner Ltd., 1934.

————. *The Game Of Skiing*. London: Butler and Tanner Ltd., 1937.

Editors, Ski Magazine. *The Skier's Handbook*. New York: Harper & Row, 1965.

Elkins, F. A. and Harper, F. *The World Ski Book*. New York: Longmans, Green and Co., Inc., 1949. 310 pages.

Eriksen, Stein. *Come Ski With Me*. New York: Norton Press, 1966.

Estin, Peter. *Skiing The American Way*. New York: The John Day Co., 1963. 96 pages.

Fairlie, Gerald. *Flight Without Wings*. New York: Barnes, 1958.

Fawcus, Arnold. *Swing Into Skiing*. New York: Harcourt, Brace and Company, 1947.

*Finds Of Skis From Prehistoric Time In Swedish Bogs and Marshes*. Stockholm: General-stabens Litografiska Anstalts Forlag, 1950. 158 pages.

Firsoff, V. A. *Ski Tracks On The Battlefield*. New York: 1943. 158 pages.

Fraser, Colin. *The Avalanche Enigma*. New York: Rand MacNally.

Freund, Franz and Campiotti, Fulvio. *The Delux Book of Skiing*. New York: Sterling Publishing Co., 1963. 124 pages.

————. *The New Skier*. London: Arthur Barker Limited, 1960.

Gemsch, Norbert and Julen, August. *Modern Skiing*. New York: Barnes & Noble, Inc., 1965.

Georg, Hans. *Modern Ski Systems*. New York: Hastings House, 1954. 64 pages.

Gereghini, Mario. *5000 Years Of Winter Sports*. Milan: Edizioni Del Milione, 1955.

Golden Press. *The Golden Guide To Skiing*. New York: The Golden Press, 1966.

Gritscher, Helmut, and Halbwidl, Fritz. *Skiing, A Pictorial Handbook Of Instruction*. New York: Taplinger, 1968. 84 pages.

Hall, Frederick A., and Benson, Nathaniel A. *Improve Your Skiing*. New York: Dodge Publishing Company, 1936.

Hallberg, F., and Muckenbrunn, H. *The Complete Book of Skiing*. New York: Greenberg Publisher, 1936. 317 pages.

Harper, Frank. *Military Ski Manual*. Harrisburg, 1945. 393 pages.

————. *Night Climb, The Story of the Skiing 10th*. New York, 1948. 216 pages.

————. *Skiing For The Millions*. New York: Longmans Green and Co., Inc., 1945.

Hoppichler, Franz. *Neige Et Style*. Hachette, 1960. (French.)

Hoschek, Dr. Fritz. *Die Naturliche Lehrweise des Schilaufens*. Wien: Deutscher Verlag fur Jugend and Volk, 1933.

Huber, Eddie, and Rogers, Norman. *The Complete Ski Manual*. New York: Prentice-Hall Inc., 1946.

Hutter, Clemens. *Wedeln. The New Austrian Ski Technique*. New York: Hanover House, 1960. 96 pages.

Inter-Association For Skiing. *The Technique of Skiing* (Swiss Skiing Handbook). Rapperswil: Ra-Verlag, 1960.

Interverband-Schweiz. *Ski In Der Schweiz*. Bern: Ra-Verlag, Rapperswil/SG., 1965. Seventh Edition.

Iselin, Fred, and Spectorsky, A. C. *Invitation To Modern Skiing*. New York: Simon and Schuster, 1965.

————. *Invitation To Skiing*. New York: Simon and Schuster, 1947.

————. *The New Invitation To Skiing*. New York: Simon and Schuster, 1958. 244 pages.

Jacques, Dr. A. *Downhill Skiing*. London: Nicolas Kaye, 1948. 233 pages.

Jay, John, O'Rear, John and Frankie, and Editors of *Ski* Magazine. *Ski Down The Years*. New York: Universal Publishing & Distributing, 1966.

Joubert, G., and Vuarnet, J. *Ski ABC*. France: Editions Bressanes, 1957, 58, 59. 141 pages.

Kruckenhauser, see Palmedo, Roland.

LaChapelle, Ed. *The ABC Of Avalanche Safety*. Boulder, Colorado: Highlander Publishing Co., 1961.

Lang, Otto. *Downhill Skiing*. New York: Henry Holt & Co., 1936 & 1946. 113 pages.

Lash, Bill. *An Outline of Ski Teaching Methods*. Salt Lake City: Elbert Kirkham, 1959. 104 pages.

Loosli, Fritz. *Parallel Skiing*. New York: William Morrow & Company, 1941.

Lunn, Arnold. *A History of Skiing*. Oxford University Press: 1927.

————. *The Complete Ski Runner*. New York: Charles Scribner's Sons, 1930.

————. *Skiing*. 1912.

————. *The Story of Skiing*. London: Eyre & Spottiswoode, 1952.

Lunn, Peter. *High Speed Skiing*. Brattleboro: Stephen Daye Press, 1935.

Luther, C. J. *Der Moderne Wintersport*. 1911.

Matthias, Dr. Eugen-Testa, Giovanni. *Naturliches Schilaufen*. Muchen: Bergverlag Rudolf Rother, 1936.

McCulloch, Ernie. *Learn To Ski*. New York: Universal Publishing Co., 1955. 130 pages.

Micoleau, Tyler. *Powder Skiing Illustrated*. New York: Barnes & Co., 1949. 96 pages.

Mountainers, Inc. *Mountaineering—The Freedom of The Hills*. Seattle: 1965. Third Edition.

Nansen, Fridtjof. *The First Crossing of Greenland*. New York: Longmans, Green, and Co., 1890 (Two Volumes).

National Ski Patrol System. *National Ski Patrol System Manual*. New York: Graybar Building, 1941.

————. *Winter First Aid Safety Manual*. Denver: NSPS., 1963.

O'Connor, Lorne. *The Canadian Ski Technique:* Toronto and Montreal: McClelland and Stewart, Ltd. 1968, 153 pages.

O'Rear, Johnny and Frankie. *Skiing Illustrated*. New York: Barnes & Co., 1956. 96 pages.

Osgood, William E., and Hurley, Leslie J. *Ski Touring; An Introductory Guide*. Rutland: Charles E. Tuttle Company, 1969. 148 pages.

Palmedo, Roland. *Skiing, The International Sport*. New York: Derrydale Press, 1936.

————. (translation by Professor Stefan Kruckenhauser). *The New Official Austrian Ski System*. New York: A. S. Barnes & Co., 1958. 126 pages.

Paulke, W. *Der Skilauf*. 1910.

Pfeiffer, J. Douglas. *Skiing . . . With Pfeiffer*. California: A-to-Z Printing Company, 1963. 96 pages.

Prager, Walter. *Skiing*. New York: Barnes & Co., 1939. 192 pages.

Proctor, Charles, and Stephens, Rockwell. *Skiing*. New York: Harcourt, Brace and Company, 1936. 155 pages.

————. *The Art Of Skiing*. New York: Harcourt, Brace and Company, 1933.

Reuel, Dr. Fritz. *Neve Moglichkeiten Im Schilauf*. Stuattgart: Verlag Dieck und Co., 1929.

Richardson, E. C. *The Ski-Runner*. London: Cecil Palmer, Mackays Ltd., 1924. Third Edition.

Rickmers, W. R. *Skiing For Beginners and Mountaineers*. London: T. Fisher Unwin, 1910.

Rybizka, Benno. *The Hannes Schneider Ski Technique*. New York: Harcourt, Brace and Co., 1938 & 46. 109 pages.

Schaeffler, Willy, and Bowen, Ezra. *Sports Illustrated Book of Skiing*. New York: Lippincott, 1960.

Schneider, Hannes and Frank, Arnold. *The Wonders of Skiing*. New York: Scribner's Sons, 1933, Revised 1937.

Schniebs, Otto Eugen. *American Skiing*. New York: E. P. Dutton and Co., Inc., 1939.

Schniebs, Otto, and McCrilles, John. *Modern Ski Technique*. Vermont: Daye Press, 1936. 132 pages.

Shambroom, Rick, and Slater, Betty. *Skiing With Control*. New York: Collier Books, 1965.

*Ski Life* Magazine Editors. *Ski Pointers By The Experts*. New York: Harper & Brothers, 1961. 254 pages.

Somerville, Crichton, Rickmers, W. R., and Richardson, E. C. *Ski Running*. London: Horace Cox, Windsor House (Second Edition), 1907.

Smith, George Allen and Carol B. *The Armchair Mountaineer*. New York: Pitman Publishing Corporation, 1968. 361 pages.

Taylor, Cliff. *Instant Skiing.* Brattleboro, Vermont: Stephen Greene Press, 1961.

————. *Ski In A Day.* New York: Grosset and Dunlap, 1964.

Tobin, John C. *The Fall Line, A Skier's Journal.* New York: Meredith Press, 1969. 288 pages.

Wagner, Janet. *How To Ski,* How To Books No. 29. Derby, Conn.: Bruce Royal Publishing, 1963, 128 pages.

Yearn, Chuck, and Maranda, Vern. *About Skiing.* Detroit: Litho-Art, Inc., 1963.

Zdarsky, Mathias. *Die Lilienfelder Skilauf Technick.* Hamburg: 1897.

# INDEX